W9-BXX-970

A "REAL" guide to REALLY Getting it Together

ONCE AND FOR ALL

(REALLY)

BY ASHLEY RICKARDS

ILLUSTRATIONS BY BECKY MURPHY

{H} HARLEQUIN®

A Real Guide to Really Getting It Together Once and for All (Really)

ISBN-13: 978-0-373-89313-3

© 2015 by Ashley Rickards

All rights reserved. The reproduction, transmission or utilization of this work
in whole or in part in any form by any electronic, mechanical or other means,
now known or hereafter invented, including xerography, photocopying and
recording, or in any information storage or retrieval system, is forbidden without
the written permission of the publisher. For permission please contact Harlequin
Enterprises Limited, 225 Duncan Mill Road, Don Mills, Ontario, Canada, M3B 3K9.

Library of Congress Cataloging-in-Publication Data

Rickards, Ashley.

 A real guide to really getting it together once and for all (really)/
by Ashley Rickards ; illustrations by Becky Murphy.

       pages cm

 Includes index.

 ISBN 978-0-373-89313-3 (alk. paper)

 1. Rickards, Ashley. 2. Beauty, Personal. 3. Self-realization. 4. Young women—
Conduct of life. 5. Young women—Life skills guides. I. Title.

 RA777.25R53 2015

 613—dc23

                              2014030263

Photography: David Phelps
Illustrations: Becky Murphy
Design: Alissa Faden

www.Harlequin.com

Printed in U.S.A.

TO ALL MY FELLOW POWERB!TCHES™

CONTENTS

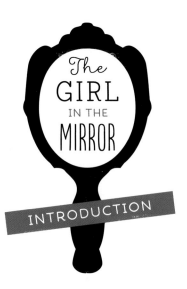

The
GIRL
IN THE
MIRROR

INTRODUCTION

I don't know when the first GPS system came out, but I do know that, growing up, I felt pretty friggin' lost most of the time. While I eventually found my way to Los Angeles to become the actress and writer I am today, it hasn't always been easy. In fact, as a teenager, I related best to my hamster, Mir, as he jumped on the little wheel in his cage and ran for hours, going nowhere.

I remember looking at myself back then; the girl in the mirror never seemed good enough. I wasn't "normal," like the other girls who wore preppy clothes and played soccer. I was overweight with a ball of frizzy hair and a bad case of acne. I liked bugs, played in the dirt with my horses and failed pretty much every math class—three times. Instead of friends, I had stuffed animals, books and Hermie, a conveniently symbolic hermit crab.

Every morning, I'd wake up and try to think of ways to escape the stinging pain I felt when people gawked at me. Whether it was my secret crush telling me I had more jelly rolls than a Krispy Kreme, my computer teacher humiliating me in front of the class after I accidentally threw up my anxiety/lunch on the keyboard, or the real-life Mean Girls throwing my stuffed animals into the woods, I felt as though I couldn't get through the day unscathed. This torment went on from eight to eleven years old, and as the feelings of self-hatred escalated with each humiliating experience, I started to shut down.

I would come home after school every day and lock myself in my pre-teen pink-and-lime-green–colored room. Moseying into the kitchen, stepping over four dogs and a constantly high-strung mother, I'd try to find some comfort in a loaf of Sarasota, Florida's best "French" unfreshly baked bread and butter. I allowed myself to fall down the dark path my bullies were pushing me toward. The way everyone at school treated me became this sort of twisted proof of all the negative thoughts I had about myself. I took one last look at the girl in the mirror, at the girl who was never good enough, and told her good-bye.

During the year that followed, something inside me went cold. I stopped crying because I thought it made me weak. I stopped bringing stuffed animals in my backpack because I thought it made me look weird. I starved myself because I thought my body was disgusting. And in the process, *I* became the bully. If I was hurting inside, I'd criticize someone else. If I wanted something, I'd manipulate everyone around me until I got it. When I felt wronged by the Mean Girls who threw lunch trays at me, I'd go to their lockers and squeeze fifteen packets of mayo inside to rot in the Florida heat as they finished their lunch. I looked strong on the outside, but I was more miserable than ever on the inside. I thought I liked myself, but I was just playing a misguided game to gain control of my life. I was praised for being skeleton-skinny, dressing like the masses and caking on makeup. But this person I had become—and the life I had—wasn't real because everything I had built it from was fake. Over time this buildup reached a breaking point and one day, out of nowhere, I found myself looking into the purple magnetic mirror of my newly preppy locker. The girl staring back at me was still the same but, in some way, more complicated. She was hidden behind more layers of shame and false identity than ever before. The minute the bell rang for the next class, I snapped out of it but I couldn't shake the feeling, or rather, the reality, that I had no idea who I was anymore.

Oddly enough, what helped next was being able to take a break from myself entirely. It was that superpower—the ability to escape who I was and explore any character I chose—that initially attracted me to the idea of becoming an actress. While my first role as a spandex-clad singing eel wasn't my no. 1 choice of identity theft (aka it was a role forced upon me

in a school opera), it did lead me to discover what made me truly happy. I remember being backstage one night, applying makeup in a dusty mirror and thinking to myself, *I've never been happier than I am right now, in this moment, about to perform onstage.*

I eventually decided to sign up for a Florida-based competition called Talent Rocks. When I got there, I looked around at the three thousand divas-in-diapers and singing contortionists standing in line with me and thought, *That's a lot of people who all want to do exactly what I want to do.* I was incredibly intimidated and, before I knew it, the typical insecurities took over. *There is no way I'm going to win this competition,* I said to myself. Rather than withdraw, I thought of how embarrassing it would be to go back home and hide in my room again. So I stayed. And while my Tyra-inspired runway pose didn't win me top honors, I knew I couldn't give up after my first try.

After convincing my parents that a career as an actress was a good idea, I set my sights on LA. What was supposed to be a simple two-week trip turned out to be a complicated whole new life. After a few meetings and getting a manager onboard, I mapped out my own perceived path and just gunned it.

I became a union worker at fourteen, and my first big break was a pilot for ABC called *American Family.* But being a Hollywood newbie, I had to go through a really long casting process first. I started by auditioning in front of the casting director's assistant, then the casting director, then the producers, then the director and then, finally, I did a screen test in front of the network execs. A half hour before the screen tests started, I made my way through the lot and into the lobby of the studio. In a grandiose setting, complete with marble pillars and forty-foot sculptures, little old me (well, little young me; I was fourteen) sat in an awkwardly spacious waiting area in a stiff, oversized leather chair directly across from the two girls I'd be competing against for the role. One girl, in the neighboring leather chair, was drop-dead gorgeous (and knew it). The other girl was already famous (and knew it), and just when I couldn't be more intimidated, it was my turn to test. I did the scene and looked around for laughs, but the men in suits just wore their poker faces. Of course, shortly after I'd finished, the already-famous girl came out laughing to herself. She walked with such absolute confidence, commanding the huge lobby (an impressive feat for any pubescent teenager), that I was sure that she had been given the role in the room. While she stuck around to talk to the casting director, I joined Ms. Drop-Dead Gorgeous Girl on the longest elevator ride ever. Ding . . . Ding . . . Ding . . . Ding . . . A million floors or so later we reached the parking garage. A disingenuous and forced smile crossed her face. "Good luck!" she said, breaking the uncomfortable silence. In more silence, my mother and I rode home in our pre-owned Saturn SUV. As soon as I got home, I went straight to the kitchen. I started to pick out some comfort food (my old guilty pleasure of bread and butter), when my phone rang. It was *the* call. I picked up my bedazzled flip phone and, before I could even say hello, my manager screamed emphatically, "YOU GOT IT!!!" I was ecstatic. As I jumped up and down in my kitchen on the old floors in a crappy apartment, I knew that this was the beginning of a new life, a new me . . . a new *everything*.

This "new life" seemed like the perfect happy ending. Time went by and before I knew it, I had a successful acting career, friends and even a boyfriend. But it still wasn't enough. I wanted to be the best at *everything*, and when I saw other actors doing cooler projects than I was, it reminded me of my old life when I didn't think I was good enough. I was scared all the time—as if someone was going to discover this significantly less appealing version of me; just Ashley from Sarasota. After three years in LA, that fear really started taking its toll. Tired and depressed and desperately trying to control the sinking fear that the girl in the mirror was going to come out and ruin it all for me, I let that fear and darkness escalate with each day. I willingly altered *who* I was in *whatever* way I had to in order to be exactly what *everyone* else wanted me to be.

This insidious trial and ever-error eventually came to a head when I found myself sitting in my room after another breakup with another boyfriend and another movie role that I didn't get, and I realized something. Up until that moment, my journey to this "happy ending" had been nothing more than the crescendo of old scars, and I was right back to square 1. I hadn't moved on from my past; I'd just been running from it, once again letting myself go to that familiar dark place. I hadn't changed at all. So, three thousand miles from Florida, I realized I had lost myself yet again because I had never fully found myself to begin with.

> So, three thousand miles from Florida, I realized I had lost myself yet again because I had never fully found myself to begin with. So I set out to get my sh!t together, for real this time—and it wasn't easy.

So I set out to get my sh!t together for real this time—and it wasn't easy. Occasionally there would be a specialized book to help me, like the comfort I found in the various paperbacks about acne "cures," but I never had any clarity on the important things, like how to live my life without being a slave to my own self-doubt. Sometimes well-meaning friends would offer me advice, but it always turned into a mass of conflicting dos and don'ts. I'd pick up a magazine that promised a cover star who was finally "opening up" about her insecurities, but I'd finish it only knowing what she ordered for lunch. All I wanted was someone to give me honest advice without the bubblegum bullsh!t. Those magazines, books and chain emails made me feel like a first-generation Siri was guiding me through life, with the language setting on Elfin.

Then I realized: The only surefire way to work out a path for my life was if I worked on myself—*my real self.* I looked at the girl in the mirror, thinking about her past, and I knew I wanted something better for her future. She wasn't broken—she was just human. *I* was just human. While I wasn't perfect, I knew I didn't have to miss out on life any longer. I no longer had to hate myself or change myself, nor did I have to be anything less than the person I wanted and deserved to be.

The truth is, I can't ignore the past and I can't just *hope* for a better future. I needed to (and still do) work on the little things every day in order to impact my life in a big way. Once I knew who I was at the core, I had the tools to guide myself from the inside toward being the best I can be on the outside. This inspired (and required) me to design some tools and tricks to help myself live every day as best I can. Each one of my tried-and-true methods reflects this idea of creating simplicity out of our complex lives, unique paths and individual challenges—while digging deeper than the surface.

Today, with my own methods and great mentors around me, I can be the best and truest version of myself. I no longer need GPS to search for happiness, because the power to find that happiness lies within myself. From the deepest self-acceptance to a simple, customized daily routine and plan, I feel at peace knowing my outside is a reflection of my truth on the inside. Now, I can say that I love myself for who I am: *the girl in the mirror*. I am who I am and where I am meant to be, simply because that is where I am in this moment. I'll never regret the past, because who I was then helped me evolve into exactly who I am today and gives me the ability to share with you, real girls just like me, how I was able to start getting my sh!t together for good. (Really.)

PART

1

YOU LOVING YOU

Lookin' at (You) in the Mirror

CHAPTER 1

INNER SELF

YOU ACCEPTING YOU

MY EXPERIENCE: THAT ONE TIME
WHEN I FOUND MYSELF

AS YOU MIGHT'VE GUESSED FROM THE INTRO, the amount of time I've spent bashing myself is unbelievable. And you thought I was done sharing? Oh, get ready. I'm going deeper.

Another way you could define those younger years is that I had major control issues. While it's not a bad thing to be accountable for your own actions, I don't think I'm alone when I say that I've taken it way too far. It would go something like this: set huge expectations for myself, carefully outline all possible consequences for failure, neurotically (#MonkStyle) work down to the most minuscule details of the task at hand, ignore all other aspects of my life while doing so, eventually complete the task, search desperately for any hint of failure and torture myself in my own cell of perfectionism (which normally included lots of sighs). My reasoning was well-intentioned—learn from my mistakes in order to do better next time. However, in my usual extremist way of life, the punishment at the end of these perceived failures—not getting the part in a movie, a botched paint job during a home decorating project or another breakup with another guy—escalated.

At first it was as simple as staying in for the night and replaying the situation over and over in my mind until I found a foolproof way to do it better. But a few years of these self-esteem–slaughtering sessions turned into total self-sabotage, laziness and depression. I thought, *Why try? I'm such a f!ckup anyway*.

So, I stopped trying.

I no longer followed my instincts surrounding each role I was cast in; I just played it safe (aka predictable). I refused to put myself out there socially, because I felt worthless and didn't want to burden anyone by befriending them. What was the point anyway? I felt I wasn't worth it, let alone being worthy enough of all my grand plans for my future. I thought my hopes and dreams were just as much of a time-consuming fantasy as my wasting time trying to accomplish what I thought was impossible for someone like me. So I stopped dreaming.

My perspective was askew and because I knew I'd been a negative person for so long, I had no idea how to turn my poor outlook into a positive one.

> The turning point for me came on the heels of these words: "When we realize that our true self is one of pure potentiality, we align ourselves with the power that manifests everything in the universe." My mind was blown and my eyes were opened to a new way of thinking and being.

Yet, I was fortunate enough to come across the works of Deepak Chopra. The turning point for me came on the heels of these words: "When we realize that our true self is one of pure potentiality, we align ourselves with the power that manifests everything in the universe." My mind was blown and my eyes were opened to a new way of thinking and being. A week or so later, I went outside on an unusually cold Los Angeles night and looked up at the sky. Then, in an absolutely cheese-tastic moment, I was struck by a Carl Sagan–style (he was an astronomer) epiphany.

Within this vast universe lay countless celestial bodies far beyond that which we are able to see. In the observable universe reside an estimated (by scientists and stuff) 100 billion galaxies. In each of those galaxies there are over hundreds of millions of stars and another, still estimated, 100 billion planets. Out of those planets, only 10 billion are in a precise position to theoretically support life. And then there is Earth—home to more than 6.5 billion people. As I looked around that night, I imagined the world and its inhabitants.

I realized that I am part of an inconceivable reality that is the result of perfectly timed chaos, which gave birth to the possibility of this entire planet.

So to think that the only reason I "am" is because of some sort of perfectly timed coagulation of seemingly random events—that's a miracle. Simply that I exist.

Suddenly, I saw the world I previously thought I knew, the world I hated and thought hated me . . . change. It was working with such intricacy that there was no mistaking that age-old idea—destiny. If the universe and its players (I am *not* referring to that guy who broke your heart) were in the exact place, at the exact moment, exactly as that moment is, there was a reason I'd made it to this point. Against all dorky, scientific odds, not only was I part of the seemingly inexplicable reasoning of the universe, but simply by changing my thinking, I had the power to decide my destiny. I had nothing to worry about because I couldn't control anything other than how I *chose* to be in each moment.

You Accepting You

This truly is the core of which all *genuine* change is built; it is the foundational first step of all the chapters to come. Once you have these basics down, you are ready to begin the book. If you feel as if you haven't aced this chapter, just remember: *It's not a test and it's not a race.* (And I'm not your intimidatingly loud/always screaming PE teacher.) You don't have to be perfect or even close to start reading more right away. It's OK to make mistakes and even more OK to make this your own! You know yourself and are familiar now with the tools you will need moving forward. And since I'm not a Barbie doll writing this book with plastic hands and fingers that don't separate—I am a real human who's gone through a lot of sh!t—I will not censor myself with you guys. In fact, not only will the word *tampon* be in this book but I'm also going to actually explain my advice in depth, sometimes with pictures, sometimes with words (never with tampons). Then you will finally have the answers you need, make the improvements that are right for you and even #FollowMeOnTwitter! (I'm kidding.)

DEEPAK CHOPRA, a really, really famous spiritual coach

His Philosophy on Life: I have only one mantra: "Easy come, easy go." I just take it easy. I just flow. I want to have a joyful, energetic body, which I do. I want to have a restful, alert mind, which I do. And I want to have a lightness of being, which I do. My purpose, my ultimately big goal is to reach 100 million people who will personally transform, so the world will transform in a good direction—toward peace, social justice, economic justice, sustainability, and good health and happiness. That's it.

From Deepak: Demystifying Spirituality
(IT'S COOLER THAN YOU THINK!)

Spirituality only means self-awareness; that's all. It doesn't mean anything more esoteric. If you don't know yourself, then you'll never know the world, because in every situation you bring yourself into that situation. If that's clear, then spirituality as self-awareness will give you true self-esteem—depending on others for your self-image won't.

And there's a big confusion between *self-image* and *self-esteem*. Self-image is what other people think of you. Self-esteem is knowing yourself and seeing that you are empowered just as you are. Many of the problems that teens have is because of this one confusion. They confuse how other people see them and label them with who they truly are. If you know yourself, you can harness your intuition and creativity and imagination in a way that you never would be able to otherwise.

You're Special and I Know It

Spoiler alert: You rock. Whoever you are, whatever you look like—you're perfect. Who you are in this moment is exactly who you are meant to be right now. Every little quirk you have—be it a cowlick or a mole—makes you unique. Freckles? Awesome. I have freckles on my arm, and if I connect them all with a Sharpie they make the Big Dipper. I've also got a freckle on my boob, and while it doesn't outline an ancient map of the gods, it's mine. It's part of me, and therefore I love it. An old woman in CVS once told me, "You're like a snowflake—one of a kind." And while I had to go buy some Pepto-Bismol to control the sudden cheese-induced nausea, I understood her point. I'm just fine as I am because it is who I am in this moment and, for better or worse, I should embrace it. And no, you don't have to give yourself a bear hug or a weird pat on the back; you just have to know that you're unique. Freakin' own it!

From Deepak: How to Start Loving Yourself

The first thing to keep in mind: It's such a waste of time to be hard on yourself—so many other people have the opportunity to do that for you. Look at the statistical probability of you existing—out of 300 million sperm, one made it. Then there were all kinds of obstacles along the way before that. The fact that you exist is a total miracle of the total universe, so just enjoy it. You're a winner to start with.

Now, observing yourself without judging yourself is the highest form of intelligence. When you observe yourself without judging yourself, you have insight into your own motivations and into your own behavior and by and by you change. There's nothing more valuable than observing yourself, as I said, without judging yourself. That's the first step. Ask yourself the questions we ask everyone: . . . The answers to these questions will unleash your creativity.

1. Who am I?

2. What do I want?

3. What's my purpose in life?

4. What am I grateful for?

5. What are my unique strengths?

6. How do I help other people?

How *I* Learned to Love Myself

After reading lots of Deepak, and a few e-how articles, of course, I wrote down a list of all my quirks, positives and fun facts about who I am. A few minutes later (OK, it took a little longer . . .) my little Q&A morphed into the following "Me Me Me" list. This helped me really delve into who I am and discover some of the little things about myself that I hadn't realized made me unique. Being part of the masses is fine and frankly inevitable in the macro scheme of things, but there's a certain je ne sais quoi that makes me feel, at the risk of sounding blunt, valued for my uniqueness. When I feel unique, I feel worthy of happiness. So, this is just a fun worksheet for you guys to really solidify who you are before we get started. And unless you're a fan of constant self-loathing and sabotage (#snoozefest), I promise you'll have fun doing this. As with all the worksheets, feel free to expand on your answers in a journal.

THE "ME ME ME" LIST

ABOUT YOU

List five positive things about your personality.

....

....

....

....

....

List five things you would like to improve on.

....

....

....

....

....

List ten things that make you unique (not just physical things like boob freckles).

....

....

....

....

....

....

....

....

....

....

Where were you born?...

What is your zodiac sign?...

What is your heritage?..

What color is your hair?................. What color are your eyes?.......

Do you have freckles?................... How tall are you?...............

What schools have you gone to?..

Have you ever had to move? Where?...

Where do you live now? Do you like it?..

....

If you have a full- or part-time job, what do you do? Do you like it?..

....

....

How would you describe your personality?..

....

Which personality trait is your favorite?...

FIRSTS

What is your very first memory?...

....

If you've taken some trips, when and where did you go on your first trip?..

....

When was the first time you drove a car?..

When was your first kiss and who was it with?..

Who was your first significant other? ....

If you have, when did you lose your virginity and to whom? How did you feel about it?..

....

When did you first fall deeply in love? ....

....

When was your first breakup and who was it with? Did it end amicably? ....

....

FAVORITES

What is your favorite color and why? ....

What is your favorite food and why? ....

What is your favorite song and why? ....

What is your favorite movie and why? ....

What is your favorite book and why? ....

What is your favorite time period and why? ....

What is your favorite car and why? ....

What is your favorite topic of conversation? ....

HOBBIES AND INTERESTS

What is your favorite subject and why (fashion, philosophy, etc.)? ....

....

If you could start studying something new, what subject would you choose? ....

What are your hobbies? Name three. ....

....

Do you enjoy practicing your hobbies alone or with friends? ....

What is one hobby you have yet to try but would like to? ....

What are four other hobbies that entice you? ....

....

BEST AND WORST

What was the happiest moment of your life so far? What made it so? ....

....

....

What was the worst moment of your life so far? What happened? ....

....

....

Who is the most inspiring person you know? ....

Who is the most inspiring person you have yet to meet? ....

What is the best dream you've ever had? Why? ....

....

....

What is the worst nightmare you've ever had? What happened in it? ....

....

....

What is the weirdest coincidence you've ever encountered? Do you think it meant something? ....

....

Describe what a perfect day looks like to you. ....

What is the sweetest thing anyone has ever done for you? How did it make you feel? ....

What is the sweetest thing you've ever done for someone else? ....

PET PEEVES

What is the single most annoying habit a person can have? (We all have one super-irrational pet peeve, mine being when everyone on the freeway slows down to a snail's pace to look at a car accident.)

Do you have any pet peeves about inanimate objects (for example, logo T-shirts)? ....

DISLIKES

What are you allergic to? ....

What's your least favorite food? ....

Which song annoys the sh!t out of you? ....

What's the worst movie you've ever seen or just hated? Why? ....

What's your least favorite book? ....

What's your least favorite topic of conversation? Why? ....

IF . . .

If you won the lottery, what would you do with your winnings?

If you could be any superhero or have a superpower, what would it be? Why?

If all your dreams came true, where would you like to be five years from now?

If you found "the one" tomorrow, would you want to get married?

Do you want to have children someday?

What does your dream house look like?

At what point in your life do you feel that you could die happy?

What goals would you like to accomplish in order to feel fulfilled?

BELIEFS

What is your basic philosophy of life?

Do you believe in reincarnation? Why or why not?

Do you believe in ghosts? Why or why not?

Do you think aliens exist? Why or why not?

Do you believe in soul mates? Why or why not?

What do you think happens after death?

If you follow a certain religious denomination, what is it and does it resonate with you?

If you don't follow any one denomination, what are some of your basic spiritual beliefs and morals?

What are the most important values of your belief system?

How do you define ethics and morals?

Do you believe that you practice your own ideals?

POLITICS

What political party would or do you subscribe to? ....

Are your political beliefs different than those of your parents? ....

What are your most strongly held political beliefs? ....

....

Do you think the world will be a better place in fifty years? ....

If not, what do you think you could do to make it a better place? ....

....

NEVER DONE BEFORE

What is something you have always wanted to try, but haven't been able to do yet? What's stopping you? If you could travel to a place you've never been before, where would you go and why?

....

....

What's an activity that interests you, but you haven't pursued yet? Why do you think you haven't yet? ....

....

....

Affirmations: I'm Confirming That Affirming Works

With all of your quirks, I know it can be hard to love yourself as is. I used to say horrible things about myself. In fact, I didn't even realize just how much I talked myself down until I started talking myself up. So, with that, I'll bet you don't even realize how many negative things you say to yourself on a daily basis. We all make fun of ourselves here and there (and hey, it's good to be humble), but you shouldn't habitually make your butt the butt of your jokes. The spoken word holds a lot of power—literally. Whatever you put out into the universe—verbally or physically—is manifested, and with that great power comes the great responsibility not to misuse it. If you keep saying negative things about yourself, you're going to end up believing them—and so will those around you.

So the next time you find yourself being your own hater, take a step back and (to yourself) counter your own verbal b!tch slap with an opposing comment. For example, let's say you pigged out at Outback Steakhouse and afterward you said to yourself, "Ugh, I look pregnant." Immediately say or think to yourself, "I am a beautiful person, that meal was the sh!t, and thank God I am not actually preggers because college sounds effing awesome." Or let's say you're with friends and calculating a tip. Maybe you got the percentage wrong and are tempted to say something to the group like, "I'm an idiot with this math stuff." Take a metaphorical step back from the table and say (out loud) "I'm not an idiot. Math just isn't my strongest area."

Affirmations are a great way to kick off the practice of thinking more positively. These are my affirmations, made into a guide to help you fill in your own blanks. When doing these, do not be self-conscious. Dream big and be honest! There is no need to share your affirmations with others—you have nothing to prove to them. Your affirmations are for *you* and you alone, simply to give yourself the gift of truth. Use this system, or customize one of your own, and you'll also confirm that affirmations work.

> **EXPERT SECRET:** More important than affirmations are self-reflection, self-awareness and stillness. But affirmations work because you introduce a thought that influences your perception, your thinking and your behavior. The more you create a groove for that in your brain, the more that will influence who you become. It's just a groove in the neural networks of your brain. —Deepak

AFFIRM THAT (GOOD) SH!T

DISCLAIMER: These are my personal affirmations. Feel free to switch things up and add your own! All you need to do is think about your wants, beliefs, hopes and dreams—**then begin each with "I can and will" or "I am."**

I AM...

I am perfect right now, for right now.

I am strong (for my size).

I am intelligent.

I am unique.

I am beautiful.

I am funny.

I am caring.

I am talented.

I CAN AND WILL...

I can and will succeed.

I can and will successfully balance all the aspects of my life (sans unicycle).

I can and will do little things now that shape the bigger aspects of my life each day.

I can and will accept and survive anything that comes my way (sharp objects aside).

I can and will treat myself with respect.

I can and will treat others with the respect they deserve. (Sorry about my road rage, Los Angeles.)

AWAITING ME...

If and when the time is right, an award for my acting awaits me. (Critics and voters: I'm not arrogant, this is every actor's dream!)

If and when the time is right, a successful literary career, full of screenplays, poetry and books awaits me.

If and when the time is right, my very own jewelry line awaits me.

If and when the time is right, a wonderful family of my own awaits me. (Relax, I'm gonna take the necessary precautions for a while.)

If and when the time is right, my own production company awaits me.

If and when the time is right, anything I desire awaits me (mostly talking about some shoes I saw at Bloomingdale's).

ADD YOUR OWN...

....

....

....

From Deepak: Meditation Isn't Just for Old Yogis

On an immediate level, meditation decreases stress, lowers your blood pressure, boosts your immune system, gives you better-quality sleep and harnesses your creativity and intuition. It's science—seriously! But that's just the beginning.

The long-term benefit is that you shift your identity so it expands. You realize you are more than who you thought you were and that you are actually a spiritual being having a human experience for the time being. You lose your fear of death and basically you have lightness of being.

TO DO A BASIC MEDITATION

Sit quietly and be aware of your breathing. Then tell your mind to settle into your breath. Tell your mind to become one with your breath. Any time your mind starts to wander (as it naturally will), bring yourself to the present moment by bringing your attention to your breathing. Your breathing is always in the present moment. It's not in the past or the future. Your thoughts are either in the past or the future, but your breath is now, so bring your attention to your breath.

. . . Back to Me! My Meditation Strategy

I find almost every type of meditation practice to be helpful, but the idea behind my favorite method is something I call *activation*. (I do at least thirty minutes of meditation in the morning, and twenty minutes at night.) Ninety percent of it is about visualizing. It could take many, many sessions, but eventually the insecurities that inspired your affirmations will go away, because you'll no longer believe in them. It's like what Deepak said earlier—positive thinking helps create a "groove" in your brain. The more you exercise those positive thoughts, the stronger they'll become. You will enter a field of pure potentiality, relax in the most effective way and learn to live in the present. It takes a while to come to that peace, but you will.

Before you begin, find your list of affirmations and place it beside you. Then write down a comprehensive list of people you want to wish well and what you selflessly want for them. It could be as simple as happiness for a stranger you saw that day.

LET'S GET STARTED

Note: If you have any thoughts or distractions during the meditation, visualize those distractions moving into a cloud, and watch that cloud drift away.

Begin by playing some soothing music—soundscapes, perhaps. Focus on your breath. As you clear your mind, visualize your lungs. Imagine them inflating and deflating as you inhale and exhale. Do this until your mind is cleared of everything going on in the outside world. Focus on your body. As you delve into this quiet and intimate place, imagine yourself in a white space. Feel yourself weightlessly held there. Take in this space and, in your mind's eye, look down. Visualize a metallic sea below you. As you gradually lower yourself into this space, cradled in safety by a feeling of comfort, visualize a light. This light somehow guides you into this sea, the field of infinite possibility.

As your feet begin to sink into this field, you will feel a physical sensation, much like the sensation of love. (I think of it almost like butterflies taking over your feet.) Focus on that physicality as it moves over your ankles, your legs, up your torso and slowly over your head. While each part of you enters this field, notice how your physical body dissolves. Soon you are no longer constricted by the physicality of your body, but are now one and completely connected to and enmeshed in this field. Your body floats in the universe as a moving part. Focus on this oneness. Think of your affirmations. As they float into the infinite possibility that you are now part of, they become fact. Focus on the people you wish good thoughts to. Think of these wishes now, as they also become fact. Breathe. Now release into the field of possibility the dreams for your future. Now released, they are no longer dreams, but working parts of the universe—bound to come to fruition. Stay in this peaceful space for a few moments, and then come back to the present. Find yourself back in your physical space and open your eyes.

Now, I know you might be sitting there feeling way skeptical. And I get that—meditation can be tricky and takes some practice and getting used to, but by practicing this method, I know I've become a better person (a side effect of the obvious relaxation benefits). After my first time, little things no longer frustrated me. I was in a state of acceptance and inner peace because I was still connected to the universe throughout the day. As an actress, I'm better able to feel every emotion and each one is more intense. Meditation has not only changed my life, it has saved it.

Belief: The Inner Joy and Outside Suppressants

There are those wonderful days when you wake up in a peaceful state of mind and feel ready to take on life . . . and then you inevitably step outside and cross paths with a hater and everything turns to sh!t. I knew I couldn't always avoid the randos yelling at me in traffic or a coworker gossiping behind my back, but these hater gators started to gain power over me. I would listen to them, even if I knew it was just their insecurity or negative outlook (they were probably just jealous of my awesome sweatpants). Each time I did that, though, I lost sight of my potential. No longer did I fully trust what I believed in my heart, so I had to find a way to expose myself to this negativity while maintaining an unwavering confidence. It wasn't easy; however, after a little practice and building a metaphorical firewall, I found a way to protect the happiness I felt inside, regardless of what anyone said or did to me. I focus on who I am and remember that the only way someone can rob me of my natural-born right to be happy is if I *let* them. When I listen to my own gut, my own positivity, I am indestructible. And to be unwaveringly confident in who you are and what you can be, well, that's a pretty freakin' powerful feeling.

From Deepak: How to Deal with Sh!tty People

Start with the presumption that you can't change another person, ever. The only person that you have influence over is yourself. When you deal with difficult people, there are certain rules you can follow:

1. **Don't try to prove another person wrong.**
   Use emotional intelligence, which means you feel what you feel, but it's important to try to feel what they feel, too.

2. Communicate consciously.

Ask people what they are observing, what they are feeling, why they are feeling threatened. How can you help them? The less insolent you are, the more likely you are to get your own needs met. Always end your request with a question mark and not with an exclamation point. You might say, "I observe that you raised the volume of your voice. I felt threatened. I need to feel safe. Will you please not raise the volume of your voice?" Don't get angry.

Be Your Own Yes-Woman
(AND GET A FEW OTHER BACKUP YES-WOMEN)

Seek motivation from within yourself. The secret to achieving this is by never believing anyone who tells you "No" or "You can't do that." I'm not talking about your mom's warning against bungee jumping without a cord; I'm referencing the bigger things. Hell, I was just fourteen years old when I packed my bags for California with little to no guarantee of success. But I did it anyway, because I knew I could. I didn't ask my friends, "Hey, do you think I should leave my life here and try to become an actress like the thousands of other people who have tried with only intermittent measures of success?" I knew what they would say ("Hell, nah!"), and they would've had every right to say it—my idea was crazy. I didn't care, though. I wanted it, and I searched within myself for the motivation to do it. I gave myself permission to take a risk. I said yes on my own.

The same goes for the most difficult times in life—the times where we didn't choose what was given to us. Whether it's a horrible breakup with the man of your dreams, a cataclysmic school crisis or a death in the family, you have the power inside to will yourself through whatever life throws at you. With each day, a new challenge may arise, but you can say yes and muster the strength to get through it. We only know how brave we are when we are forced to be brave. If you go through each day knowing that you are absolutely capable of handling whatever that day may hold, you will become stronger than all your yesterdays combined. All you have to do is say yes and go forward.

Now, I'm not suggesting you *only* listen to yourself or that you solely rely on yourself forever. There will be times when you need help. Asking for help does not mean you are incompetent or a failure. When you need help, ask for it, but make sure you ask someone who supports you fully in your journey or whatever the task is at hand. In this sense, make sure that in times of need, when you struggle to be your own yes-woman, that you have a backup yes-woman. If you can't find a backup yes-woman in a friend or family member or coworker, think of a few people who've inspired you. Print out some of your favorite quotes to motivate yourself in the morning to have a great day. Some of mine are on the next page.

Listen to the Positive
TONY LITTLE SAYS YOU CAN DO IT

I know how hard it is to take a compliment. It is so easy to read too far into a well-intentioned one and look for a hidden insult. The key is just to take a compliment for what it is (to do that, before you're tempted to say anything else, just say "thank you"). Even if someone compliments you on something that embarrasses you or touches on an insecurity, be flattered. They see a beauty inside you, whether or not you appreciate it yet. Take those kind words and run with them. I suggest keeping a mental note of these compliments. If they come in a card, keep the card, especially the really great ones (drug store shout-out!). When you're having a hard day and can't snap yourself out of it, think back to all those people who believe in you. If they can believe in you, you can believe in yourself. Appreciate the positive and let it help you.

Humble It Up!

By now, you probably (hopefully!) have more confidence, dreams and hopes. The next step is being humble about it. While you're destined for something amazing, it doesn't bode well to share these things willy-nilly with anyone with ears. Remember, these things are for *you*. Think of them as a secret truth that only you know. That being said, there are some people you *should* feel comfortable sharing your deepest thoughts and desires with, but make sure that they value you enough to respect your privacy. Share them with your mom, unless you feel that she will lecture you. Share them with your best friend, unless you think she will blab. Share them with your boyfriend, and even if he doesn't understand quite what you're talking about, that's OK (boys are dumb), just as long as he respects you and who you are enough to keep from mocking your intimate dreams.

*You must be the change you wish
to see in the world.*
—MAHATMA GANDHI

*Be who you are and say what you feel
because those who mind don't matter
and those who matter don't mind.*
—DR. SEUSS

*Live as if you'll die tomorrow. Dream
as if you'll live forever.*
—JAMES DEAN (Not the guy dressed as the sun in those
commercials—that's Jimmy Dean)

*Life is not futile. You may find love,
serenity and action in every moment
along the beautiful journey.*
—ASHLEY RICKARDS (Yup, I say smart things, too.)

*An eye for an eye leaves
the whole world blind.*
—MAHATMA GANDHI (Plus the eye shadow
industry would totally go out of business.)

*Don't judge each day by the harvest
you reap, but by the seeds you plant.*
—ROBERT LOUIS STEVENSON

Discipline comes from within.
—CHINESE PROVERB (I heard it on *South Park*, though.)

*This is as it is meant to be. That is
meant to be what it is. Because this
and that are all there is.*
—ASHLEY RICKARDS (Wow, I'm, like, deep.)

*History repeats itself, but each time
the price is higher.*
—PROVERB FROM SOMEWHERE
(but I saw it on my dry cleaner's whiteboard)

*A successful man is one who can lay a
firm foundation with the bricks others
have thrown at him.*
—DAVID BRINKLEY

*You must know you can swim
through every change of tide.*
—THIS WAS ON MY YOGI TEA
(but apparently my dry cleaner had the same tea)

*Nothing is ever late. Everything that is
meant to be is exactly on schedule.*
—ASHLEY RICKARDS (excludes periods)

*That which does not kill us
makes us stronger.*
—FRIEDRICH NIETZSCHE
(Yeah, Kanye publicly nabbed that one, too.)

*Comparing yourself to others is
to compare your insides to someone
else's outsides.*
—OLD ADAGE

*Life isn't a problem to be solved
but a mystery to be lived.*
**—A LOT OF PEOPLE HAVE SAID THIS A LOT
OF DIFFERENT WAYS.** (They're dead now.)

Just remember that you're doing this for yourself. You have nothing to prove!

BELIEVE IT, BUT DON'T BRAG (FACEBOOK STATUSES ARE NOT A DIARY)

Remember that you bought this book for you. Think of it as a diary of sorts. The deepest parts of you will be unveiled so that your own true light can shine through. You'll get to a point in this book where you feel so good that you'll want to tell the world how confident you feel. Hold back—part of becoming the best version of yourself is to be humble. Instead, recommend the book so that others can benefit from it, too. This is neither a competition nor a guide to perfection. There are no scores or winners; there are only those who "do." All you need to do is try. There is no need to brag about everything you are feeling, learning and improving on.

Fearlessness: Be Afraid…Be Very Afraid…of Being Afraid

There was a time (many times) when I was so afraid of failing or possible pain that I stopped trying anything—from getting on the scale, to doing a screen test (because I probably wouldn't get the huge role after all), to just going out with a friend in case I said anything wrong. I would be stuck in fear of what might happen or that I wasn't good enough. Whether or not it was rational didn't matter at the time. There wasn't anyone who could console me or quell those fears. So I became a flake. If the stress became overwhelming and I got scared, I'd cancel whatever I had that day and sit at home watching TV under a blanket, hiding out from things that hadn't even happened.

That fear kept me from some amazing experiences and left me pretty much alone—with only a feeling of worthlessness. Which I now know, thanks to a gazillion dorky articles, is due to a few things—including the ways fear is interpreted in the brain, aka "fear conditioning" and "fear extinction." (Relax. You don't need a deep-repair mask for your fear follicles.) The idea is that not only do we have fears based on our life experiences so far but we can also develop new fears every day by conditioning our brains to react a certain way toward these (real or imagined) stimuli, and our unconscious brain activity that makes it so.

OK, I'm going to go out on a metaphorical limb and guess that what I just said only made a little sense to you. So for the sake of "Why, Ashley, why?" let's just get all technical up in here. Don't worry, you don't have to be a brain surgeon to understand this—and don't freak if you can't pronounce some of the words ahead right away (I tried and it's really hard).

FEAR RESPONSES: OMFG!!! AND WHATEVS

Your brain interprets fear in two ways simultaneously. This first one, which I'll just call the "OMFG!!!" response (that will not be on the SATs), is a bit messy and impulsive. Let's say you're walking down a crowded street, and you think someone is following you. You look behind you and see a few sketchy-looking people—they're your "stimulus." Your brain sends this sensory data to a part of your brain called the thalamus. There, inside the part of your brain that you are probably thinking must look like a llama, the thalamus processes that information and tries to determine if it is, in fact, danger. Then your OMFG!!! response would initiate the thalamus to assume it *is* danger. The llama-looking brain part then passes it along to another part of your brain called the amygdala. This amygdala will get a bit panicky, so it'll just press the insta-fear button in order to protect you from the original stimulus and alert the hypothalamus to activate the fight-or-flight response. Then, in a much faster fashion than this paragraph would suggest, you immediately see the creeper as dangerous and think—you guessed it—"*OMFG!!!*" Then you either run or, like, hit the dude with your purse while yelling "Fire!!"

While your brain is busy with the OMFG!!! response, it is also processing fear in another way at the same time. I'll nickname this the "whatevs" response. Rewind back before you hit the stranger over the head with your purse, cuz we're gonna take it back and show how the whatevs response works in the same scenario. OK, so you're walking down the crowded street and you think someone is following you. You look behind you and see a few sketchy-looking people. These people are, again, the stimulus. As you look at them, your brain sends this info to the thalamus. The llama-thing then spits out that information to the sensory cortex, which interprets the info. Your sensory cortex will be all rational and determine that there's probably another side to the "stranger-danger" fear it received. So it passes that info along to the hippocampus to establish context. The hippocampus then thinks back to any other times that resembled the stranger-danger scenario, factors in those past responses and comes up with a conclusion. The hippocampus will deduce that you should chill because the creepers are probably just normal dudes, and send a memo to the amygdala, which then goes back to the hypothalamus and tells it to turn off the fight-or-flight response and just be, like, whatevs.

The whatevs response isn't a totally dismissive douche and the OMFG!!! response isn't a crazy b!tch, because they happen simultaneously and give you two very different (some might say complementary) options when gauging your fear factors. Regardless of which response kicks in, both of them lead back to the hypothalamus, which is the portion of your brain that controls your fight-or-flight response, which is governed by something called fear conditioning, which can be alleviated by fear extinction.

FEAR CONDITIONING AND FEAR EXTINCTION

I don't want you to feel self-conscious or confused about your fears, so before we get to killing some of them off, I'm going to explain how you may have gotten those fears in the first place. In the 1920s there was this dude named John Watson (please do not picture Jude Law right now . . . ugh, #distracted) who did something kind of crazy but proved a point by doing it. He taught a small child to fear mice. That little kid had no prior fear of mice. In fact, during the experiment, he really liked the mice and tried to pet them a lot. But John Watson (STOP THINKING ABOUT JUDE LAW!!) used classical Pavlovian conditioning and paired a neutral stimulus, the mice, with a negative effect. In this experiment, when the child would reach out for the mice, that motion would be accompanied by a loud noise right behind him. This little kid (his name was Albert) started to associate what he saw (the neutral stimulus) with the noise that scared him, and soon he saw the whole sitch as terrifying and began to fear mice and did so throughout the rest of his life. What Jude Law did here—sh!t, I mean, what John Watson did here—was exploit the idea that fear is a product of conditioning. To put that into context, if a bee had stung you in the past, you may still fear bees to this day. This is because you associate the sight of bees with the painful sting you encountered in the past and therefore recoil as a result of that negative experience. You've been conditioned to fear it.

On the flip side, you can also use this method of conditioning to sort of reverse-condition your fears in a process called fear extinction. Eighty years later, there was another dude who also experimented with mice (not the child; he was in retirement at this point). Mark Barad, a scientist at UCLA, performed an experiment in which he created a fear in lab mice by producing a sound in the mice's cage that was followed by a small electroshock. The mice, of course, began to condition themselves, and upon hearing the sound that Mark produced, they would immediately brace themselves for the shock. Then Mark started the process of fear extinction. He did so by applying the now-feared sound without the electroshock. After the mice heard the sound without the shock many times, they stopped fearing the noise. So, the idea behind fear extinction is creating another conditioned response to counter the original conditioned fear response. A bunch of studies (like a lot, which I don't care to list), note that the amygdala seems to be where the fear memories are located—the same memories that are formed through fear conditioning and play a big part in the different fear responses your brain goes through. However, scientists are now theorizing that the new fear extinction memories are transferred from the amygdala into your medial prefrontal cortex for storage, which then attempts to override the old fear memories in your amygdala and instead helps you overcome the fear with your new positive, or neutral, fear extinction memories.

Now, you've got a lot of info right now, so I'll give you the CliffsNotes version: your brain has two simultaneous but different reactions to fear (OMFG and whatevs), both of which lead back to the hypothalamus. The hypothalamus governs your fight-or-flight response, based on brain chemistry but also fear conditioning—what you've learned to fear in your life so far. The good news is that you can overcome this conditioning by practicing fear extinction and recondition yourself not to fear the things you once feared as a conditioned response.

PRACTICING FEAR EXTINCTION

OK, so, let's all just focus on me right now. Specifically, thinking back to that time I was lying on the couch when I was hiding from my fears. At any given time, I would let my fears control me. Whether it was when they told me to avoid the screen test for *Awkward* (which would become an international hit) or when they told me I was fat and food was the problem (I wasn't and it wasn't).

When you give up without trying, you might as well have failed. Your mind overcompensates with a rationale: "I'm glad I skipped that. It would've been a disaster." By chickening out, you end up feeling even more useless and depressed. And the next time a situation similar to the one you avoided occurs, again you flake—and who can blame you? You've never tried it before.

But you need to learn how to move through the fear and expectations and just f!cking do it. Once you push yourself that first time, and realize that you didn't die just from, like, talking to someone sort of intimidating, you'll learn to shake off that fear. Good news: Right here, right now is the moment you can begin to conquer your fears with a little fear extinction, aka exposure therapy. (Flashing of genitalia not suggested.)

CLOSURE WITH EXPOSURE

Remember how the mice we talked about earlier were trained not to fear the thing they were taught to fear through fear conditioning? Well, don't think of yourself as a lab rat, but keep that scientific breakthrough in mind. The added negative stimuli of the past triggered fear conditioning, but, as later proven, when we replace the fear and its association with past negative stimuli with positive stimuli, our fears can be reversed, starting right now. Here's how:

1. **Identify the fear.**
   Make sure the fear you choose is not blatantly dangerous to you.

2. **Determine the severity of your fear, between 1 percent and 100 percent.**
   Think of three reasons for, or benefits of, conquering this fear.

3. **Approach your fear.**
   While first confronting your fear, approach it at a level you are "comfortably uncomfortable" with. If you could rate your panic on a scale of 1 to 10, start at a 3.

4. **Once you have confronted your fear at the level you are "comfortably uncomfortable" with, stay there.**

   As you approach your fear, remind yourself that this time is a new experience and void of any past negative results or feelings.

5. **Take in and accept the fear you are now facing.**

   Stay present, and while dismissing the past rationale for this fear, observe the surroundings or details/circumstances of what you are facing now.

6. **If you become nervous or scared, remind yourself that these feelings will pass and, in of themselves, are not harmful.**

   As you stay in this space, identify three positive things about what you see/feel.

7. **Work through it.**

   If a negative result or feeling should arise, take action to solve it.

8. **If panic arises and keeps you from battling any potential negative result, take a deep breath and remind yourself that you are stronger than you know and are getting stronger throughout this process.**

   Identify how to change this negative stimulus into a positive, or neutral, one and identify the actions needed to do so step by step. Follow through, one simple step at a time.

9. **Release yourself from the fear.**

   Stay in this moment until the negative feelings that were associated with your past fear conditioning have been counteracted by 10–15 percent with this new experience.

10. **Do not leave this space until you understand that this is a new interaction with your (soon-to-be-old) fear.**

    Remember that this is an exercise that must be repeated, possibly many times, in order to fully conquer your fear.

11. **Reflect.**

    Journal the experience and write down what happened, how you felt and what DIDN'T happen.

12. **List five things you are proud of doing or improved upon during this exercise.**

    Do not criticize your performance. That will only add another aspect to this fear.
    Be patient with yourself.

FEAR B!TCH SLAP

Remember, whatever your fear is—emotional, physical, work or love—you can eventually overcome it. (Especially because 99.99999 percent of the time, the feeling of fear is worse than what you actually fear.) It's as simple as working smart, working hard and working for the right reasons with pure objectives. Before you know it, you will have pushed past your fear and into an inspiring sense of strength. If it doesn't happen right away, that's OK. You took a step toward freedom and that's what matters. Just proceed to live in the moment, and in this moment only. With time and practice you'll develop a life where you can conquer any fear or setback with flying colors. Soon you'll end up with more than you could ever know . . . I promise. The only reason I have what I have right now is because I stopped letting my fears control my life. Simply put: I chose to conquer the fears before they conquered me.

What is your biggest fear?

Describe three outcomes if that fear came true.

Describe how you would handle each scenario.

Describe what you would do post fear consequences.

Describe how that would make you feel.

Describe what you're feeling now? Like, right now.

Describe three reasons you hate this exercise.

Describe what you thought this exercise was going to be.

Describe three reasons your brow is furrowed right now.

Describe why you are still doing this exercise.

From Deepak: Read This When Sh!t Gets Rough

Every experience that we have, even if it seems very toxic or hurtful or dark, if we are aware of who we are, it moves us to a higher level of consciousness. You should say that even the bad experiences, in some way, are helping you to become who you are.

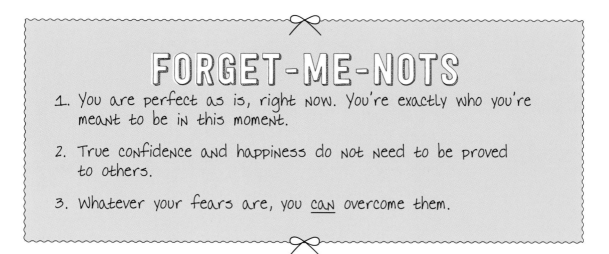

FORGET-ME-NOTS

1. You are perfect as is, right NOW. You're exactly who you're meant to be in this moment.

2. True confidence and happiness do NOT need to be proved to others.

3. Whatever your fears are, you _CAN_ overcome them.

YOU CARING FOR YOU

Roomba Doesn't Have a Line of Loofahs

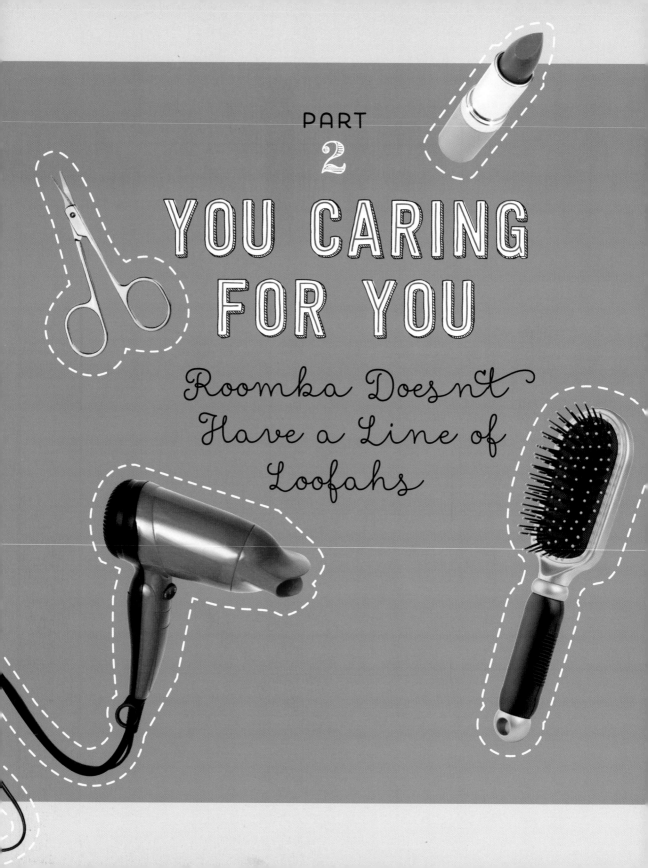

CHAPTER 2

SKIN

LOVE THY PORES

MY EXPERIENCE: ROOMBA DOESN'T HAVE A LINE OF LOOFAHS

WHEN I WAS FOURTEEN YEARS OLD, I developed a habit of staring into the bathroom mirror for hours, searching for things that were wrong with my appearance: pale skin, giant pimples, frizzy hair. For every fault I found, I made it my personal mission to find a product or trick that could magic-eraser it. There would be nights where I stood there over the sink, my face covered in a pond-scum-green peel-off mask, my arms buried under gobs of self-tanner and my hair covered in an entire jar of mayonnaise (yes, mayonnaise) and wrapped in an infomercial hair wrap. I might've smelled like a chemically altered container of diet mayo, but once I removed all that crap, my hair and skin looked absolutely stunning—for a day. I'd soon realize that the mask peeled off part of my eyebrows, and when I proceeded to apply some vitamin E lotion to soothe my peeling skin, my pores clogged up, causing me to break out faster than One Direction. Not to mention that my body was shedding layers of orange-looking dry skin more efficiently than a turbo juicer and my hair *still* smelled like mayo (which killed any chances of a successful hair flip).

Despite these results, I kept putting myself though an endless cycle of product/outcome/product because some dumbass once said, "Beauty is pain."

Then, one day, my friend's mom dropped a bomb on me. "If you keep exfoliating," she said, "you won't have any skin left!" While that may be the worst thing you can say to an overly self-conscious teenager, it *did* resonate

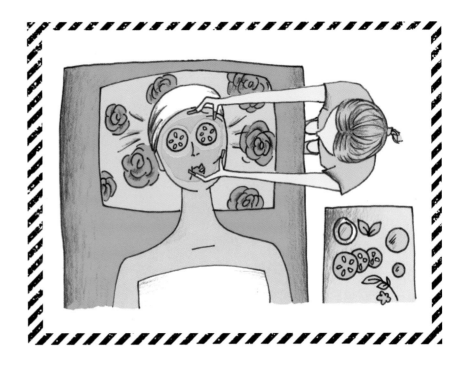

with me. It gave me the genius idea that maybe if I stopped torturing my skin, it would stop torturing me. So I tried something that may be the most difficult thing I've ever had to do—nothing.

I started to notice that my face didn't sting when I put on makeup and that it didn't feel scaly and dry when I went to bed. When I stopped stressing out so much, I realized how easy it was to take care of myself. I stuck with my simple, hardly anything routine for a few weeks and, sure enough, I looked noticeably better on the outside, but more important, I felt a million times better on the inside. Once that harmony fell into place, it allowed me to become the best version of the girl in the mirror: the real girl.

DR. HOWARD MURAD,
award-winning dermatologist and author

MEET YOUR
EXPERT

His Philosophy on Skin Care: I always say that if there's one thing you can do right now to make your skin more beautiful, it's to smile. I encourage an attitude of happiness; and the way I look at happiness, it's returning to the toddler in you—to the girl who wasn't concerned about what others thought of her, and who was also not critical of others . . . someone who enjoys life so much her belly hurts. Return to that mind-set and you'll create a healthy life.

Unclogging the Mystery of Your Own Skin

Everyone's skin is different. But Dr. Murad and I aren't just going to strap you into a pickup truck, drop you in the desert and leave you to figure out all your specific skin care needs on your own. We have an easy, twenty-minute test that will start you on the right path. (For just $29.99, plus shipping and handling! Kidding.)

Essentially, there are three basic skin types: normal/combination, dry and oily. To find out which category you fall into, all you have to do is wash your face with a gentle cleanser) without putting on any moisturizer afterward—but just this one time! Check back twenty minutes later. You have dry skin if your skin feels noticeably drier than it was before you hit it with a washcloth. If your skin feels oily, you have oily skin. You have normal skin if your skin goes back to—you guessed it!—a normal state (neither dry nor oily) at the end of those twenty minutes. And combination skin is, of course, a mix of things: you're typically a little oilier around the middle of your face and drier on the cheeks. Here's a breakdown of each type.

Dry Skin

Your friends may be struggling with pesky pimples, but you probably aren't. People with dry skin may not ever have to worry about acne, acne scarring or enlarged pores because this skin type produces less sebum (oil) than average. Overall skin sensitivity and itching are some of the common characteristics of dry skin (as long as that itching isn't on your lady business, you don't need to worry). Keep in mind that your skin's lack of sebum (god, that word is gross) compromises its ability to absorb lipids and water, which can cause the aging process to start (or appear to) a little earlier on in life. But this type of skin is actually pretty manageable and easily treated.

BREAKDOWN

Instead of relocating to a humid environment, here are some things you can try first:

Lipids: We all know what water is, but lipids are a type of chemical compound-y thing that contain many nutrients, including vitamin E and essential fatty acids, and are found naturally in your skin. As the paramedics to your skin's outermost layer, lipids help these tissues process and absorb moisture.

Exfoliation: Your skin is pretty sensitive and already has a hard time replenishing moisture naturally, so beware of exfoliating with anything even remotely harsh. It could make the next face washing all stingy and burn-y.

Hydrate: You should always try do this from the inside by drinking a lot of water and regularly taking fish oil supplements. In terms of your skin care regimen, keep your face "damp." This will keep that taut, squeaky feeling you get after washing at bay before your moisturize. Make sure to immediately (and I mean immediately) apply moisturizer or serum to your skin. Try a lightweight serum with natural ingredients so as to reduce any product-related sensitivity. Let this light coat of moisture absorb into your skin (you shouldn't at any point feel that your skin becomes drier than prior to washing) for one to two minutes before sealing the deal with a creamy moisturizer that is heavier in consistency than your serum. For extra-dry skin, test a moisturizer's

heaviness by placing a dollop in your hand and moving your hand. If
the cream keeps its form and doesn't drip, that's a sh!tload of moisture
(a good thing).

Normal/Combination Skin

Factors: What the hell is normal? Well, nothing is, but I'll save my phil-
osophical rant on majority and expectation for a long road trip with my
boyfriend. Normal/combination skin is characterized by being periodically
both a little dry and/or a little oily. The reason this category of skin types
has a slash is because you either got lucky with the genetics and have no
concerns right now or by treating your skin type incorrectly, you are causing this dry/oily flux.

BREAKDOWN

If you don't have consistently oily or dry skin, don't treat oily or dry skin.
Because by using the same ingredients people with these skin types have,
you're aggravating your skin and creating the problem you were trying to
solve or preemptively strike.

KEEP IT SIMPLE

Having a very simple skin care regimen doesn't mean you aren't taking
care of your skin as much as you could. It simply means you have less to
treat and therefore less to do.

EXTERNAL CAUSES

No matter what, you may still get a pimple or have dry skin. It's not uncom-
mon to have drier skin in the fall and winter. Take appropriate, not drastic,
measures to counteract the dryness. If you have a pimple or even a breakout, understand that stress or diet may be the culprit. Stay away from greasy
foods and do your best to ease your anxiety.

DON'T FUTZ!

If your skin is fine, do not use it as an excuse to experiment by using different products or treatments. Your skin is like a baby: if it just went to sleep,
don't throw a rattle in the crib and expect it not to wake up crying.

Oily Skin

Thanks to plenty of Emo punk songs, I'm well aware that we are already dying as soon as we are born. That being said, as the aging process of your skin begins, which can start as early as your late twenties, those with oily skin are probably going to notice a delay in that process and even fewer wrinkles down the road than other skin types may experience. Now, you'll probably be the envy of your friends later in life (at least the non-Botoxed ones), but right now your skin type has a few specific tendencies that tend to be specifically not so fun. Because your skin produces more sebum (oil), you're more likely to experience or already be experiencing acne. But don't freak yet. There's some stuff you gotta know.

EXPERT SECRET: Just saying to you, "Don't pick your skin" doesn't work (because I know you will anyway!). Instead, look for ways to minimize it. *When you pick at your skin, you're introducing surface bacteria that can go beneath the surface, which causes those red bumps.* You end up making your skin look worse than it really is. The next time you're tempted to pick, at least put a warm towel over your face first. Then cleanse the skin—I make a clarifying cleanser that kills 99 percent of all bacteria, which will help prevent bacteria from getting into the open pimple once it has popped. —Dr. Murad

BREAKDOWN

Just think of each zit as a snowflake, uniquely different. Each type has a different cause: hormonal, genetic, psychological, infectious (calm down; it's not twenty-eight days later on your face) and/or diet. These all require a different understanding and approach to treatment, which Dr. Murad will explain.

MOTHER EFFIN' ACNE

While the whiteheads on your face aren't as pretty as the white-crested mountains of Aspen, they are very, very, very different from the other pimply members of your breakout zone. First, look at where the pimples in question are popping up (at the worst possible times, I know . . .).

TEENAGE ACNE

Surfaces in the middle of the face—they are violent, harsh, red pimples.

ADULT FEMALE ACNE

Appears from the nose down to the mouth, but it's not as red and aggressive as teenage acne.

CAN YOU POP THE THING OR NOT?

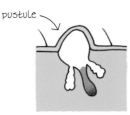

pustule

papule

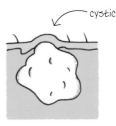

cystic

POP IT!

A pustule contains pus and will generally turn into a whitehead the night before a first date.

(Fun fact: Those are dead white blood cells in there!) If done correctly, you can extract these with little to zero scarring. To extract: Prep skin by placing a warm cloth over the zit for three to five minutes. Then, cover both index fingers with tissues and press down and *away* from the head of the pimple, which puts enough pressure around the pore to release its buildup safely. (Pushing into the zit can damage your skin tissue. Don't do it!)

LEAVE IT!

A papule, on the other hand, doesn't contain pus—it lives beneath the epidermis (the outermost layer of your skin) and is hard and stubborn as hell.

With this type of pimple, it can be difficult to tell whether you should "pop" or "stop." The bottom line is this: if you don't see an obvious whitehead on the surface of *any* breakout, it's not safe to extract at home and could lead to scarring if you cave to the temptation and try to pop it. Instead, use acne cream containing salicylic acid to help unclog pores.

CALL YOUR DERM!

If you've got a set of pimples that are sore and inflamed, you're dealing with cystic acne.

They're large bumps—also known as nodules—that are filled with a weird liquid (come on, I know you've tried to pop one before...) and form deep inside the skin. While these types of pimples can take a painstaking three weeks to go away, they should never be popped—they cause the worst post-pick scarring. If you need to get rid of one ASAP, call your dermatologist about a "cyst injection," which contains cortisone and reduces inflammation. It takes about two minutes, costs 10 or 15 bucks, and your pimple will clear up within a few days.

P.S.: There are imitators that *look* like acne, but don't be fooled. Rosacea can look like acne, but if you don't have a comedone—that white center—your skin may be irritated by something else, such as your hair spray or shampoo.

HORMONAL ACNE

It will give you large pimples around your jawline that last for an eternity. These suckers can occur at any age, but most often occur during your period, when you're lacking estrogen and are more likely to break out. (Pearl-clutching moms of America: That's one of the reasons why birth control works so well for acne—because it's mostly estrogen—so your daughter's doctor is not so crazy for suggesting it!)

And now for the million-dollar question: Can you pop the thing or not? Unlike books (no offense to mine, obviously), you *can* judge a poppable pimple by its cover.

Three Things You Can Do to Help Your Skin
(WITHOUT BUYIN' A THANG*) *ALMOST

Hydrate: **Eat plenty of water-rich foods throughout the day.** I even cheat a little by taking fish oil supplements. (Dr. Murad explains that the omega-3 essential fatty acids found in fish oil supplements help strengthen your cell membranes, which is what helps them hold on to water. So as your body becomes more hydrated, your skin does, too!)

Exfoliate: **You're refreshing your complexion by getting rid of dead skin cells and allowing buildup to safely escape before it becomes Zit City.** The trick here is to limit yourself to exfoliating one night a week (MAX, people, or else you'll irritate your skin and cause even more breakouts).

Eat well: **Pimples are often caused by stress and/or poor eating habits.** Stay away from greasy foods and do your best to ease your anxiety. (Yes, that means I'm giving you permission to unfollow those shady b!tches on Facebook.)

Four Things to Note about Any Skin Care Product Label

OK, so chances are you've never swallowed your exfoliator and "contacted a Poison Control Center right away." However, if you're like me, you've found yourself wasting two hours in a beauty supply store trying to figure out the difference between the "rejuvenating face wash" and the "clarifying face wash," when all you really wanted was some clarity on rejuvenating your skin. Since the list of ingredients on the back tends to be more confusing than Nicki Minaj's wardrobe, there's no easy guide to what's what in skin care products. But fear not, help is here! (And no, you won't need your AP chem book for this.)

> **EXPERT SECRET:** Acne on your back is difficult because it's tough to apply topical agents. (Just like when you have an annoying scratch, it's hard to reach back there and deal with it!) Taking a relatively low dose of vitamin A by mouth is helpful. (Accutane, which is the harshest drug for acne, is a very strong form of vitamin A, but also has many side effects.) Zinc is also a very good anti-inflammatory and can by taken as a vitamin. Of course, always consult with your doctor about what's best for you. —Dr. Murad

1. **The Food and Drug Administration (FDA) has only approved four ingredients to treat acne.**
   Those are salicylic acid, benzoyl peroxide, resorcinol and sulfur. When you're making a plan to clear up your acne, your solution needs to include one of those four ingredients. What will work best for you depends on your skin, but here are a few things to note about each one: benzoyl peroxide tends to be a little irritating and drying (so use a moisturizer with it), sulfur tends to be a little more calming, salicylic acid is sort of in the middle, and resorcinol is almost never used anymore.

2. **The list of ingredients is organized from the ingredient with the highest percentage to the one with the lowest percentage.**

So when a company advertises a certain ingredient in its product, be sure to check the back and see if you're actually getting what you're paying for.

3. **Water is almost always first when ingredients are listed, and that's pretty standard.**
   (P.S.: Yes, I'll totally judge you if you're looking at the Evian mineral water spray and wondering where the water in that product is.)

4. **Some ingredients may be trademarked and therefore not totally disclosed and explained in layman's terms.**
   Companies usually go with something scientific-sounding, like HydroBioLux eye serum. This isn't a scam or an illuminati conspiracy, per se, but rather a way for companies to keep their own unique "recipe" a secret from other companies.

Frequently Asked (Skin Care) Questions

SO WAIT, IS THAT CRAZY LIST OF INGREDIENTS TRYING TO TRIP YOU UP ON PURPOSE?!

Again, you're mainly looking for one of the four basic acne treatment ingredients—salicylic acid, benzoyl peroxide, resorcinol and sulfur—but you also want some helpers. One example would be glycolic acid, which helps exfoliate the skin a little bit and allows better penetration of other ingredients. There is also something called INCI (the acronym for International Nomenclature of Cosmetic Ingredients) names, which are approved by the FDA, so some of the funny-sounding exotic names are chosen because they're using INCI names, instead of common names. Manufacturers aren't necessarily putting anything horrible* into their skin care products. When we treat our skin with respect, and work with it rather than against it, our skin will have an easier time naturally combating acne on its own.

---

* "The only thing that really does harm your skin is pomade. A lot of my African-American patients use pomade for their hair and unintentionally get it on their face. That tends to clog the pores more than anything, which makes acne worse. Pomade is fine to use, just try not to get it on your skin." —Dr. Murad

For a complete list of skin care ingredients for each skin type and their purpose, take that list with you next time you shop!!

SHOULD YOU WASH YOUR FACE EVERY DAY?

Yes! Washing your face daily is important. It ensures that you are removing any dirt or grime that may have accumulated during the day.

IS WEARING MAKEUP EVERY DAY BAD FOR YOUR SKIN?

Not necessarily. There are many options for makeup now and some of them even have benefits for the skin, according to Dr. Murad. See chapter 4 for more suggestions.

ARE MORE EXPENSIVE PRODUCTS EVER WORTH IT?

Yes. In many cases, high-quality ingredients typically cost more and this, in turn, affects the price of the product, according to Dr. Murad. I usually "splurge" on moisturizers and serums.

WHAT THE SPF?!

If you don't know what *SPF* stands for, then I strongly suggest you stop whatever you're doing and immediately keep reading. *SPF* stands for sun protection factor. It's a measure of how well a skin care product protects against ultraviolet rays from the sun in an easy-to-understand rating system for consumers to make the best choices for their own skin. You probably know by now that tanning is not only bad for your skin, but potentially deadly. For now, though, I'll stop being so vague/terrifying and talk about shopping.

As far as choosing the right sun protection product for you, it's a matter of lifestyle factors and preference.

FROM DR. MURAD: Why You Should Never, Ever Go to a Tanning Bed (Like, Ever)

A tanning-bed tan doesn't look like a real tan—that's because it's a fake tan (hence the orange-y afterglow). You're also aging your skin, making your skin more susceptible to pigmentation, wrinkles and skin cancer. You can get a safe tan without the harm of the sun or UVA rays by using a bronzer and washing it off at the end of the night, or getting a spray tan that will last for about five days. Some people think, *Well, if I don't get enough sun, I'll lack vitamin D!* Vitamin D comes in vitamins that you can swallow. I'm not telling you to sit in your basement all day, but using a tanning bed is causing yourself unnecessary harm.

Moles: Check Yo'self!

Go with the "ABCDE" approach.

A stands for asymmetry: one side of the mole looks different than the other.

B means irregular borders: instead of an oval or circle, the mole has an irregular shape.

C is variation in color: instead of solid red, brown or black, there are all different colors in there.

D is a diameter bigger than your pinky nail, or five millimeters.

The most important one is E, for evolving. Let's say you look at all your moles, even the ones that have been there forever. If there is a mole that looks larger than it has before or is beginning to have a different color or is changing in shape, it's potentially harmful and you should see a dermatologist immediately so she can make a diagnosis. Ideally, what you should do is look in the mirror (or when you're taking a bath or shower) and check all your moles for changes or irregularities at least once a month.

EXPERT SECRET: You're never going to be somebody else, but you can be the best you, and make the best of what you have to offer. Acne itself at some point will be gone, but just because you have terrible acne doesn't mean there's not a beautiful person inside. Don't be so hard on yourself. I know it's hard, I know it's painful, but any acne can be improved. Even if you don't have the financial means to afford prescriptions and topical creams, everyone can eat more fruits and vegetables, exercise and get more sleep. —Dr. Murad

Dare Ya 'Diem Style!

I would never ask you to do something pointless that I wouldn't do myself.

In fact, the following dare is one I personally found incredibly comforting as I tried to move forward from my own skin issues.

1. **Without makeup on, without any primping at all, observe your face in the mirror.**

2. **Now smile—even if you are upset, anxious or angry by how the reflection makes you feel.**

3. **Look at your smile and the way each muscle in your face moves to express joy.**
   You may need to fake it at first, as I know this can be emotional, but just watch as you smile. Feel free to play around with your expressions as well.

4. **Just observe your ability to express emotions.**
   The more you do this easy little trick, the more accepting you will become of whatever your skin looks like. Your skin and face are doing their job by letting you express yourself. The rest is a surface matter and will take care of itself now that you know the basics, you know how to use them, and you have started to let go of your lingering negative perceptions.

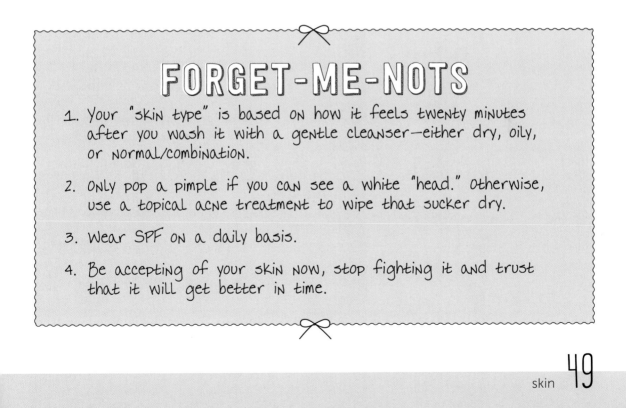

FORGET-ME-NOTS

1. Your "skin type" is based on how it feels twenty minutes after you wash it with a gentle cleanser—either dry, oily, or normal/combination.

2. Only pop a pimple if you can see a white "head." Otherwise, use a topical acne treatment to wipe that sucker dry.

3. Wear SPF on a daily basis.

4. Be accepting of your skin now, stop fighting it and trust that it will get better in time.

CHAPTER 3

HAIR

BRUSH SUGGESTED

MY EXPERIENCE: PUTTING MY HAIR'S HEALTH FIRST

I'VE NEVER BEEN CALLED A SKANK ON TWITTER SO MANY TIMES in one twenty-four-hour period as the day I went blond. The lighter look was an impulsive decision, yet when I think back to the day I decided to take the plunge, I'm forced to wonder: *What the f!ck was I thinking?!* My intentions were good—I wanted to explore a different side of "Ashley," but my execution? Not so good.

I hired a colorist I'd worked with recently on a movie. She agreed to brighten my bob and I agreed to do it in her backyard. I also agreed to go with the lightest possible shade of blond *and* OK'ed the use of some cheapy bleaching-ammonia crap to do so (very bad idea). When the color didn't come out quite right, we decided to bleach it again . . . and again (*very, very* bad idea). Then came the post-color trim, which wasn't much of a trim since a lot of my hair just fell out (I sh!t you not). By the time we got to the "big reveal," I was already nervous, my scalp had endured some pretty severe burning sensations and what I saw in the mirror *did not* help.

My reflection, more abrasive than Joan Rivers on *Fashion Police*'s worst look of the week, confirmed my new, near-ghostly state. *Oh my god! THAT is my hair?* I didn't pick my jaw up off the floor until I felt a desperate need for approval coursing through my colorist's veins. "It looks . . . AMAZZZIIINNNGGGG!!!" I said with a smile so overcompensated that my welling eyes looked more like tears of joy. I didn't want her to ask me any more questions about it, so I just got out my checkbook, tipped her double her salary (I was guilt-tripping, I still don't know why . . .) and walked out of that lady's backyard with white roots, orange undertones and hair that was kinkier than *Fifty Shades of Grey*. The damage was real, the color was unreal and my reflection in the mirror was surreal.

In an effort to moisturize the madness, I used a deep conditioning treatment with keratin in it—and left it in for *three days*. Turns out, while keratin is a protein that can strengthen your hair, in large quantities it can also make it super-brittle. I realized this when I finally washed everything out of my hair, and another four inches came off, falling to the floor in broken, shattered pieces. There I was, with short, damaged blond hair and a really pissed-off expression to match. I needed help.

Thankfully, my friend Demi spotted that mess from a mile away (OK, we were in my kitchen, but whatever) and recommended I go to Nine Zero One salon in Los Angeles. When I got there, I noticed all the stylists talked like scientists and looked like fashion models. My colorist Nicole shouted out things like "40r mix with 623n and a light glaze of 54b!!!!" I still have no idea what that meant, but I soon learned that there are much better, easier ways to care for my hair.

Turns out, if you treat your hair well (with only slight doses of keratin), it will work for you in any way you want.

Nicole's "Get Your Sh!t Together" Story

I was sixteen years old when my parents made me register for cosmetology school, and I had no idea what I was getting myself into. I dreamed of going to college at the University of South Carolina Beaufort and becoming an international journalist. I wanted to be the female version of Anderson Cooper, or at least his sidekick. However, my life would unfold a little differently.

I started cosmetology school during my senior year in high school. I became a licensed hairstylist four months after graduating from high school. I hit the ground running and never looked back. My career path has allowed me to travel all over the world, teach other hairstylists how to be better professionals and work with some pretty awesome celebrities.

MEET YOUR EXPERT

NICOLE LEAL, colorist at the famous Nine Zero One salon

Her Philosophy on Hair Care: My main focus is keeping the hair healthy. I have this little catchphrase: *Beautiful hair is healthy hair.* It's your biggest accessory—you wear your hair every day!—so it's important to invest in it and take good care of it.

So many times in my career I've been faced with a situation that has helped me understand that, when it's meant to be, all the pieces flow together effortlessly. I get to help people enhance their natural beauty every day and listen to all their life stories, and it is truly rewarding. There is truly never a dull moment and after so many years in the industry, I stumbled upon Nine Zero One salon. I've been a hairstylist there since the day we opened and every day I feel just as excited as the first day I walked through the doors.

I constantly reflect back on my career and couldn't imagine doing anything else. Who knew that cutting my friends' hair before soccer practice when I was in junior high would end up being training for my lifelong career? They say, "If you do what you love, you'll never work a day in your life." I couldn't agree more. If someone would have told me that my career would be where it is today, I would never have believed them. I believe anyone can conquer the world, and have gorgeous hair while doing it!

No Ends Left Behind

Whether your hair is colored, curly, straight, thick or thin, at the end of the day, the products you choose to use *matter*. Ignoring that fact will leave you in an unfortunate blond burnout situation (see above). You have a specific hair type that requires specific attention. So, Nicole and I came up with a few easy ways for you to ID, treat and love your hair—no matter what it looks like when you wake up in the morning.

First, a Few Rules from Nicole
(NO MATTER WHO YOU ARE)

RULE #1

Never buy shampoo and conditioner in a set—you want to customize what's appropriate for your type of hair. Ninety percent of my clients are mismatched. A volumizing shampoo and a moisturizing conditioner is a great combo.

RULE #2

You don't need to wash your hair every day. Shampooing can often remove natural oils from your hair that are necessary to keep it from getting dry and brittle. Rinsing your hair on days in between shampoos will do the trick.

RULE # 3

The best way to tackle hair breakage is through a combination of protein and moisture. You can get that in your shampoo and conditioner, but you need to switch it up. Your hair will adjust to whatever product you use, so if you've been using one kind of conditioner for two months, your hair is already tapped out on it. By changing it up, your hair gets a refreshed set of benefits.

Getting to the Root of Your Hair Type and Its Needs

Wash your hair as you normally do, but don't apply any leave-in products. Then, towel-dry your hair and let it air-dry the rest of the way. Now your hair is doing whatever the eff it wants and is ready to be ID'ed.

FINE/STRAIGHT

If your hair dries with no visible curl or wave, then you've got straight hair. (Duh.) Straight hair is usually on the shinier side—since light is able to reflect off it—but it also has a tendency to be on the thinner end of the volume spectrum, so use a volumizing shampoo. It fattens up the hair shafts with protein, making them bigger. Embrace layers during maintenance cuts and always blow-dry hair upside down to gain maximize fullness.

> **EXPERT SECRET:** This goes for everyone: Always run conditioner through the ends of the hair—avoiding the roots—otherwise it'll end up feeling greasy. And every so often, you'll find you don't even need to add conditioner at all and can just use a light leave-in conditioner before styling. —Nicole

WAVY

You'll see slight bends in the hair when you air-dry it, but no official curls. To give your natural texture a boost, sleep with a braid in your hair overnight. It will dry like you curled it and hold better than if you used an iron. You can also embrace the beach-y look you've got by using a beach spray product or volumizing mousse to enhance texture. Diffuser attachments for blow dryers work great to help push your waves into place.

CURLY

Curly hair can range from loose spirals to tight ringlets, but the most important thing is not to shy away from conditioning (that's what will give you shine). Use a lightweight conditioner to prevent any weighing down and to leave your hair feeling light and bouncy. If you're on the corkscrew end of the spectrum, you can avoid frizz with a light gel or a leave-in conditioner, which will lock in moisture and make your hair more malleable for straightening.

> EXPERT SECRET: Your conditioners in the shower are purely for giving you surface shine. They're not actually penetrating the hair shaft, so you're not going to get any kind of treatment from that. However, with deep conditioners, the molecules are smaller and able to deeply penetrate the scalp, which will give you a long-term repairing effect and maximum shine. —Nicole

Ingredients Breakdown

Hair-care ingredients have been pretty much the same for decades—the only difference is the renaming or recategorizing every so often to keep things fresh. The most notable ingredients to look for are proteins, oils and moisturizers, and, of course, some random good-for-you and not-so-good-for-you ingredients.

TEN HAIR TOOLS EVERY GIRL SHOULD OWN

- Shower cap
- Wide-tooth comb
- Fine-tooth comb
- Round-bristle brush
- Flat-bristle brush
- Thinning shears
- Tourmaline blow-dryer
- Flat iron
- Wide-barrel ceramic curling iron
- Small-barrel ceramic curling iron

FIVE HAIR PRODUCTS EVERY GIRL SHOULD OWN*

*Besides the obvious shampoo and conditioner.

- Leave-in conditioner. It's a detangling magician.
- Deep conditioning treatment. Regular conditioner only gives you surface shine, ladies!
- Heat-protecting styling serum. It'll protect your hair against torturous blow-dryers, straighteners and curling irons.
- Hair spray, to keep your handiwork in place.
- Dry shampoo, for days when a shower is just too overwhelming.

CUTS WITHOUT CHAOS

One of the biggest ways to highlight your features is through your haircut. But there are hundreds of options, so it can be somewhat of a daunting task to determine which one is right for you. Since the dawn of scissors, a few styles have remained classic. (Fine, maybe not since the dawn of scissors—Marie Antoinette's hair was pretty funky—but it sounded good, OK?) Within these chops for your mop are slight variations that, when taken into account, add up to the perfect style, based on the shape of your face, the length of your hair, your tresses' texture and how much time you can devote to maintenance.

LET'S TALK ABOUT YOUR FACE SHAPE

Discovering your face shape is a key first step in determining the best hairstyle for you (and, like your social security number, it's something you'll need to recall for life). Here's the breakdown.

SQUARE

Equal width both ways, but with a structured jawline.

Shoulder-length hair or longer looks great on you. And since you have strong, angular features, try a cut that's soft and natural (going too bold could make you look masculine).

OVAL

Longer than wide, but with a smooth—as opposed to rigid—structure.

Oval face shapes have the neutrality to rock almost any cut and style, you lucky duck! Go as far as a spunky faux hawk, if you'd like, as long as it feels like a good representation of *you*.

ROUND

About the same width the entire way around, with no major corners around your jaw.

Focus on styles that will frame and thin your face— like an asymmetrical cut, where your hair is angled and longer in the front, shorter in the back. Minimal layers will help you avoid too much volume.

 **OBLONG OR RECTANGLE**

Longer than it is wide, with a structured jawline (if you have a curved jawline, your face is oblong).

The key here is to go for a style that doesn't elongate the face too much. Try fluffy bangs and a cut that's shoulder-length or shorter. Add volume to the hair with lots of layers.

DIAMOND/ TRIANGLE

You have a narrow hairline, and your jawline comes to a point around your chin, starting below your ear.

Keep hair sleek and sexy with a shoulder-length cut or long hair and wispy bangs that soften the face.

HEART

You have a widow's peak and cheeks that are slightly wider than your hairline, and drop to the chin.

You could rock a pixie cut, which would draw attention to your jawline; however, long hair also looks great with lots of layers around the chin.

Color Decoded: So, You Want to Dye Your Hair?

AT HOME VERSUS AT THE SALON

The main difference between coloring your hair at home versus going to a salon is that at-home color doesn't give you as much flexibility to customize your color. If you decide to become a salon-goer, you'll get a customized consultation about your hair color, plus higher-quality treatments and hair products. (I swear no one is paying me to say this.) So if you've got the cash (or your parents do), save some time and mistakes and utilize the experts in their natural habitat.

But for those of us who consider $50 bills an endangered species, at-home hair color can be done successfully. You've just gotta be savvy about it and you can become your own expert! Nicole and I have your back.

PIGMENT

Hair color—aka melanin—is divided into two types of pigment: eumelanin and pheomelanin. Eumelanin is more common and causes dark hair, whereas pheomelanin creates lighter shades of hair—blonds and reds. (FYI: The *absence* of melanin causes white or gray hair, aka no pigment.) Given the fact that almost 75 percent of Americans color their hair eventually, becoming familiar with coloring basics is key to preventing a hair-related meltdown. Here is a DIY on color from the salon to the dorm bathroom.

HAIR COLOR COMMITMENT LEVELS

Hair dye is generally broken down into three (well, sometimes four) categories.

Temporary
Best known as "spray-in color," this trial option washes out with shampoo (or sweat if you're at Mardi Gras). It can add a bright pop of color for rando switch-ups and unexpected mood swings.

Semi-Permanent
This category is made up of smaller molecules that penetrate a hair strand's outer layer. It won't drastically change your hair and is often used when you

TRIM YOUR OWN BANGS

Bangs grow like weeds, so I get it—you don't want to schlep to the salon every time they start messing with your ability to see things. While you should always go to a salon for your initial set of bangs, here are my secrets to pulling off a maintenance trim. (Note: I recommend first investing in a pair of high-quality hair scissors and a pair of thinning shears for blending.)

Step 1 Always cut your bangs dry, since your hair shrinks as it dries (and is longer when it's wet).

Step 2 Using a fine-tooth comb, separate your hair into three horizontal layers—top, middle, bottom.

Step 3 Starting with the bottom layer, trim no higher than the corners of your eyes. For the top layer, trim no higher than the point where your eyebrows meet in the middle of your face. Blend, being careful not to chop any severe length off.

Step 4 Holding shears upright in a vertical motion, snip to soften any bluntness in the hair. Again, this should be done very carefully. You're not chopping off any real length here—simply blending.

Step 5 Brush through with your comb. Then step back from the mirror and check for any inconsistencies. If need be, go back and lightly address the askew pieces a bit with your scissors.

want to enhance your natural color, go a touch darker or cover a few grays (word to your mom).

Demi-Permanent
This type of color enters the hair cuticle at its core, where it forms the kind of molecule that takes up to twenty-six shampoos to wash out. This color won't help your brunette tresses go blond, though, as it lacks ammonia, a key ingredient in going lighter. However, the small amount of peroxide found here does allow for a pretty noticeable color change.

Permanent
Don't worry—this no-going-back method doesn't need to be feared. (It's not like you're getting married!) Itty-bitty molecules seep into the hair's outer layer and move deep into the core of the hair, expanding it in a way that can't be washed out easily or faded. (BTdubs, both ammonia and peroxide are generally found in this dye.) If you're trying this at home, it's a good idea to test this color out on a small clump of hair before dumping your entire head in the sink, just to make sure you two are a good match.

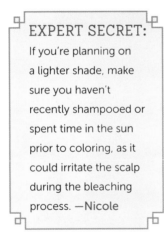

EXPERT SECRET: If you're planning on a lighter shade, make sure you haven't recently shampooed or spent time in the sun prior to coloring, as it could irritate the scalp during the bleaching process. —Nicole

CHOOSING THE RIGHT SHADE OUTTA FIFTY

Picking a color from an aisle of boxes isn't as simple as pointing into thin air and proclaiming, "That one!" (which I've done). I've learned that it's a smart idea to choose your color based on your natural hair color, as well as your skin's undertones and overtones.

Levels of Color
It's pretty simple. Natural blondes are going to be levels 8–10 and dark blondes/light brunettes or redheads (gingers, holla!) will be levels 5–7. Dark brunettes will be levels 1–4. Whatever your natural level is, you should only move one or two levels up or down the spectrum. Is there a time and place for crazy colors and purposeful rule bending? Hell, yes. But if you're going for a statement like that, heed my advice and let a professional colorist do it in the salon.

Overtones
Generally, your skin's overtone (light-skinned to dark-skinned) corresponds

with the hair color that best complements you, be it blond, brunette, red or black. So, lighter skin will look great with a lighter shade of hair color, a medium skin tone will look most natural with a medium shade and dark skin looks very lovely and rich with dark locks. Again, this is *generally speaking*, so please don't send me hate mail. Feel free to mix and match as you please.

Undertones

Your skin can be one of two undertones: warm or cold (there's more on this in the next chapter). That should be your guide to your hair color's "temperature," meaning warm skin tones = warmer hair hue (yellow-red) and cool skin tones = cooler hair hue (a bluish green-purple). You can avoid brassy undertones while lightening your hair by staying within one or two shades lighter than your natural color.

Get a Highlighter!

If you've been reading this entire time (thank you!) and just want highlights, we have now reached that point. Highlights are used to complement your hair color—not look like a ton of spider legs on your head. Know that when you buy boxed hair dye, it's made to have highlights included—and not just be one solid wash of color. But if you don't want to do a total head dive and instead just want to perk yourself up a bit, read on.

1. Assess your base color.

At-home highlights are easiest to accomplish for those with lighter hair that isn't overprocessed or chemically relaxed. Your highlight color should only be one shade lighter than your base color. Light to medium brunettes should look for a deeper golden hue. If you have hair like mine, though (super-dark!), your best bet is to head to the salon, as it's more of a challenge to make your highlights look natural.

2. Do your prep work.

If you have short- or medium-length fine hair, use a highlight cap, which is best for applying all-over highlights. If you have long or thick hair or just want highlights to frame your face, choose a kit that has a highlighting brush. Most boxed sets have a few variations of this nifty tool included. Either way, it's wise to practice first by replacing the bleaching agents with a conditioner and applying it to the hair as if it were the real deal. You'll avoid a frosting freak-out later.

3. Let the bleaching begin.

The next and simplest step is just to follow the instructions on the box. After all, years of research went into this product and taking matters into your own hands is like driving with your eyes closed (meaning: a really bad idea). When applying the bleach, start from the bottom of the strand and apply the color moving up. Your roots process color faster and this application trick will ensure that you don't end up with sloppily tapered highlights.

4. Play hair monitor.

Once you've finished applying, keep a close watch. Frequently check that the hair isn't getting too light by using a paper towel to remove the color on a small strand. If you've reached your goal, rinse it out. If it's still too dark, reapply the bleach and check back after another two minutes.

5. Switch things up.

When the time comes to touch up your highlights, usually in six weeks, avoid reapplying the bleach to the same parts of your hair. Stick mostly to the roots and add a touch more bleach to the longer pieces here and there. Otherwise, you could end up with all your highlights blending together and looking flat.

Tips for the Aftermath

Make sure to use a color-saving shampoo and/or conditioner. If you're a blonde, ward off the orange burn of your local water system by using a purple shampoo—it purifies the lighter hair colors and prevents you from getting that nasty bronzing effect. After a coloring session, fully shampoo out all the color; any remaining dye can continue to fry the hair. On the flip side, a deep conditioning treatment helps seal in your color. Maintaining a major moisture effect is essential in colored or treated hair, as it is especially prone to damage. And use a wide-tooth comb to avoid undue breakage.

Touching Up

The process of gauging when you need to touch up your hair can make you feel a little obsessive-compulsive disorder-ish and leave you with crazy blond straw.

Nicole's general recommendation—mine, too—is every four to six weeks for lighter levels or blondes because this will prevent any kind of color banding (when you start to see different lines of color). Brunettes and redheads can wait as long as six to eight weeks for touch-ups—you won't notice your roots as easily since they're a lot closer to your natural color. But as Megan Fox has proved, dark brunettes and those with sleek black hair can push it to anywhere between eight and twelve weeks.

If you confused Willow Smith's "I whip my hair back and forth" advice with Kanye West's "I'm just trying to change the color on your mood ring," and find yourself with an ever-changing hair color, you're going to notice that your hair lacks shine and doesn't style as well as it used to. Give you hair (and your heart) a break once in a while, because there's only so much it can take before it's unable to grow any longer.

DO! Enlist a friend's help.
She can tell you if you missed a spot.

DO! A strand test.
A quick test is a lot safer than dousing your hair in color all at once and finding out the hard way that it's the wrong shade.

DON'T! Strand-test in the bathroom.
Your bathroom lighting isn't a universal truth—double-check how a shade looks on you by going out in the sunlight (natural lighting!) to finalize your strand test.

STYLE YOUR HAIR LIKE A PRO

Being an actress means people are constantly styling my hair in all different kinds of ways—from crazy updos to trendy braids (I hate that *Awkward* braid . . .) which take a *minimum* of forty-five minutes to "perfect." In real life, though, when I am my own hairstylist, I just don't have time to do all that every day (sometimes multiple times a day, if you include touch-ups). So I like to keep things fairly simple. These are my favorite styles for an everyday look, nighttime fanciness and emergency fixes when I've got some serious bedhead.

GIVE-IT-TO-ME-STRAIGHT HAIR

(TIME: 30–45 MINUTES)

Divide your hair into three layers, and use a flat iron to straighten each section. (Always straighten hair that is *completely* dry, folks.) Add a sexy side part to create a bit of drama.

Step 1

Step 2

Step 3

Step 4

Step 1 **Step 2** **Step 3**

Step 4

BOMBSHELL WAVES
(TIME: 30 MINUTES)

I *love* this look for a date—it looks effortless and sexy, but not like you just rolled out of bed. Divide the hair into three sections and—again, making sure the hair is completely dry—use a small-barrel curling iron or wand, always pulling your hair away from your face and over the iron, rather than slipping the hair under and around the iron. Leave the curling iron on each section for about ten seconds before moving onto the next one. After you're finished, let the hair set for about fifteen minutes and then tousle or brush through it, adding just a touch of a lightweight hair spray throughout.

Step 5

"It's Actually Not Complicated"
THE ^BRAID (TIME: 5 MINUTES)

Chances are you already know how to do a standard braid, but a more modern update is to keep the braids loose. This will prevent you from looking like an awkward teenager on an MTV sitcom (yes, I hate that braid). Divide your hair into three strands and twist from top to bottom into a braid, as you normally would, and secure with a band. Once you're finished, start from top to bottom and gently tug outward on the folds, loosening up the style.

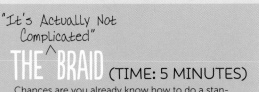

THE "CAN'T BE TAMED" PONY

(TIME: 10 MINUTES FOR TEXTURED HAIR; 45 MINUTES FOR STRAIGHT HAIR)

Prep your hair to give it some added texture by blowing it dry and even going through it quickly with a curling iron. In one swift motion, pull the hair up into a high ponytail and secure it with a hair band that matches your hair color. Piece the hair apart and spritz hair spray throughout, then tousle it with your hands.

For a More Formal Version
Take a section of hair from the ponytail and wrap it around the band. Secure it with a few bobby pins. Pull a few extra pieces of hair down around the front of your face as well.

Step 1

Step 2

Step 3

THE SWEET SIDE PONY

(TIME: LIKE, 2 SECONDS)

This simple hairstyle looks great the day after you've gotten a blowout or curled your hair, when it has a nice amount of relaxed texture to it. Tousle the hair a bit to add a touch more volume before starting. Leave a wispy bit of hair on one side, and bring the rest around and through your ponytail. There, done. Time for school or work.

Step 1 Step 2 Step 3

Step 4

THE SPICY BUN
(TIME: 10 MINUTES)

You know how to do a bun, and you definitely
know how to do a braid (see page 67). Put them
together, and you've got yourself a spicy bun.
Start by separating your hair—pulling three-
quarters into a ponytail and leaving the bottom
layer behind. (Take all the hair at once if you just
want to do a regular bun.) Twist the ponytail up
and around, securing it into a bun. Then, take
the bottom layer and braid it. Wrap it around the
bun, leaving it a little loose, and secure the end
underneath the bun with a bobby pin. With the
opposite end of a comb, pull out a few wispy
pieces to frame your face.

Step 5

IN MY LINE OF WORK, IT'S NOT UNCOMMON TO BECOME A CHAMELEON, CHANGING FOR EACH CHARACTER.

However, in real life, always stick to who you are on the inside. Changing your hair color shouldn't change your identity, but rather amplify it. So unless you've got Tyra's hairstylist on standby for spring break—or even your next road trip to Aunt Donna's house— leave all your styling products at home and go natural. Becoming comfortable with your birthday hair will come in handy, especially when you aren't that girl who is forty-five minutes late for a date because you were curling your hair into oblivion.

Style Notes

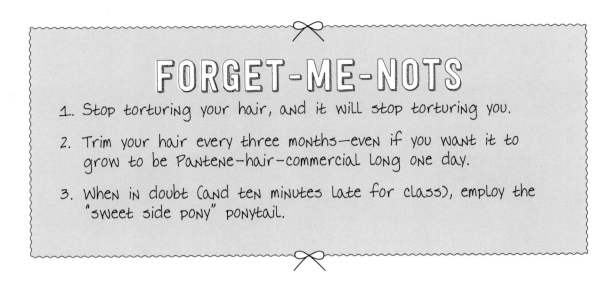

FORGET-ME-NOTS

1. Stop torturing your hair, and it will stop torturing you.

2. Trim your hair every three months—even if you want it to grow to be Pantene-hair-commercial long one day.

3. When in doubt (and ten minutes late for class), employ the "sweet side pony" ponytail.

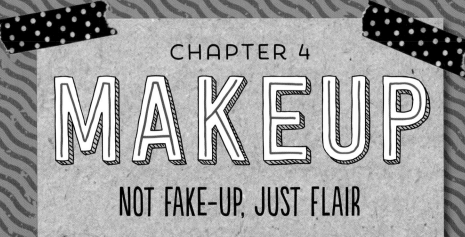

CHAPTER 4

MAKEUP

NOT FAKE-UP, JUST FLAIR

MY EXPERIENCE: A SYMBOLIC
AND LITERAL MASK

TO CAKE OR NOT TO CAKE? That was the question on the night of the 2012 Critics' Choice Awards. It was my first major nomination and my nerves were on fire. That, combined with bad lighting in my bathroom, led to an unfortunate concealer clusterf!ck.

It all started with a power outage. After the first season of *Awkward*, I was nominated for my role by the Television Critics Association for best actress in a comedic series. I'd gone to my favorite showroom to pick out my dress for the evening and was shaved and ready to go (I don't shave if my legs don't show—#dirtysecret). Well, at about noon on the day of, just as I was about to put on my primer, the lights went out.

WTF, I thought. I paid that! And then I remembered: I actually had *not* paid that. FYI, you actually have to send the electric company money when you pay a bill. Guess I was too busy playing a normal girl on TV to remember to do normal things, like paying bills.

After a completely unwarranted screaming match with the electric company, I had to find a backup plan. I called one of my guy friends and asked to use his house. I packed up my face and leg makeup (hey, legs need bronzer, too), and as soon as I stepped into his bachelor pad, my shiny new heels and expensive dress got the attention of his roommates, and got my attention back on the real issue at hand: my pimple-spotted skin. As I walked up his stairs, I was reminded of how amazing it felt to have all eyes on me. I wanted that feeling to last—I felt so powerful! So, I decided to make myself look as perfect as possible for those boys. They wouldn't see "Ashley with acne" come down the stairs again; they would see a hot-ass girl strutting her stuff on the way to an awards show for totally kicking ass at work.

I started with primer, then added foundation. I looked at myself in the mirror and I could still see my pimples. I added a bit of concealer while promising myself I wouldn't look like a pimply imperfect teenager at this awards show—I wanted to look more Helen of Troy (Spoiler: That didn't happen). When I looked at myself in the mirror again, I could see how tired I was. So, I put on more concealer. Then I looked at myself in the mirror AGAIN: I couldn't move my face without feeling like it was cracking with translucent powder. I was striving to achieve Angelina Jolie–like perfection, but I overshot it. By a lot. So much so, that when I arrived, nobody took pictures of me. Yup, that's right. One of two things happened next: I was (a) being purposefully ignored by the paps to save myself embarrassment or (b) they didn't recognize me. The latter is more likely. And, thank god, I didn't win. It would've been so embarrassing to give my first acceptance speech in that scare-drobe, with that makeup (that's what I tell myself). I overdrew my lips so much that I made wax Halloween lips look like a subtle accessory.

Sadly, that wasn't my first faux pas with makeup. I'd always thought of my love for concealer, blush and mascara as a way to change what I looked

like and hide behind some sort of "worthy" attractiveness that I didn't believe I possessed naturally. But I had it all backwards. Makeup isn't about trying to fix your insecurities or changing your face structure—it's about flattering and highlighting your favorite features. When viewed like this, makeup helps you portray your inner beauty on the outside while gaining a confidence that'll help you feel like the best version of yourself—the real one.

MEET YOUR EXPERT

KATHLEEN FREEMAN, celebrity makeup artist
(including mine on *Awkward*!)

Her Philosophy on Makeup: My approach to beauty and makeup is to keep it looking as natural as possible. Beauty starts on the inside with a good diet and lots of hydration, which gives your skin a radiance that cannot be achieved by topical products alone. I think everyone has something they like about themselves, and everyone has stuff that they dislike, but the key is to play up what you like and focus on that. Make that your focal point and go from there.

Warm versus Cool Skin Tones

Your skin's undertone, or "temperature," is one of two simple categories: warm or cool. But surprisingly, determining your skin's undertone has very little to do with your skin tone (pale, olive, dark, etc.). A quick way to decode whether you're "warm" or "cool" is to look at the veins on your wrist. If they have a slightly blue/green color, you've got a warm skin tone. Blue/purple represents a cooler skin tone. Know this, and you'll have a much easier time selecting makeup that works with your complexion.

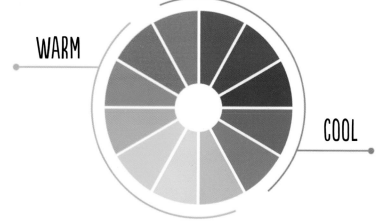

WARM

COOL

FIVE MAGICAL MAKEUP PRODUCTS EVERY GIRL SHOULD OWN

- Moisturizer with sunscreen. A two-in-one that will help prevent sun damage and wrinkles.
- Chapstick with SPF. To keep your lips soft (and yes, they can get sunburned, too!).
- Lip gloss, for an added bit of shine.
- Mascara. It makes you look more awake even on two hours' sleep.
- Bronzer (but not the orange-y kind). It adds just enough warmth to your skin—especially during the winter.

FIVE MAGICAL MAKEUP TOOLS EVERY GIRL SHOULD OWN

- A basic, fluffy brush (for multiuse, including blush and bronzer)
- A concealer brush (for under the eyes)
- A blender brush
- Sponges (also good for blending)
- An eyelash curler

Your Skin's Foundation

Truth: If you've got relatively good skin, you likely don't need to be wearing foundation every day. (And even if you have acne, piling on foundation can clog the pores even more, so it's best to resist wearing it 24/7.) But for special occasions, foundation is a nice way to fully even out your complexion.

That said, the fluorescent lighting in department stores won't shine a light on which foundation is best for you. All you gotta do is this: dab three different options on your jawline and step outside in natural light. Whichever one disappears into your skin best is your perfect match.

KEEP 'EM CLEAN!

If you've been breaking out a lot lately, it may be due to dirty makeup brushes. They rack up tons of bacteria, so not giving them a shower once in a while is like asking for a pimple party on your face. Wash your brushes every week, using a gentle soap and warm water. Let them air-dry overnight.

Expert Secret

You don't have to spend a lot of money to get a good product that works for you. You can find good products that are gentle enough for your skin at the drugstore.

—KATHLEEN

WHAT'S-HER-FACE

You identified your face shape in the last chapter (I told you you'd need to remember it!). While a lot of the tips below can work for anyone, understanding your facial structure can also help you apply makeup in a way that best flatters your face when you have a big event—like a prom, a job interview, or any time you need to take a selfie (#kiddingbutalsonotkidding).

SQUARE

Recap: Equal width and height; a structured jawline.

To add roundness, take a shading color (could be a foundation one or two shades darker than your regular foundation, or a taupe-color powder) and contour under the cheekbones, chin and forehead, then blend, blend, blend. You shouldn't be able to see where one foundation starts and another ends. Draw attention to your lips with a soft gloss.

OVAL

Recap: Longer than wide, but with a smooth—as opposed to rigid—structure.

Your eyes are the main focus if you have an oval face shape. Accentuate your brows by filling them in with an eyebrow pencil (go one shade lighter than your hair color). Then apply a luminescent highlight powder just below the brows and blend with a nude eye shadow. (See page 81 for which color eye shadows look best with your skin type.)

DIAMOND/TRIANGLE

Recap: Narrow hairline, and your jawline comes to a point around your chin, starting below your ear.

Contour the sides of the face (temples) and blend toward the hairline, the tip of the forehead and the very tip of the chin. Use a highlighter or a lighter foundation along the jawline. Apply peachy/bronzy-color blush to the apples of your cheeks. Groom brows a little apart from the center, giving a wider appearance in that area.

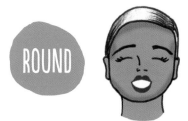

ROUND

Recap: About the same width the entire way around, with a smooth jawline.

Lucky you, you've got a face shape that screams youthful. Take a shading (contouring) color and apply to the temples, jawline, forehead and chin, blending. For a playful, natural look, add a pop of color to the lips or eyes, ditching any makeup elsewhere. (You'll be surprised how much a red lip can brighten up your complexion. Plus it looks super-French.)

OBLONG

Recap: Longer than it is wide, with a structured jawline.

This sleek face shape is sophisticated *and* easy to work with. Contour cheeks, corners of the forehead and jawline, and blend well. Lightly dust bronzer over the same areas to add dimension.

HEART

Recap: You have a widow's peak and cheeks that are slightly wider than your hairline and form a "V" at the chin.

With this classic face shape, focus on highlighting your cheekbones and jawline. Contour under the cheekbone and temples, but skip your cheekbones, as they are usually already pronounced.

EXPERT SECRET: When someone is saying, "Oh, you look like you're not wearing makeup," it's not necessarily about the eyes, the lips or anything else. It's about the skin. You want to make your skin look like you're not wearing makeup. —Kathleen

CONCEAL THOSE UNDER-EYE CIRCLES

Everyone has a little bit of puffiness under the eyes—especially during stressful times like finals week. Concealer will help. For people with more of a blue under-eye, your concealer should be just a tiny bit orange/yellow—it's the neutralizing color for blue. For those with more brown-gray under-eyes, your concealer should be a little bit pink, since pink is the neutralizing color for browns and grays. Placement is also important. You can't just put it under your whole under-eye and rub it in—you'll look like a raccoon! It has to be placed specifically and blended, blended, blended, blended.

blue under-eyes = concealer that's a bit orange/yellow

brown-gray under-eyes = concealer that's a bit pink

Step 1 I put it on under the eye where it's needed and then blend it out into the cheek.

Step 2 On your more prominent indentation, such as the under-eye hollows, I take a little bit more of the lighter concealer and dot it so that it's concentrated there.

Step 3 Then I blend it in with the general and slightly darker under-eye concealer I used to cover the under-eyes originally. What ends up happening is a reverse contour effect; your hollows appear plumped and the puffiness around them appears flattened. Then, voilà! You look like you've slept for eight hours.

Bronzer, Blush and Your Cheeks

Just as with concealer, the most important thing to remember about bronzer and blush is to blend. You shouldn't be able to see where it starts and where it stops. Bronzer especially should be used very sparingly. After dabbing my brush in a bronzer or blush palette, I always tap the brush against my wrist to get rid of excess powder. Then, lightly apply bronzer to the forehead, nose and cheeks—everywhere the sun hits—and top with blush on the cheekbones.

EXPERT SECRET:
Do not put a cream product on top of a powder product, ever. It never works. —Kathleen

All Eyes on Eye Shadow

Your eyes are the first thing people notice about you, so you want them to pop. The secret is to never choose an eye shadow that matches your eye color. Then your eyes will get lost, and that's not something iPhones can fix. Instead, use a contrasting shade to make your eyes stand out.

For a surefire natural look, go to your makeup counter and find a brown with *hints* of these colors, a bluish-brown or black for brown eyes, a maroon-brown for green eyes, or a goldy-brown for blue eyes.

Blue eyeshadow works well with brown eyes.

Purple works wonders on green eyes.

Browns and rusts look great with blue eyes.

Your Best Lip Color

There are always exceptions to the rule, but here is a general guideline when you're standing there, helpless in the middle of CVS:

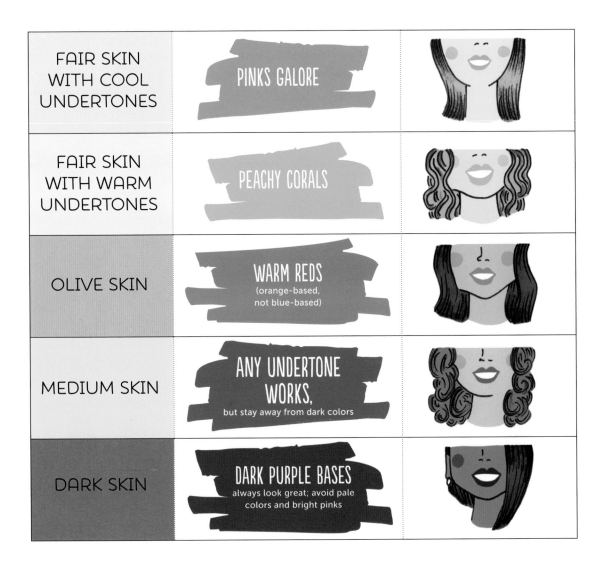

FAIR SKIN WITH COOL UNDERTONES	PINKS GALORE	
FAIR SKIN WITH WARM UNDERTONES	PEACHY CORALS	
OLIVE SKIN	WARM REDS (orange-based, not blue-based)	
MEDIUM SKIN	ANY UNDERTONE WORKS, but stay away from dark colors	
DARK SKIN	DARK PURPLE BASES always look great; avoid pale colors and bright pinks	

Special-Occasion Makeup

Whether you're the outgoing type who loves to wear loud makeup, or an understated type who prefers simple earth tones, there are a million ways to have fun with your look. Here's an easy guide to live by.

THE ALL-NATURAL SCHOOL LOOK

Keep it light. Apply a layer of mascara, a pink or nude lip gloss and, if needed, a quick dab of foundation or concealer over any trouble spots.

THE RISING-STAR WORK LOOK

When mentors encourage you to "stand out," they don't mean with your makeup. (You don't want to seem like you put more effort into your look than your work.) Keep your makeup natural by using primarily neutral shades. I like to use a golden brown over my eyelids, and blend with a darker brown, blending it out a bit to align with my eyebrow. I don't use eyeliner here—just a touch of mascara, a dab of lip gloss, and I'm good to go.

THE DREAM GIRL DATE LOOK

Of course you want to look hot, but you also want to look like yourself. *Don't* cake on the makeup—you've already got the date, so there's no need to hide behind a bunch of foundation. Go with a light lip gloss (soft for kissing but it won't get all over him) and waterproof mascara (sometimes the regular mascara smudges and you don't want to accidentally rock raccoon eyes).

THE IT-GIRL EVENING LOOK

Go all out here: try new trends and experiment. My personal favorite is a classic cat's eye and smoky shadow. The trick is to go slow, just layering a bit of color at a time. Start by framing the eyebrow with a highlighter or shimmer just underneath the brow. Then take your lightest color and go over your eyelid, not too far above the crease. Now that you've highlighted both your brow line and eyelid, it's time to contour your eye crease. Slowly trace your darker shade directly into the crease above the area you just highlighted. After your first brush-over, do a once-over and then continue blending this darker color toward the outer corner. If you're feeling wild (but a bit tired) dab a small amount of highlighter on the inner corner of the eye to help blend (this also makes you look more awake!). Apply eyeliner to the top and bottom lids, smudging the bottom just a bit to smooth out the look. Blend it into the corner of your eye to meet that gold shimmer in the corner around your eye. Lastly, add a few individual false eyelashes to the outer corner of your eyes. If you're having a hard time with the smoky eye, that's OK! It takes practice. Another evening look that I love is natural eye makeup and blush, but with just a pop of bright pink or red lipstick.

Expert Secret

It is never, ever OK to sleep with your makeup on. Your skin has to breathe—it's the largest organ in your body. Clean skin is just better-looking skin.

—KATHLEEN

Your Alarm Clock Hates You

If you've got a big event to go to and *zero* time to do your makeup (been there!), I've learned a few high-speed makeup tricks that'll help you win the war against your alarm for good!

STICK TO POWDER

Applying liquid foundation in a hurry can end up looking cakey. Instead, quickly dust a powder foundation over the skin after applying daily moisturizer.

DOUBLE YOUR BRONZER VALUE

Dash a bit of bronzer over the cheeks, nose and forehead and use it as an eye shadow, too.

LAYER THE GLOSS

Instead of rifling through piles of lipstick and gloss, apply a tinted lip balm. (And if you don't have time for foundation or bronzer, this can double as a last-minute bit of color on your cheeks.)

MASCARA

Skip the eyeliner and apply a double coat of black mascara.

Ingredients Breakdown

As with skin care products, it's important to know about the ingredients you're slathering on that pretty little face of yours. The Food and Drug Administration takes great care to regulate what goes into the stuff you're buying, but with so many different labels and promises and colors and everythang, the important stuff can go unnoticed. Remember these names and you'll be able to waltz through the aisles of any store with that educated-buyer confidence that you once thought only Oprah's makeup artist could have.

NONCOMEDOGENIC

This is a label that the FDA will only give to a product that was independently tested and proven not to clog pores and/or cause blackheads. Usually listed on the front or back of the product's packaging. *Won't clog pores* is saying the same thing, but that product has not gone through this FDA-regulated testing process. Look for this guarantee on your foundations and concealers.

NONACNEGENIC

Another FDA-awarded title, but a bit trickier to find. As it implies, this label means that it was tested by a contractor not affiliated with the company and proven not to cause acne—papules or cystic. Look for this on your foundations as well, but if you can't find it, don't worry. Not all products that lack this designation cause acne, nor should you think they're ineffective.

OIL-FREE

This is a good thing to look for if you have oily skin. Luckily, most makeup lines have a foundation that is oil-free nowadays. But if you've found your perfect shade with a product that isn't sans oil, try the manufacturer's pressed powder foundation. That'll be your oil-free option!

SYNTHETIC FRAGRANCES

There's no doubt that these umbrella ingredients will make your makeup smell less like sh!t, but always test out products with synthetic fragrances on a small area (like your wrist) before applying them to your face. You'll avoid any rashes or irritations that can come from an allergic reaction to this stuff.

A Final Tip

Makeup can be a great confidence booster, but it's important to stay confident in your natural beauty, too. Instead of automatically putting on makeup every day, brave the wild once in a while and go bare—it'll relieve your skin and build your confidence. Start with a low-key outing, like running errands. If you start to feel self-conscious, call a friend to occupy your mind and give you an extra ego boost. The more often you go out without makeup, the more comfortable you'll feel in your own skin—and you won't need constant concealer to feel your best.

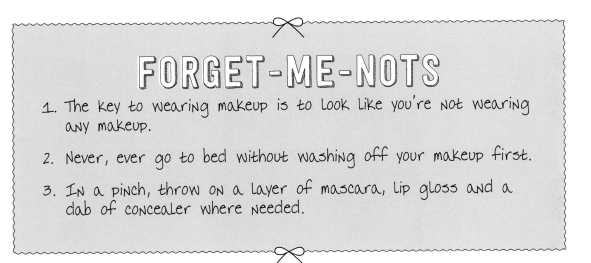

FORGET-ME-NOTS

1. The key to wearing makeup is to look like you're not wearing any makeup.

2. Never, ever go to bed without washing off your makeup first.

3. In a pinch, throw on a layer of mascara, lip gloss and a dab of concealer where needed.

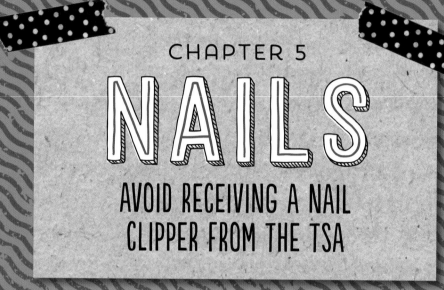

CHAPTER 5

NAILS

AVOID RECEIVING A NAIL CLIPPER FROM THE TSA

TOPCOATS ARE OVERRATED

THEY CALLED ME "GOOP GIRL." At around nine years old I was (OK, I totally still am) very into cosmetics and girly things to sort of "topcoat" the way I felt on the inside. I'd started buying the OPI versus the discount store nail polish and even dedicated one whole day each week to this DIY indulgence—Spa Sunday. Needless to say, I'd had my fair share of trial and error, but even more impressive was the amount of cosmetic products, tools, gadgets and hair masks that I had not just acquired, but used. EVERY DAY. Well, five drawers of exfoliating scrubs, nail buffers and hair dryers were never really easy to travel with. But they called me Goop Girl for a reason, and when it came to camping with my family, I didn't leave one nail clipper or cuticle softener in any of the drawers. The Goop Girl was about to go camping.

But then we entered the campground. The ranger showed us where to go on the map, and we made our way into the thick of it. We passed by the huge RVs, luxury hitch trailers, but right before we headed into the section for tents and small pop-up trailers, I looked around from inside the safety of my parents' cool, dry car and saw something so shocking, so traumatizing, so foreign, that I had no words for it. My parents started laughing as they watched their (kinda spoiled) only child react to what I now know is an outdoor communal shower. Then it hit me: I would have to use that and even with a swimsuit and cute flip-flops the grimy mix of mold and other people's suds made me freak. My parents were giving me a serious Goop Girl wake-up call.

But right before my girl plans started to chip away at my manicure, my parents burst out laughing. "We're kidding!" they said, as my mom began to snort-laugh. "But, wait . . . We aren't going camping?" I asked hopefully.

"Oh, no, we are still going camping. We rented a cabin, but we thought this would be a funny pit stop." As my dad started the car and got back on the traffic-filled freeway, he asked me a question: "Would you rather stay at the Grand Wilderness Resort in Disney for the weekend, and leave your spa stuff in the car so we can spend time together as a family? Or would you like to keep your goop stuff—and stay in that campground?" Well, duh, I thought. But, I didn't want to be stuck with my parents while we asked strangers to take awkward family photos (when I was *not* camera-ready) the whole time without any mud masks to hide under. But I chose the hotel, and thank god I did.

That was the best vacation I ever had with my family. We really bonded. We'd come back at night and order room service and look at the pictures from the day. Even though my hair was a mess, only three nails still had color, and I was makeup-free, in a lot of ways, I'd never looked better. Go figure, being with the ones you love really puts things in perspective. I didn't need to spend an hour and a half getting ready on vacation as a nine-year-old. My parents knew that, too, and that if I kept spending so much time focusing on beauty, I would miss out on the beauty of life. So, these days, I dig my hands into anything life gives me . . . because now I have gel nails. (That sh!t doesn't chip!!)

We've all had a run-in with the Chick Who Has the World's Longest Fingernails, but I'll go out on a limb and assume that is not the look you're going for. Nails are sort of like icing on a cake: just a few coats will make even the biggest mess look polished (pun intended). Luckily, this effect isn't restricted to salon VIPs. There are some easy tricks to getting a great mani at home—so settle in. It's about to get *really* girly here.

Go figure, being with the ones you love really puts things in perspective. I didn't need to spend an hour and a half getting ready on vacation as a nine-year-old. My parents knew that, too, and that if I kept spending so much time focusing on beauty, I would miss out on the beauty of life.

—ASHLEY

Bathroom? What Bathroom? You're at the Spa, Dahling

Because acrylics are never OK, I'm about to give you the lowdown on the ultimate spa experience that you can do at home. You'll only need about $40, a trip to the drugstore and a deep *ahhh.*

1. Let there be water.

Fill a small bowl with warm water (read: not boiling-hot) and add a splash of sesame oil. Soak your hands in the bowl for up to five minutes. This softens the nails and makes trimming less painful.

2. Snip, snip.

Start with clippers if you've got some major length to take care of—same if you prefer short nails, which are best for those of you ladies who play the guitar. Either way, make sure your nail clipper is sharp. (You'll know you've got a crappy clipper if your nail doesn't snap off after the first go at it.) Be careful not to trim beneath the end of your fingers, as that could lead to ingrown nails or hangnails, which sting like a b!tch. Just get rid of the obvious excess, and let a nail file take it from there.

3. Single file lines, please.

When filing your nails, always think of One Direction (but don't get distracted by that thought!). Go left to right, lift, and left to right again. Don't switch it up. This is gentler on the nail and won't handicap future nail growth.

4. Not your momma's skewers.

I'm talkin' about BBQ skewers, Willis! This is my cheap daily trick for clean nails. Since I use baby oil at night to remove my waterproof mascara (extra tip!), the black residue gets under my nails and makes it look like I've been playing in the mud all day. Take a wooden BBQ skewer and gently maneuver it under the nail, being careful not to push much deeper than where white meets pink (otherwise, you'll see blood—ew), and set the day's gunk free.

AUTHOR SECRET: A cheap pack of nail files goes a long way. Almost every drugstore will carry some great sets of twenty or so. Throw one in your purse, one in your makeup bag, one in your car, one in your locker—really go wild here. Scientific studies show that the most severe nail chipping happens an hour before a date, so it's best to be prepared. (My lawyer wants me to tell you that there's actually no evidence of that, but you get my point.) —Ashley

5. **The skinny on cuticle clippers (buyers beware).**

   You don't need to cut your cuticles unless you have hangnails (this goes for when you're getting a professional manicure, too). I know you're thinking, "Well, WTF, Ashley! What if my cuticles just keep on growing?!" Quit fearing some creepy cuticle skin is taking over your entire Coral Escapade mani because that's never gonna happen. As Dr. Murad says, "The cuticles are protecting your skin—for example, the water that you wash your hands with can have microbes that can lead to infection, so your cuticles act as a barrier." Basically, healthy cuticles take care of themselves. You can push them down, sure, but no need for you (or someone else) to cut them to shreds.

6. **Get buffed up.**

   Most drugstores sell these convenient four-way buffering blocks. Pick one of these babies up, and once the nails have been trimmed and the hands have been thoroughly washed and dried, gently use each side of the buffer. (Keep all buffering away from the cuticles to avoid aggravation and bloodshed—#SpartanSalon.)

7. **Exfoliate.**

   Use a salt scrub to shed any dead skin and make hands super-soft, or make your own scrub by combining granulated sugar with your favorite body wash in a small bowl for the same effect. Rub gently—just a few circular motions will do the trick.

8. **Behold the pumice stone.**

   Soak your feet in warm water (bubbles are encouraged) for five to ten minutes. Dry thoroughly. Buff off the hardened skin on your heels by scrubbing with semi-deep pressure for about forty-five seconds. P.S.: Steer clear of blisters. Don't try to pop or buff them—simply apply a Band-Aid to help protect them while your body heals itself.

9. **Moisturize—feet, too.**

   Massage cuticle oil onto—you guessed it—your cuticles, and lock the moisture in with a happy-smelling lotion. What is a happy-smelling lotion, you ask? Why, any scent that brings you relaxation or whatever mood you need.

The ⭐ VIP Upgrade

Throw in these add-ons and you might as well call yourself Beyoncé.

1 AROMATHERAPY LITE

Go to a mall, any mall, and choose a candle that suits your (desired) mood:

Citrus: uplifting and energizing

Lavender or eucalyptus: relaxing

Ylang ylang or patchouli: romantic and comforting

Vanilla or chamomile: sleeeeppppyyyyy

2 SOAK YOUR HANDS IN WARM TEA

This sounds like a certain breed of crazy, but believe me, it works. The antioxidants in black tea will absorb into your skin, and soaking your hands in green tea can even reduce excessive sweating in your hands. I promise, detoxing your digits will make you feel as pleasantly ridiculous as those ladies who put caviar on their face. *Note:* Don't try this at tea time.

3 FIND DEAD SEA SALTS

Go to your local health store for a holistic twist on your at-home exfoliating routine. According to Eastern medicine, there are amazing detoxifying qualities to this mix.

4 GIVE YOURSELF A HAND MASSAGE

Once your hands are plenty moisturized, press your thumb into the space between your (other) thumb and index finger, applying medium to strong pressure. Move farther out on the hand with gradually softer strokes. Or, make your mom do it for you—and return the favor . . . tomorrow.

The Art of Nail Art

1. **Kick out any stage-5 nail polish clingers who've over-stayed their welcome.**
   Choose a nonacetone nail polish remover and cotton balls (tissues take forever) to get rid of any old color. Acetone removers can be too harsh and strip the nail of its natural moisture. Anywho, you want a clean nail so that the new polish can fully adhere to the nail and dry properly.

2. **Layer with a base coat.**
   You're allowed to skip this step if you only want to keep the color for one night or just have a few minutes to spare. However, if you want your manicure to last for a few days, it's best to apply a clear base coat first. This will help bind the polish to the nail and prevent chipping.

3. **The main event.**
   Painting one hand at a time (which allows for fewer mistakes and butterfingers), apply two coats of color, giving it a minute (literally) between the first and second coat. For the first coat, put a bit of pressure on the brush so that the bristles fan out and apply the color in one stroke. The second coat is for covering any gaps and creating even color. Apply a third coat only if needed, making sure the nails are almost dry before putting it on.

4. **There's always that one hot-mess nail . . .**
   To wipe away any excess polish on your fingers, wrap a piece of a cotton ball around one of your handy wooden BBQ skewers, dip it in nail polish remover and carefully remove. If you smudge a nail, dip a fresh skewer/cotton ball in nail polish remover and—keeping your newly manicured hand at a safe distance from the liquid—clean your nail and reapply your polish.

5. **End with a topcoat.**
   Even if you've only got a second, don't skip the topcoat. Once your nails are mostly dry, apply a fast-dry clear polish, being careful not to apply too much pressure. Topcoats will harden your polish and add a touch of shine (#worthit).

Tips for the Salon

You may have breezed through this chapter if you frequent the nail salon weekly, but there are still some things you need to know before offering your hand for a manicure.

BYOP (BRING YOUR OWN POLISH)

Especially if you've noticed that your salon's polishes look older than your grandma. That could also be a sign of unsanitary situations all around, so if you haven't noticed anything soaking in blue Barbicide, run for the hills and find another, safer salon.

WHIP YOUR SPF BACK AND FORTH

The UV drying lamps used for shellac manicures are basically small versions of tanning beds; therefore, they hold the same dangers. Bring sunblock and apply it to the top of your hands before you enter the light. The UV rays are harmful to your skin.

BREAKS FOR BREAKAGE PREVENTION

Give your nails a break from all the polishes, gels and glues once in a while. Without at least a week's rest every month, your nails won't get enough moisture or oxygen to grow thick and healthy.

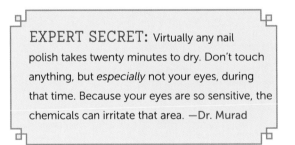

EXPERT SECRET: Virtually any nail polish takes twenty minutes to dry. Don't touch anything, but *especially* not your eyes, during that time. Because your eyes are so sensitive, the chemicals can irritate that area. —Dr. Murad

FORGET-ME-NOTS

1. Never cut your nails below the tips of your fingers. That could cause ingrown nails or hangnails, which sting like a b!tch.

2. Wooden BBQ skewers, often found in and easily steal-able from your mother's pantry, make great under-the-nail cleaners.

3. It's OK to skip the base coat when you're painting your nails, but it's always worth applying the topcoat.

PART

3

YOU:

As Seen on You

CHAPTER 6

NUTRITION

MICROWAVE AND DISHWASHER SAFE

MY EXPERIENCE: WAR AND FOOD

IF YOU'D MET ME TEN OR SO YEARS AGO, you would've gotten to know a little girl whose once curly blond hair had turned brown and straight, and who liked to sit alone in her room, playing with dolls because they couldn't hurt her the way people could. Being so young, my coping skills were still forming—in fact, my brain was still forming, literally—and eventually I grew out of dolls and instead found great comfort in food. Sugary food. I cried, my tired parents handed me treats—which filled up a metaphorical hole inside me—and by ten years old, I'd gained *a lot* of weight. I was chubby.

Kids made fun of me because I wore adult sizes (which seriously got in the way of my ability to wear those dresses that matched my American Girl dolls, but that's probably a good thing, looking back). The bullying got so bad that my parents pulled me from the accelerated learning school I was attending in Florida (which was also probably a good thing, as we were studying for the SATs in fourth grade) and plunked me in a basic Montessori school.

Luckily, there was a summer break before the big move, and I'd lost the weight in one of those strange growth spurts (that, and my parents stopped giving me two bowls of ice cream for dessert every night). But on the first day of fifth grade, I walked in and felt the familiar stares of judge-y peers. I assumed they could tell how fat and ugly I felt, so within my first few hours of being there, I decided to become a b!tch. I made it my mission to try to control *them* first, so that they couldn't hold any power over me.

Once I realized my power over people, I extended my reign to food. It was a weird thing for me to be so young yet still capable of causing such harm to my own body. It started with binge eating, which eventually grew into full-blown anorexia. I think I was just repulsed by the food that had made me the fat kid. I felt that this new school was a second chance, so I snubbed my nose at anything that risked making me feel "less than." By fourteen, my eating disorder and I moved to Los Angeles, which definitely did not help. Quite the opposite: I was *praised* for being so skinny by stylists, casting directors and even fellow actors. In LA, anorexia became less of an emotional coping strategy (at least it seemed that way) and more of a lifestyle choice.

I went to a cocktail party for a magazine launch once, and I remember arriving to the swanky hotel rooftop, all ready for the red carpet with this great, tight dress on.

I also hadn't eaten in two days.

I wouldn't let myself eat anything until I got those stupid pictures taken of me looking just as "perfect" as the other celebs on the carpet. I finished the photo ops and walked around pretending to belong. I was starving and now I could eat. As I was juggling my clutch, I started eyeing all the delicious hors d'oeuvres pass by on expensive trays held by ridiculously good-looking servers. I grabbed a bite-size appetizer just as a waiter passed by my other side. I grabbed another one from his tray (some fancy-looking ice cream cone with cheese inside), and just as I was about to eat it, I heard a familiar voice. It was a girl I knew from various auditions and acting classes. I said hello and went to hug her, which soon felt very awkward, as I was clutching my clutch under my armpit and juggling two hands full of food. She laughed before I even finished my hug.

"Doubling up?" she asked. Her friend, who appeared out of nowhere, looked over at her and they smirked. I was humiliated and felt like a total fat ass. Before I could think of a joke, she'd spotted someone else she knew and walked away, her friend trailing behind her, but not before giving me a b!tchy, sympathetic once-over.

"Bye," I said, but their backs were already turned. I felt as if I was back in grade school, stuffing my face to feel full inside. I felt heavy, even though I wasn't. And I hated the fact that my enemy of the past—food—was still haunting me. Eager to save face, I quickly gobbled up the bite-size pieces. As a bit of that cheese stuff stuck to my lip, I felt the sinking feeling that everyone was looking at me, made worse by the fact that my stilettos were literally sinking into the fake grassy patch near the entrance to the restroom. Instant shame pulled me up and I headed to the bathroom. It was empty.

Without thinking too much about what I was doing, I went into the stall and made myself throw up. Afterward, I felt better. I had been able to have my cheese cone cake and eat it, too. *I could eat and never be fat*, I thought!

From that point on, this twisted logic ruled me. Soon I was eating three meals a day or more, gorging on set and escaping to my trailer afterward to throw up.

It worked for a while, until one day at home I had eaten so much and purged so quickly that I felt incredibly weak. I couldn't see straight and it was hard to breathe. I felt light-headed, and I was freaked out. I called my doctor. Luckily, I was able to drag myself to his office and got checked out.

He explained to me that I had become so dehydrated and malnourished that my body was simply shutting down. I left that office scared as hell, and I vowed not to make myself throw up ever again. But two years of bulimia was a difficult habit to break. Eventually I did cut myself off, but only by eating the bare minimum—enough to keep me functioning without feeling bloated or gaining weight. I was still anorexic. I still fasted when I put on a pound or two and, frankly, it was working—on the outside at least.

Around the same time, I met some girls my age who were also "recovering" from their eating disorders. They knew I wasn't really recovering, but rather clinging to mine for dear life. But I didn't listen to their advice. I was convinced I was fine and that eventually I would be normal again or at least just learn to live like this. I thought, in a way, I had recovered.

Until this book came about. I knew I'd touch on the eating disorder bit, because I didn't want any other girls to feel what I felt, but I was under the strong impression that no matter what my weight—skinny or too skinny—I could always claim to eat however someone wanted me to. I'd just lie to the press. And the plan was basically to lie in this book. But I can't do that because I got help from a professional.

As I write this now, I'll confess, I am happily working through my eating disorder. I do my best every day to nourish my body, to show it respect so that I can continue to do what I do—inspire and make a difference. Some days I do well, and some days I don't. I am still in recovery, a daily battle at this stage. However, that won't be the case much longer. If I keep doing my best, I can soon be, really and truly be, fully free of disordered eating and live a healthy, fulfilling (and filling) life.

A major part of my diet plan is, well, a freakin' plan. By setting myself up with all the right goodies, I know that I have a better chance of getting the most out of life (and lunch). Take a look around: we survive on food and too much or too little may be the reason some of us age less gracefully, suffer from various physical ailments and eventually die before our time. The good news: All of that is preventable, treatable and in some cases reversible—if you start now. Diets that provide sustainable energy aid in physical appearance (Hail to the omega-3s) and improve life span through clean, mindful and enjoyable eating. They are key to increasing not just your health but your quality of life. It's really simple to start eating your way to a better and more productive life. Staying focused in a world of distractions and emotional setbacks is hard, and food is one of the easiest things to use as a coping tool. But eating a bucket of ice cream (yeah, I've eaten a whole BUCKET) isn't going to get my ass any farther off the couch or any further into actualizing a solution. So I try to keep in mind what is MINE.

Wait! What Is MINE?

MINE is a way through life, an acronym to remember when you're at risk of forgetting what the purpose of food really is. For example, when I think about what I want out of life, be it career success or a family of my own, I begin to visualize it, internalize it and then start the process of actualizing it, as MINE. Not only will it improve your willpower (or help you rediscover it), but MINE will also help to quell both your conscious and subconscious destructive habits. It's simple.

Mindful: Be mindful of your motivations for eating or craving certain foods; feeding your feelings only makes the feelings grow. Be aware of how your body responds to certain foods, the quantities and the situations that trigger negative responses. Does pasta give you a tummy ache? When you multitask and eat do you notice your hunger diminishing or do you have a sudden and distracting feeling of being bloated? If you go to work, school or even out running errands, will it be easy to find healthy food or will you just forget to eat? Asking yourself questions like these gives you the power to be honest and mindful of what to eat or not eat, when to snack on the job and how to prepare yourself (and your Tupperware) for any situation.

Intuitive: Use your intuition to guide your eating choices. Your body's cues on hunger can be surprisingly tricky to interpret. Giving your body what it actually needs only requires a few extra seconds of "checking in" with your system. For instance, if you got enough sleep but are running low on energy, instead of grabbing a cup of coffee or an energy drink, feed your body what it needs—calories. The same thing applies if you're just thirsty; sometimes you may get the munchies, but there's a good chance you may just be dehydrated. On the other hand, you may experience cravings for sweets or carbs. The good news: You can trust your body on that! If you want sugar, your body is sending messages to your brain that you need sugar to maintain your blood pressure. Eat what you want, as healthy a choice as possible, when your body tells you it needs fuel. Be sure to distinguish your body's *sensations* from your mind's *feelings*. It's easy to zone into the feelings and allow them to cloud your decision making. But this habit leads you to eating when you aren't hungry, eating things that can harm your body and ultimately setting up a habit of merely addressing those temporary feelings, rather than finding a solution to the problem.

Nutritious: There's no way that you can get 100 percent of your daily vitamins and nutritional needs exclusively from your food. In addition to taking supplements and vitamins (see my website), it's very important to pack your diet full of superfoods. For example, let's say you have a cheese stick; the bonus would be calcium and some of your daily dairy, and the downsides would be that it's high in fat and, per serving, not filling. If you had a bag of chips, the bonus would be sodium (not a great bonus), and the downsides would be that it was high in fat and low in protein, had no vitamins or minerals and was full of preservatives and chemicals. Try to compare your food choices based on what has more bonuses than downsides. If you have a toss-up between two foods, choose the snack that has the fewest additives or, super-bonus, is USDA-certified organic.

Enjoyable: Food is primarily a fuel for your everyday functioning, but having a boring, tasteless diet can lead to an eventual binge on junk food, minor depression and irritability, and limits in social situations. I have the same breakfast (banana) and afternoon snack (protein-and-greens smoothie) every day, my favorite snack food is trail mix and my main diet principle is organic/natural foods. But I don't eat that every day or live by the organic principle 100 percent. Being too strict would limit my dining-out options, keep me in a constant state of PMS and eventually lead me right back into bad habits. In addition to focusing on the pleasure aspect of a diverse diet, choose foods that are physically engaging to eat or to prepare. Wherever there is more involved in the preparation or consumption of your food, there's more attention devoted (indirectly or directly) to really absorbing each and every sensation (smell, taste, texture, aesthetics) your meal has to offer.

MY KINDA HEALTHY PLATE

This is a standard guide—and what I try to shoot for—when creating a healthy, but still kick-ass meal.

⅛ HEALTHY FATS

like avocado or nuts. Yes, some fats are good for you! They help you digest your food, boost your brain-power, and can keep you full longer.

ABOUT ½ VEGGIES

steamed broccoli or carrots, roasted red peppers or eggplant. In general, the more colorful your plate is, the more it's filled with a diverse set of nutrients. Veggies are where you can have a lot of fun with this!

¼ LEAN PROTEIN

like lean, grilled chicken

¼ WHOLE GRAINS

brown rice counts!

When time is of the essence, here's what I like to have in a hurry:

THE PARFAIT OF CHAMPIONS	Greek yogurt, banana or regular granola, organic strawberries and blueberries.
THE GREEN-WITH-ENVY SMOOTHIE	2 scoops of Non-GMO dairy-free protein powder, 1 mini can of pineapple juice, 5–6 ice cubes, ½ frozen banana, a pinch of chia seeds, ¼ cup rolled oats, 1½ cups of various frozen fruits (either mango, pineapple, strawberries, blueberries, raspberries or kiwi) and 1½ scoops of powdered greens. (It's like eating your veggies without, well, eating them.)
TOTAL NUTCASE	I make a huge 60-ounce canister of this at least every other week. It's a great snack that's sweet (chocolate), salty (nuts) and filling without making you feel bloated. Put equal parts diced cranberries, roasted and salted cashews, almonds and shelled pistachios and milk chocolate baking chips into a sealed container and shake it until it's evenly mixed. I recommend keeping a snack bag–sized portion in your purse at all times, just in case you get hungry.
THE FROZEN-TO-TABLE TREAT	Don't fear frozen veggies. Because they're flash-frozen at peak ripeness, they contain more nutrients than the fresh stuff. Kale; frozen carrots, broccoli, red pepper (or yellow/orange) and peas, sautéed with just a touch of olive oil, salt and pepper.

Understanding How
Your Body Works

The next few pages will give you an understanding of some natural body processes. (If that made you think of farting, it's OK because the same thing happened to me.)

METABOLISM

Metabolism is a collection of chemical reactions that convert the energy from food (calories) into energy that your body needs to perform daily activities, including necessities like shopping and dancing around the room to Beyoncé. There are two types of metabolism that are always occurring in your body.

1. **Anabolism:** the building of body tissues and energy stores. Anabolism naturally occurs during adolescence when we are growing into classy women and also during pregnancy (don't forget to take your pill today).

2. **Catabolism:** the breakdown of body tissues and energy stores to create more fuel to carry out bodily functions. (Yep, thinking about farting again.)

Naturally,

If anabolism = catabolism then weight stays the same

If anabolism > catabolism then weight gain occurs

If anabolism < catabolism then weight loss occurs

BMR

OK, so your basal metabolic rate (BMR) is the number of calories that your body burns each day while at rest. It takes energy (calories!) for your heart to beat, blood to pump and organs to function, so even when you're just hanging out, bingeing on Netflix, your body is always burning calories (#Science). Each person's BMR is different and is calculated using height, weight and age.

BMI

On the other hand, the body mass index (BMI) is a simple equation to measure fatness (don't be scared) that is calculated using height and weight only. BMI classifies people into four different weight ranges: underweight, normal, overweight and obese. Some people believe that BMI is an accurate indicator of "what's healthy and what's not" in terms of weight, but this is FALSE. BMI doesn't take into consideration bone or muscle, which both weigh more than fat. (See, I told you I was smart.) So a person with strong bones and good muscle tone will have a high BMI. Because of this, athletes and fit, health-conscious people who work out a lot tend to find themselves classified as overweight or even obese. Not cool! A high BMI does not mean an individual is even overweight, let alone obese. It could mean the person is fit and healthy, with very little fat.

Powerb!tch-Approved Healthy Eating Styles

ORGANIC

First off, unless it says *FDA-certified organic* on the label, it may not be 100 percent organic. *Organic* basically means that, from start to finish, the food was grown, processed and preserved using only natural ingredients and is free of human-made or manufactured ingredients (I'm talking about preservatives, genetically modified organisms [GMOs], and artificial dyes and flavors). As I have found by living in a really progressive city (yay, LA!), many options are available to me that make it easy to eat organic, but they're not necessarily cheap. In my experience, my body seems to function better with an organic diet, even though humans survived for many thousands of years without companies like Montecito, it's really a matter of preference.

VEGETARIAN

You know this already—we're simply talking about the dietary lifestyle that excludes meat. While some vegetarians consume no animal meat whatsoever, some (called pescaterians) do eat fish. It's possible to eat a balanced diet as a vegetarian because many nonmeat items are full of protein.

VEGAN

This is a diet free of any animal products—meat, cheese, butter and even eggs. But thanks to Whole Foods and a ton of smart hippies, there are many vegan "substitutes" for those foods and nutrients. Even if you don't buy into this, some would argue that it may be healthy to eat vegan. I disagree with that—the vegan diet is extremely restrictive and it's often hard for vegans to consume a balanced diet—but it's your decision to make. If you do decide to try a vegan diet, consult with your doctor or nutritionist to make sure you're getting all the nutrients your body needs.

SUPPLEMENTS

I admit that I take a ton of supplements, everything from arnica (herbal) to biotin (amino acid) to zinc (a mineral) daily. Most people would argue that too much of a good thing is a bad thing, but I'm careful to monitor my intake so as not to overload on vitamin K (which can be toxic if overconsumed), while pounding the water-soluble vitamins (such as vitamin C) and utilizing herbs for specific concerns (such as arnica when I have a bruise). As long as you're careful and work with your doctor, you, like me, may find that supplements offer a lot of benefits to your overall health. I premake my vitamin packs weekly; that way I can grab a pack and go if I'm in a rush. If you prefer a liquid option, go to your local health food store and invest in a powder drink. Most of them taste pretty good when mixed with juice or into a smoothie, and can offer additional nutrients, such as powdered greens or red fruits. Just be sure to eat first. Vitamins tend to make you nauseous if you take them on an empty stomach.

Dos and Don'ts

(DO!) **Try your best to erase the past positive associations you made with the food or goodies in question and focus on how they make you feel now.** It's easy to eat something out of habit or because your peers are consuming something and bonding over it. But focus on an alternative. Maybe switch to decaf coffee if caffeine prompts frequent anxiety or insomnia, and if pasta or sugars cause fatigue, bloating and digestive issues, go gluten-free or sugar-free for a bit. If it makes a difference, stick to that! There's no need to suffer because something tastes good. You'll find an alternative for every craving, every allergy and every restriction in the world of food.

(DON'T!) **Avoid eating as a secondary task.** Whether you're studying, watching TV, Internet browsing or doing anything else you can do without using your hands, you're bound to eat too much if you multi-task while eating. If you're on the go, pack snacks that are utensil-free and full of nutritional benefits, like trail mix, veggie chips, sliced fruit or bite-size veggies.

(DO!) **Set yourself up for a consistently healthy diet by packing lunches, snacks and even your own beverages.** Lunch boxes today are way cuter than that light-up Power Rangers lunch box your little brother had five years ago, and bringing your own lunch is also a great way to start to go green. Try a recycled lunch box: Ukonserve. com has some freakin' sweet options that are recycled, reusable, BPA-free and, most important, matchy-matchy.

DON'T! Feed your feelings. Feelings and external stimuli can easily manipulate us into ignoring our body's signals. In reality, events happen, we experience them, we internalize those experiences, we react and, finally, we cope with the events' effect on us. While this is the actual time line of events, oftentimes we don't even notice what event happened or how it triggered certain emotions. Instead, we find ourselves working backward, sitting with a feeling of anxiety or frustration and automatically coping with the feeling as opposed to the trigger. We try to subdue the feeling with a comfort food as a means for avoiding facing the emotion and finding a productive solution to the problem.

DON'T! Push yourself to maintain a perfect diet 24/7. Try to find the balance between a consistent flow of nutrition and the starring role in *Supersize Me 2*. Give yourself at least one meal a week with absolutely zero boundaries. If you want a chocolate cake for breakfast on Tuesday, have it. But be careful not to do an entire day of cheating. Such a drastic change in nutritional intake every six days is essentially a mini-yoyo diet. So don't cheat yourself into taking the easy way out or you'll end up completely obsessed with food and come up with different excuses to bend this rule or that rule. Remember, it's about balance, which takes hard work, but it does pay off, not just in the way you look, but in the way you feel.

THE FOOD LOG

At times, I've found it helpful to keep a daily food diary. On page 206, you'll find a larger checklist to help you manage your day. Here's how to use the "Food Log" section of it:

Write down how you're feeling before you eat. If you're just hungry, write that down.

Write down what you ate and at what time. This doesn't have to be super-thorough; it just gives you a better idea of your eating patterns. You also don't need to write down nutritional info, such as calories or carbs in the food, unless you're told otherwise by a doctor or nutritionist.

Write down how you felt after you ate it. This can include anything from an emotion (guilty, calm, focused, better) to the state of your hunger (that is, whether you're still hungry or crazy full) to what you did next. (Did you get back to the next task of the day or did you obsess about the food and get distracted?)

Reflect on your patterns each week. This will help you better understand your relationship with food.

HOW I FELT BEFORE EATING	WHAT I ATE	TIME	HOW I FEEL AFTER EATING

FORGET-ME-NOTS

1. Practice MINE: Mindful eating, intuitive guidance, nutritionally packed foods and enjoyable variations in your diet.

2. Your body is your best indicator of what to eat and when.

3. Find a diet that complements your lifestyle, steers clear of your allergies and is also easy to sustain. Balance is key, so don't overdose on rice cakes!

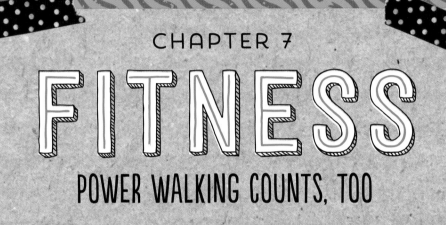

CHAPTER 7

FITNESS

POWER WALKING COUNTS, TOO

MY EXPERIENCE: MY INSECURITIES
DIMINISH IN THE WAKE OF EFFORT

AS I WRITE THIS NOW, I'm forced to think back to yesterday. I woke up and, as usual, fed my cat, had breakfast and went to put some pants on—except I couldn't because they were too tight (unusual). I thought to myself, *Here I am, working out four to five effing times a week, and yet I'm still bloated and unable to fit into my pants.* (I could've also thought to myself, *Here I am, fresh from a horrendous breakup.* Or: *Here I am, working my ass off writing this book.*) I knew I'd put on weight and had been avoiding these very pants for this very reason. But here I was, in a Texas stare-down with what I thought was the root of all my problems . . . and I was about to freak on the pants.

So I did. I started raging harder and louder than ever. Sort of like a '90s Looney Tune, the blood rushed to my face and steam might have even come out of my ears. I yanked every single piece of clothing out of their almost painfully perfect places. Ripping them out of drawers, off hangers, from compartments and whatever else, I threw them with all my might on the floor, cursing at them as if they were going to apologize for "everything I've ever gone through." I felt as if I had no control over myself, as if all my pent-up anger was directly caused by this one pair of pants.

Eventually, I exhausted myself and fell asleep. When I woke up, I realized there were a few factors that contributed to this episode. First, I expected that I would magically be better the minute I decided to take action (with the breakup, the eating disorder and my plan to get fit). Obviously, none of those things have a quick fix. Second, I felt as if my body wasn't mine any-more—I'd been focusing on the exterior to prove to the outside world that

And nothing makes you feel more powerful, more in control, and just generally badass than when you feel strong and in shape.

—ASHLEY

I was OK, when the only real way I was going to get healthy was if I did it for myself.

Fitness is the most literal metaphor and one of the clearest rewards for putting in hard work. I believe fitness is a very spiritual thing—you're taking care of yourself, training your vessel to be more capable and also learning how your body works naturally. Everyone has a special skill—mine is running and punching (aka kickboxing and martial arts). I'd never done martial arts until about a year ago, but it comes naturally to me, so naturally that, as I write this now, I am dying to do it again. I'm the karate kid but I am enjoying myself—it's challenging, it's poignant and it's in my nature.

I've also learned that my body responds best to what I call "journey fitness," which is all about incorporating nature and/or engaging in methods of fitness that feel fun and can actually teach you something about yourself, as opposed to rep after rep of a rigid routine. My fitness journey has led me to start regaining control, acceptance and, most important, balance in my life. I know that logically I have to eat every day and work out to be healthy, but now, I'm beginning to *feel* that significance. I may have put on fifteen pounds, but fasting or purging won't help get me in balance—not in the long run. Instead, I have to work through my metabolism, since it's been damaged after so many years of disordered eating, and show up for a workout to keep my body strong and functioning in an optimal way. And nothing makes you feel more powerful, more in control, and just generally badass than when you feel strong and in shape. Luckily, I have the help of Lalo Fuentes, my trainer. I met Lalo at seventeen and wasn't ready to face my real issues yet, so I didn't work out with him for a long time. (Plus I had a crush on him. And makeup is no good at the gym; you just look vain.) Lalo has taught me so much more than the importance of balance and health—he's helping me get my sh!t together and, most important, letting me kick the sh!t out of him during kickboxing.

Exercise Your Body *and* Spirit

I've learned firsthand the benefits of mindful treatment of my body and its endless payoffs—mostly in shopping confidence and styling the best me. Your body is a vessel that does its job simply by being treated respectably for optimum performance, so that it can best serve your missions in life.

MEET YOUR
EXPERT

LALO FUENTES,
celebrity personal trainer

His Philosophy on Fitness: Never take your health for granted. Fitness and wellness are a journey, not a destination.

Lalo's "Get Your Sh!t Together" Story

I remember my days back in high school very well. I used to go to class with just a pen and a blank piece of paper, folded into four parts in case I needed to take notes. Maybe the lack of control over kids should be blamed on the system, where you can choose your own classes and plan your future as if you were an expert. When my family and I moved from Peru and I got that freedom in America, things went south for me. I chose two fitness classes (which came in handy later on), wood shop, computers and, I believe, two more that were requirements. Oh yes, I also chose art. I remember that class because it was on Fridays, and on Thursday nights the Hungry Sailor had twenty-five-cent beer specials. I remember coming to class either hungover or still buzzed.

I think you know how things went for me. Bad grades, expulsions and I even got into bigger problems that I prefer not to remember. After a few months of summer school mixed with night school later, I graduated from high school. That's when I decided it would be great to take a break and be a bartender. You know, too much work and stress. Some of my friends got into college—one to be a lawyer, another one a doctor—and I started to feel not so good about my situation. I started working at my dad's store, pulling twelve-hour days, seven days a week, and I was getting burned out quickly. But sooner rather than later, it struck me. One day I woke up and I decided to get my sh!t together and go to college. After too much monotony, your brain suddenly starts to dig new information and education.

After debating a few careers, including nutrition, I decided to study business. Finance, to be specific. I was so excited once I made my decision that I ran and told my dad about it. His response was quite the opposite reaction I expected. He said, "Who are you going to fool?" and he told me that I was going to waste my time and money, and that I was a bad student and always had been. He said if I wanted to learn business, he could teach me at his store. Those words, though painful, were the ones that fueled my desire even more to prove to him, myself and everybody else that I was capable of succeeding.

Long story longer, I got accepted to college, and from the very beginning all my grades where As and Bs. I finished school with finance and advertising degrees and then moved to NYC for an internship with an investment banking firm. It was in New York that I discovered my passion for fitness. I quit my finance job and continued on with the fitness industry.

One of the things that helped me, and still helps me every time I feel stuck on something, is to type out my short-term goals as well as my long-term ones on a computer, print it out and tape it on the wall next to my computer. Every time I finish a goal, I highlight it. Every day, I take a look at them and try to finish or at least work on each one of those. Getting your sh!t together is a work in progress. It's like sailing across the Atlantic Ocean. You need to enjoy the ride, but you need to have a desired destination in mind and a plan of action.

Today I know I don't need to prove to my parents or anybody else that I'm capable of doing something. Now, no matter what people say or think about me, I do things because I want to better myself as a human being. I'm happy and comfortable the way I am. I'm complete.

Understanding What Your Body Was Built For

Some people look in the mirror and think, *Why am I this way?* It's because, as Lady Gaga says, you were born this way. From an anthropological standpoint, we put people into three different categories: ectomorph, mesomorph and endomorph. And, across the board, everybody has the same potential to feel really good about who they were created to be.

MESOMORPH

Description: You're right in the middle—not "petite" per se, but your bone structure is still relatively narrow.

Remember these pluses: Your metabolism is somewhat predictable. As with most people, it will show when you've been over- or undereating. When you work out, rely on being very in tune with any and all physical cues your body tries to send you.

Avoid these pitfalls: Because your body is kind of "in between," it can be really easy for you to mistake yourself for a more definitive type, driving yourself crazy because you think you're an "out-of-shape ectomorph" or because you want to look like Sofía Vergara. It'll never work to aim for something you're not. Adopt a healthy diet and exercise program and your body will naturally become the best version of itself.

ECTOMORPH

Description: You're narrow-boned, with smaller wrists and a smaller neck.

Remember these pluses: You're one of those (freakishly lucky) girls who can eat whatever she wants without easily putting on weight.

Avoid these pitfalls: You have less ability to build muscle and you're probably never going to feel like you're all that athletic, but many girls want a lean, feminine figure like this.

ENDOMORPH

Description: You have a wider bone structure and defined curves.

Remember these pluses: Your ability to build strength is far superior to those in the other two categories. Rest assured, everyone will be jealous when all your hard work toward getting into peak physical shape lets you easily kick ass at the gym—sailing through dead lifts while all the boys cry. (P.S.: Please be on my dodgeball team!)

Avoid these pitfalls: You're built for power. Instead of judging your body by your current clothing size, focus on muscle definition. I say *muscle definition* because body-fat percentage is an ugly phrase, but I kind of mean the same thing.

A FITNESS PLAN YOU'LL ACTUALLY STICK TO

I'm a (wo)man with a plan. Always. Planning out your goals is the best way to create a fitness journey that holds you accountable, diversifies your workouts and helps monitor your progress. I love to look back on the hard parts and celebrate long-sought-after accomplishments. What is more satisfying than that postworkout feeling of achievement and hard work? That being said, a lot of my fitness plans have really sucked. They were too time-consuming or scheduled into time slots that just weren't realistic (like the butt crack of dawn). I finally started thinking, *Oh, wait, so if I make a plan that works with my other day-to-day plans, I can spend less time reworking my plan and spend more time actually doing my plan.* Then I thought, *OK, I think I have a plan to make a really good plan now.* I started off by asking myself a few questions, which led to me figuring out the best type of fitness for my lifestyle and personality, all of which I've typed up into a lovely little questionnaire for you to answer for yourself below.

THE PLAN-MAKING PLAN: PLAN

FITNESS
How much time per day do you have to commit to fitness, based on your current schedule?

A I have about thirty minutes a day. I have school and/or work to deal with, which doesn't allow me anything more without sacrificing QT with friends and family.

B I have an hour each weekday. Maybe weekends, too. Bring it on.

C I have no time. Sorry.

If you chose A or B, you now have your time frame for working out. Try to hit at least twenty minutes every day unless reasons of a nonexcuse type prevent you from doing so.

If you chose C, I'm going to ask you to do something that you will thank me for later. For the next week, write down every single thing you do, from putting your pants on to studying for a final. EVERYTHING. Write down how much time it took you to do that. Then, at the end of the week, look honestly at how you spent your days. Chances are you've spent at least one hour doing something that doesn't benefit yourself or others. To clarify: Taking a bubble bath or reading a book are things you can consider "rejuvenating personal time." Recategorizing your iTunes library, however, is not. Highlight each iTunes-esque task that isn't a means to an end and add up how much time you spend on those activities daily. The total is how much time you have to work out per week. Congratulations!

GOALS
What are your goals?

A **Weight loss.** I have been told by more than two professionals that I am overweight.

B **Stress release.** I might punch a baby if I don't punch a punching bag.

C **Physical well-being.** I am not underweight or overweight but I want to enhance my overall health.

D **Toning up.** I want to get fit so that I can feel as good on the outside as I do on the inside.

E **Competition.** I am already pretty physically fit and am now in training for a race.

As you can see, each reason has a specific goal in mind. Instead of focusing simply on "weight loss" or "looking sexy," focus on the reasons *why*, which will motivate you to keep going. (Sidenote: If you chose B, I don't recommend *actually* punching a baby if you can't get to a punching bag.) Here are some specific suggestions for each goal—although the benefits I lay out here can apply no matter what you want to accomplish.

If you chose A, focus on a classic mix of aerobic workouts and strength training. The cardio will help you burn calories and the weights will make you strong enough to keep going and push harder, and they'll help speed up your metabolism.

If you chose B, look for workouts that prioritize mental well-being, like yoga or kickboxing. These help you zero in on your emotions and release tension in a healthy way.

If you chose C, your job is simply to explore a bunch of different workouts and find the ones you love most (so that you'll keep doing them!). Start off with some simple strength training or daily powerwalking, which is making a comeback, I swear.

If you chose D, your motto is "feel the burn" with workouts like Pilates or a barre class. A routine that focuses on mass reps will build your muscles without bulking you up, giving you that toned look.

If you chose E, congrats! You're already a pro at the whole being fit thing. (Why are you even reading this chapter?) Try training with a like-minded friend, who will help motivate you on days when you aren't feeling it and push you to go harder.

LOCATION

How well do you tolerate working out with other people?

A I have a hard time knowing what to do on my own, but I'm too self-conscious to work out in public.

B I love working out with other people—I feed off their energy.

C I like competition but I hate the gym.

If you chose A, workout DVDs and YouTube videos are your perfect match. Most require some basic equipment, like a yoga mat, a resistance band or free weights, so do a bit of research ahead of time to know what you need before you press PLAY.

If you chose B, you're best at a gym or with a workout buddy. If you have it in your budget, consider hiring a personal trainer once a week—he or she will help to supervise you one-on-one and give you lots of motivation.

If you chose C, scrap the gym membership and instead sign up for intramural sports in your area. You'll thrive on the team effort but won't feel trapped in a stuffy weight room.

Lalo's Five Motivation Dos and Don'ts

DO! **Be patient.** If you're overweight, you won't see visible change overnight, but if you stick with it even for a week, you'll see a complete difference in your energy, and you'll want to do it more. A few weeks later, your clothes will start to get looser, your posture will be better and you'll feel stronger. Your job is to enjoy what you can from the experience and have fun.

DON'T! **Give up.** Commit to the long term. Make a decision to hit whatever your goals may be, and then have the dedication and commitment to follow through. But at the same time, we're human beings, so you're probably going to have a piece of chocolate here and there. Don't be too hard on yourself—just say *OK, that happened*, and move on. One small slipup won't erase all the work you've done.

DO **Keep your eye on the prize.** When you think you don't want to or can't work out, think about the advantages that will come from doing so. It's like, if you're a writer and need to write, how are you going to feel once you finish writing that essay, article or poem? That's what's going to drive you. In most cases, you cannot get yourself motivated to write just because. You need to have a goal in mind. So ask yourself, *Even though I'm feeling a little sluggish now, how am I going to feel if I work out today?* Odds are, you're going to walk away in a much better mood, feeling stronger and more accomplished.

DO! **Pass the twenty-one-day mark.** To see real results, I would recommend twenty minutes of exercise per day, minimum. It takes about ten minutes for most people to run a mile, and then you have time for some strength training (push-ups, sit-ups, etc.). It takes twenty-one days for something to become a habit, and then after twenty-one days it just becomes a part of you.

DON'T! **Stress over catching up.** If I go on vacation for two weeks and come back, I'm not going to be able to do exactly the same workout as I did before and I have to be fine with that. You just need to pick up where you left off—then it becomes more fun and you feel less pressure.

FOLLOW LALO'S PERSONAL TRAINING PLAN

Below, Lalo breaks down eight calorie-torching moves that you can do right in your bedroom. But first, you gotta know all about his "freeze" technique, which will help make sure you're getting the most out of each move.

FROM LALO: THE "FREEZE" TECHNIQUE

The "freeze" technique is best described as taking a second to connect your mind with the muscle(s) you want to work while doing each move. When we "freeze" at each point of a move (a squat, a sit-up, etc.), it allows us to generate more energy to change position or to finish the exercise, thereby burning more calories and making the muscles work harder! So, as you're doing the moves below, remember to "freeze" for one full second during each part of the exercise, connecting your mind with the muscles you want to work.

POWERB!TCH LUNGES

This works your inner legs, butt and core; improves balance.

Facing front with your arms at your sides, bend your left knee to a 90-degree angle and extend your right leg back. Bring the tip of your right hand over to your outer left ankle. (Be careful not to over- or underextend here. Placing the tip of your fingers right on your ankle puts your hips in just the right position.) Bring your arms back to your sides and your right leg up 90 degrees. Lock your hips and squeeze your butt and shoulder blades together. Maintain good posture. Do fifteen reps on each side.

THE OLYMPIC SKIER

This works your inner legs, glutes and core.

Bring your right leg back and behind your left foot, allowing the outside of your right foot to lean into the ground, and putting your weight into your butt. Reach your right arm out and over your chest, so it makes a straight line with your foot. With your chest now upright, bring your right leg back up and extend it out to the right side, with your foot pointing forward, toes facing out and hands in a boxing position. Make sure your weight goes on your front heel here. Do fifteen reps on each side.

x 15

x 20

PLIÉ SQUATS

This works your inner legs and glutes, and improves coordination.

You can add up to a three-pound weight here or do this without weights at all. Stand with your feet a little wider than shoulder-width apart, hands extended over your head. Bend down so that your knees are over your heels, aligning with the tips of your toes. Put your weight in your heels. Bring your arms out to the side and then scoop them in front of you. On the way up, squeeze your glutes and inner legs. Do twenty reps.

COBRA TRICEPS EXTENSIONS

x 15

This works your triceps, shoulders and chest.

Lying facedown in a push-up position, allow your chest to touch the floor. Lift up into a plank ("cobra" position with your shoulders back and chin up) for one second, then slowly come back down, squeezing your glutes to protect your back. Do fifteen reps.

RISE 'N' SHINERS

x 15

This works your shoulders, biceps and upper back.

Stand with your legs shoulder-width apart. Start with weights (up to three pounds) out to the side, making a 90-degree angle with the floor. Lift your arms up together (but don't let your hands touch; they should just be raised in parallel lines above your head). Come back down to a 90-degree angle, squeezing your shoulder blades. Then bring them out and touch them in front of your chest, maintaining a straight line and a 90-degree angle, parallel to the floor. Do fifteen reps.

Note: While doing this (and any move with weights), you should be standing in an "athletic position": slightly sitting back on your hips, while flexing just a tiny bit in your knees and your weight in your heels; abs tight, shoulder blades together.

THE 100S AND "V" POSE COMBO

This works your core.

Lie down, facing up. Bring your legs to a 45-degree angle, then move your arms from the shoulders up and down for sixty reps. Right after that, bring your body to a "V" position with your legs and upper body off the floor and hold for thirty seconds.

x 15

BALANCE-Y BRIDGES

This works your core and lower abs.

Assume a plank position (arms shoulder-width apart, extended to the floor; butt low; legs extended and back). Raise one leg, keeping your butt down and abs tight. Do fifteen reps on each side.

YOGI WITH A TWIST

Full body move.

Start in a push-up position, with your arms shoulder-width apart. Do a push-up (keeping your butt down). Kick your right leg out and to the front, keeping your arms straight and abs tight. Lean back and hold for three seconds. Keeping your hands together, twist to the side so your hands are together and your arms create a straight vertical line. Hold for two seconds. Move back into push-up position and repeat on the other side. Do five to ten reps.

x 5-10

BY THIS POINT, I'M USUALLY MAKING FAT CRY LIKE A BABY

If you want to add cardio to your routine, do a twenty-minute run outside, or on the treadmill at a 0.5 percent incline. You could also walk uphill to work your abs and glutes (putting all your weight on your heels, taking big steps and making big movements with your arms, keeping your abs tight)—or again on the treadmill at an 8–12 percent incline on 3.0 speed.

Do this workout three times a week, alternating with yoga or any other preferred workout. Get it, girl.

MY MUST-TRY WORKOUTS

When you're ready to mix up your routine and try something new—whether it's just a quick run around the block or something more adventurous—this is my personal list of workouts worth trying. You're bound to find something that sticks.

☐ **ELLIPTICAL**
(Doing it backwards will make your glutes pop—BendAndSnap)

☐ **WEIGHT AND STRENGTH TRAINING**

☐ **TREADMILL**
(Watch out for eye-guy-candy)

☐ **RUNNING OUTSIDE**
(It's like a freakin' Nature Valley commercial)

☐ **HIKING**

☐ **SWIMMING**
(Sans floaties)

☐ **KICKBOXING**
(Be careful if you're working with a partner; I have accidentally punched Lalo before)

☐ **PILATES**
(It's our generation's Jazzercise)

☐ **YOGA**
(A little Zen never hurt anyone)

☐ **ROCK CLIMBING**
(Either indoors or up a mountain)

☐ **PLYOMETRIC**
(Think P90X)

☐ **SPIN**
(Craziest sixty minutes of your life)

☐ **GYMNASTICS**

☐ **DANCING IN FRONT OF YOUR MIRROR**
(Yup, this is a workout)

> EXPERT SECRET: I would never go on a scale, but if you're the type of person who really needs to know where you're at, I would just go once a month. Women's weight tends to fluctuate more than men's because of their menstrual cycle, so the scale can go all over the place and drive you crazy. —Lalo

Lalo's Injury Protection Hotline

Q: How can I tell if I'm pushing too hard during a workout?
A: There is a difference between pain and burn, which people tend to confuse. Burn is fine up to a point, but pain is something that should be avoided at all times. A burning sensation is expected while working out. It is an external factor that you need to control with your mind in order to bring your body to its full potential. You need to listen to your body as well, because, at some point, too much burn could lead to injury. If you push your body too much through the burn, you could easily pull a muscle.

Pain (often sharp or achy) should be avoided during your workouts. You need to learn to listen to your body and stop when pain begins. That's an indication that something is wrong, and you should stop. If your knee hurts while you're doing a squat, it probably means your knee is not strong enough and needs some attention. Try doing some dead lifts instead. Not only are you still working on your legs, but you are making that knee stronger, too.

Q: What's the easiest way to prevent injury without obsessing over it?
A: Switch up your workout. Think of the gym as a playground—today you're running on the treadmill; tomorrow you're doing the elliptical. The next day you can do a yoga class. Not only does changing up your workouts regularly help you burn more calories and give you faster results, but it helps your body adapt to different situations, making it stronger. If I have a client who is a runner, I will usually make her do exercises that require a change of direction. When you are a runner, you're not used to doing movements that, say, a basketball player would do. If you don't practice different types of moves once in a while, you become more prone to injury than people who work their body as a whole.

Changing your workouts also helps your body increase bone density by a process called osteoblast. This process works as follows: when you apply stress to your limbs, bone cells run to the portion of the bone where it can create a callus to prevent fracture. This callus becomes part of your bone structure, making your bones thicker and stronger. This process usually takes about eight weeks, so a safe period of time to change out your workouts is about every six to eight weeks. If you are constantly changing your workouts, even better, because the body starts developing bone density as a whole. Running short distances like one to three miles is a good way to develop bone density.

Q: What does it mean when you tear a muscle?
A: A muscle can tear for many different reasons, including heavy lifting, a bad landing or even fast and repetitive movements. A muscle tear could also happen if the body is not warmed up properly or it is pushed beyond its limit. Sometimes we injure ourselves without knowing it and then we take our body to the edge. A good, active warm-up before your workouts will warm up the muscles you're about to work out and test the movements prior to the exercise.

Q: Is it safest to avoid any sort of physical activity when you're injured?
A: Movement is key for healing an injured body. While I agree that it is necessary to stay away from the injured spot, it is important to keep working around the injury to get the body back to normal. There are times when you have had an injury years ago and now you are experiencing some type of pain in that area. It is most likely because you haven't kept that area strong enough. The solution? To make the muscles surrounding that area strong and bring them back to their normal condition. To do this, it is important to start slow and progress accordingly.

AUTHOR SECRET: Not only will switching up your exercise routine help you engage all your muscles and keep you constantly improving (if you do the same thing every time, your body will eventually get used to it), but, more important, you won't get bored this way. Whether you're changing the number of reps, the order of the routine or starting a new sport/routine altogether, this is a must for a long-term love affair with fitness. —Ashley

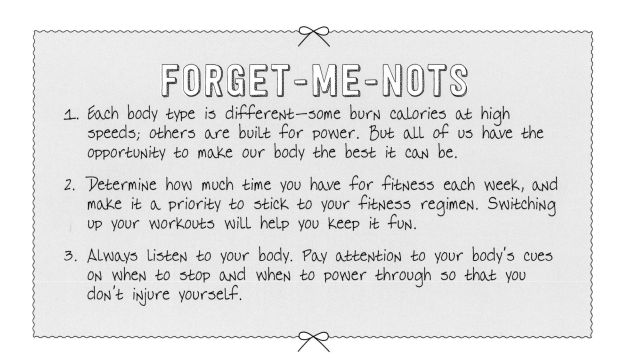

FORGET-ME-NOTS

1. Each body type is different—some burn calories at high speeds; others are built for power. But all of us have the opportunity to make our body the best it can be.

2. Determine how much time you have for fitness each week, and make it a priority to stick to your fitness regimen. Switching up your workouts will help you keep it fun.

3. Always listen to your body. Pay attention to your body's cues on when to stop and when to power through so that you don't injure yourself.

CHAPTER 8

FASHION

YOU'RE THE ONE WEARING IT

MY EXPERIENCE: RED CARPETS
GONE WILD. BAD WILD.

WHEN YOU COME TO LA, you learn quickly: lose the Abercrombie, get the miracle bra and if your shorts show your butt cheeks, that's a good thing. Luckily, I was already into the short-short-short-shorts, but the rest was a bit harder to do (a miracle bra can't do sh!t if you've got nothing to push up).

I got the hang of it after a few years. I was pulling off the hipster thing really well, got side bangs, and was wearing whatever I wanted. Truthfully, the wear-the-brand-on-your-shirt-pocket thing always grossed me out (unless it was a freebie—I have no idea why brands give me free stuff that I can't afford, but I seriously could've used that back in my Florida days). I just did my thing, which always consisted of wearing classic clothes and not listening to anyone else's advice on my personal style. But eventually I got too busy to pick out each piece of clothing I wore to every event, so I started letting people choose for me.

I will now share with you the single most frustrating moment in my fashion history.

I'm all about pushing the limits, so when I first met this particular stylist at a photo shoot, we clicked because he felt the same way. He was the definition of fabulous—still is—so having him dress me for the People's Choice Awards seemed like the best idea ever. And even though I swore I'd never hire a stylist, into the trash that proclamation went. Our first fitting was in an amazing loft downtown. It was late on a Thursday night, and I was exhausted. As I walked into the ultra-secure building, complete with really weird art, a totally bored and presumptuous doorman rang the loft. Once I was "permitted" to enter, the doorman escorted me up fifteen floors to the penthouse. I stepped inside and felt pretty damn fancy. Here I was with a herd of people, thousands of dollars worth of dresses, and all the attention on me. (Yeah, I love that. So what?) I tried on a few looks, all of which seemed either too casual or not quite right for the event. After a very extensive session, we decided the $2,000 white go-go boots and one-of-a-kind jumpsuit just weren't going to work. There was an awkward silence, and then he and his team of stylists promised to find me new options by that weekend.

By Saturday night, Awards Show Eve, the options were (I sh!t you not): a bondage-style dress made of leather straps that barely covered my (very tiny) nipples, a tube top and silk shorts that were too big and boasted a cruise ship–like pattern (think Carnival Cruise ships and old people) or a boring blue sheath dress. I was in my bedroom changing out of option three, and I had no idea what to do. I was too tired to do the math in my head, but I knew the answer was "It's too late."

I didn't want to break his heart and not wear anything of his, but I also *did not* want to wear anything of his. I texted my older male friend (no, it's not like that, but Paul really likes to throw people off and pretend to "be like that"), and I told him to come over and help me.

Meanwhile, I stayed in my room. "How are you doing in there?" the stylist asked through the door. "Uh, great. Just, uh, trying them all on, again," I said. Paul was still ten minutes away, and those ten minutes in the apartment went by like an embarrassing YouTube video in slow motion (shout-out to *Tosh.0*). Finally, Paul walked through the door and I was like, "Oh, hey guys! This is my, um, PR, agent, person."

"Yeah. Yeah. Yeah. I want to see what we're wearing here to the show," Paul commanded.

"Oh, this is my *favorite*!" the stylist said, as I had changed back into the *Fifty Shades of Grey*–inspired bondage dress. Paul looked at me, kind of uncomfortably, like when your dad sees you in a bikini, and he was like, "NOPE. That won't work. OK, she's gotta go now!"

The stylist left, after a long beat of silence. And then I cried to Paul.

"None of the sh!t I own in that stupid M$*%($&F(%&#! closet works! S*$&! Seriously, I am so f!cked! I f!cking hate clothes." (I swear when I'm sad . . . or mad . . . and I was both.) Then Paul left, and I went and cried to my then-boyfriend on the phone. He was no help whatsoever. So, I went to sleep (after more obnoxious crying over a silly dress).

On the day of the People's Choice Awards, I had a table read for *Awkward*. In what may have been the quickest read-through of a script ever, we wrapped it up and all headed home to get ready. But I still needed a dress, so my manager's assistant called ahead to a high-end department store's PR department and told them I was coming by in thirty minutes and to please help me.

What followed was one of the most glamorously chaotic moments of my life.

I walked into Bloomingdale's, and the PR woman was waiting for me at the entrance. She escorted me upstairs, where she had selected various dresses off the rack. I tried one on—the first one, a nude, floor-length beaded gown—and it was perfect. Two minutes later, I bought shoes that matched and was walking out the door (OK, running, but whatever). The rest is kind of a blur. I only remember watching TLC's *Bridezillas* while my hair stylist was prepping my curls, and then I was in the car and headed to the awards show. As I got to the red carpet, I caught my breath and found my publicist. We walked the carpet, posed for some pictures, and then the most amazing thing happened.

"Excuse me . . ."

I turned around to find the person addressing me.

"I just have to say, your dress is easily one of the best here. It may be my favorite."

My publicist looked on in shock as Tim Gunn, from *Project Runway*, finished his really long and genuine compliment to me: "I'll be naming it in my top ten of tonight."

I tried to act really cool, "Aww, thank you so much! You have no idea how hard this was to find."

And then I walked on a cloud. A fashion cloud, with my stellar dress and oddly comfortable heels. The only thing that made the night better was when *Awkward* won the People's Choice Award.

It was an amazing night, and as I got home and lay down on my couch, still in glamour mode, I savored the moment and all the bullsh!t that led up to it. I realized that not only had a middle-aged straight man saved the fashion day (thanks, Paul), but that I won't ever cede control over my image to another person again. There's no point in wearing a trend if it isn't your style. I realized that nobody knows how to best represent or portray the "real" me as well as me. Except for maybe Bloomingdale's.

Now onto some more serious things that I want you to know. While that story was light and fun and hilarious (you're welcome), the truth is, I have a goddamn hard time loving my body. Whether from bullying, loss or abuse, it is almost a given that some part of you will have been traumatized in your early life. The details are different but the sentiment is the same: I've been bruised. While overcoming deep-seated trauma is a lifelong effort, you don't have to hide in the shame of that trauma. I get deep satisfaction out of controlling the way I appear though my fashion—it's how I express myself, it's one of the ways I come out of hiding and allow myself to live life, in freedom. Fashion is *not* a superficial trip to the mall. It's an expression of who you are. And I can only hope that this chapter affects you the way fashion affected me.

Just like you, I go through ups and downs and breakups and other sh!tty situations, where my clothes feel kind of sh!tty, too. Do I buy great clothes? Yes, I am currently the proud owner of a brand-new fall wardrobe in a size that's too small. It doesn't make me feel good to try on pants that don't fit or look at another pair of pants and know that I shouldn't even try to get into them right now. Why do I do that? In the past, I thought it would motivate me to lose more "breakup weight," or what have you, if I bought the smaller clothes in advance. But that wishful action didn't motivate me to go to the gym more or eat better—it made me want to give up. I'd end up in sweatpants, but even those didn't fit. When I'd try to put them on, I could hardly get them over my ass. I don't think I am the first girl to try to wiggle into them, only to bend down and notice how many rolls would form when I bent over, only to rip those sweatpants in a hurry to get them off.

When I have to leave my house in the morning, for work or to run errands, the worst part of my day is right after I've tried to fit into those clothes. I'm breathing heavily and I look at my body in the mirror, that stupid full-length mirror. I look at it and I actually think the mirror has to be distorted or something, *How could I look like this??* And then I see my naked body, postworkout and even after a healthy breakfast, and I realize, it's not the mirror that is distorted. It's how I view myself, my own reflection, that is distorted. I get so lost in the "victim" jail sometimes that I take away my ability to see myself in the present, separate from what I've gone through. It's not as simple as toughing it out; I can't just shove down my emotions and pretend they don't exist; that would be lying to myself. And I don't want to lie to myself or lock myself down into the pain forever. It's within my power to treat myself with a care and love that is independent of circumstance or other people. And that is my best chance at being happy. After all, the only thing anger and self-sabotage do is prolong the pain of the past and keep us hidden and hurting.

It's when you're getting dressed for the day, that you're faced with that crucial moment where half of you is trying to keep on movin' forward with your day, and the other half of you is naked, aware and awake in your self-consciousness. You have two ways to go when it comes to this: one is exactly what I've admitted to doing over and over, which is a type of denial that leads you back into the past and stops you cold, in that feeling of emptiness where you get lost in negative thoughts about yourself. The other way (and I'm not going to call it the "light path" because that reminds me too much of *Star Wars*) is one that cherishes that final moment of action before you leave for the day, which makes that moment of vulnerability nothing short of divine. It becomes a moment where you're not in the past, not in the future,

> **Stop punishing yourself for what you are not and celebrate what you *are*, and what you are right *now*. Are you bigger than you want to be? Fine, but don't start off on the wrong fashion foot and start building your wardrobe around a blueprint that you don't have just yet.**

but acutely aware of the present. You want to put on those awesome pants that fit your body right *now* and make you feel special and beautiful and perfect. The ones that make you grateful for all the work you've done to get where you are, so that by the time you finish thinking those happy thoughts, you're dressed and walking out the door into a day of infinite possibility.

Stop punishing yourself for what you are not and celebrate what you *are*, and what you are *right now*. Are you bigger than you want to be? Fine, but don't start off on the wrong fashion foot and start building your wardrobe around a blueprint that you don't have just yet. No excuses here, b!tches. This is about being happy, and you WILL BE f!cking happy, dammit!! Go out and find a pair of pants or a shirt or whatever else and buy it right now, in the size that you are . . . in a color you like right now . . . in a style that expresses who you are . . . and is basically something that makes you feel like a charging Spartan at whatever occasion you're headed to. (If you don't have extra coins for this, I'll show you some tricks on working with the clothes you have and the magic of alterations.)

At the end of the day, fashion isn't just art—it's using art as a means to express yourself. But the only way to know what it is you're trying to express and make fashion work for you is knowing and owning your truth. Because, bottom line, when you *feel* great in your clothes, you will *look* great in your clothes.

MEET YOUR EXPERT

ANNEBET DUVALL,
stylist and senior fashion editor at *Seventeen*

Her Philosophy on Fashion: Fashion is about wearing what you feel good about yourself in. Everybody's got those days when you walk out of the house and think, *Wow, I really love this outfit.* That's how you should feel most of the time. Day to day, I like to feel cute but I also like to feel comfortable. I know I'm a tomboy, so I like jeans and T-shirts and sneakers. To mix it up, every day I try to wear something I haven't worn in a really long time. When you do that, you're like, *OK, this isn't so bad.* That's how you play with style and discover what you like.

From Annebet: Figuring Out Your "Personal Style"

Understanding your personal style is great because it makes you less reliant on trends and more focused on what really works best for *you*. Here's how to zero in on yours:

1. Pick out five things that you love.

Look in your closet and pull out what you really love to wear. (And if you don't like what's in there, tear out pages in a magazine or go to a store and look around.) They should be five things that you would grab in a fire if you owned them. One of my favorite things is my Helmut Lang leather pants.

2. Think about what those pieces are preaching.

Let's say there are these neon pink shoes that you've loved forever and make you feel great, and you wear them with jeans, you wear them with dresses, you wear them to church, you wear them to parties . . . wherever you're going. That says something about you and your personal style. Decide what that is.

3. Fill the holes.

From there, figure out how you want to build from those key pieces—what you want to pair them with. You'll say, I don't have a gray sweatshirt, but I think one would look great with these pink shoes. So then you buy a gray sweatshirt and add it to your collection. All of a sudden, you have this look that's totally yours.

EXPERT SECRET: Don't force yourself into thinking you have to be one specific body type—everyone is different. You just have to really get to know your body—and be honest with yourself. You do that by trying on lots of different things. I've learned to accept certain things about my body, and work *with* those things, not against them. Occasionally, we'll get photographed for something as editors, and for so many years, I just wore baggy T-shirts and fluffy skirts, and I'd see the pictures and be like, *I'm so huge.* I wasn't, I just wasn't working *with* myself. Now I'll put on a tight pencil skirt or something more flattering, and I'll see the photos and think, *Wow, I look so much better.* It's just about the way things fit. It's not about what size is written inside or covering anything up. It's trial and error—you have to go in and be dedicated to trying on a bunch of different things (things you would never usually consider!) and decide what looks best on your body. —Annebet

ANNEBET'S FIVE CLASSIC PIECES EVERY GIRL SHOULD HAVE IN HER CLOSET

1

ONE OR TWO GREAT PAIRS OF JEANS THAT FIT PERFECTLY.

The kind where you can roll out of bed and just put them on and you know that the look is going to work.

2

AN AMAZING WHITE T-SHIRT.

Whether it's boat-neck, V-neck or has cut-off sleeves. I have a million white T-shirts because they work with everything.

3

A PAIR OF BLACK PANTS.

They're good for an interview, good for running around doing errands, good for anything.

4

A CLASSIC WHITE BUTTON-DOWN.

Pair one with the jeans or black pants and you have an instant outfit.

5

A THONG.

Seriously. Panty lines are not your friend.

one

two

five

three

four

ASHLEY'S OTHER FAVORITE PIECES TO CONSIDER

one

FOUR

three

two

five

1 **BOOTS** One pair of midcalf, basic black leather boots with no metal bling. If you have gold or silver hardware on the boot, it can feel restricting when picking out jewelry (just sayin').

2 **BLACK STILETTO HEELS** If you've ever needed a quick change from school or work to a date, packing a pair of sky-high pumps is your answer. This is the shoe equivalent of an LBD.

3 **KHAKI** This isn't just for tagging along to your dad's country club outings—khaki is key. While it may not be the trendiest item you own, either a skirt or pants (some type of bottom) is a flattering and youthful go-to that matches, well, everything.

4 **A NAVY BLAZER** Blazers scream "professional!" and I think navy is the most season-neutral color there is. Make sure the blazer hugs your curves—get it tailored if you need to. This is also a piece to spend a little money on, as a good blazer will last a lifetime . . . or at least until you spill coffee on it.

5 **NICE PAJAMAS** OK, this isn't really "fashion," but there's something subconsciously great about going to sleep in something that you can wake up feeling gorgeous in. You don't need a freakin' garter belt—just a pair of satin or silk PJs that make you feel like royalty.

THE CLASSICS OVER TRENDS QUIZ

My shopping secret: Buy classics, not trends. But how to avoid ending up with a closet full of boring stuff? Ask yourself these five questions:

1. Can you think of at least three places to wear this (places you'll actually go)?   YES   NO

2. Are you able to customize this piece with accessories you already own (or would you have to purchase an entirely new outfit to go with it)?   YES   NO

3. Has this style been around for a few decades, updated with only slight variations?   YES   NO

4. Will you be able to wear this for at least three years without feeling really embarrassed about it?   YES   NO

5. Is the price of this item equivalent to the price you would pay for about five "trendy" items at a cheaper store?   YES   NO

If you answered yes to at least three of these questions, that department store hanger is holding a quality investment purchase that will look great on you now and will last you for years. Go for it, and don't look back.

> **EXPERT SECRET:** A well-dressed girl is someone who is wearing something that fits her and has the confidence that comes from that on the street. I'll always choose her over the girl in the latest trend. —Annebet

From Annebet: A Specific Guide on Shopping for the Most Difficult Thing Ever (Jeans)

There's no need to fear skinny jeans (but you should always fear mom jeans). Go forth into the jean section confidently with this countdown to finding your perfect pair.

1. **Give yourself options.**

   Go to a store that has multiple brands, and just plan on spending a looong time there.

2. **Ask yourself where you'll be wearing each pair.**

   Are you going to wear them during the day or at night? Are you going to wear them with heels or with flats? If you're wearing flats, you should probably go skinnier. If you're going to wear them with heels, a bit of flare in the jean will make you look amazing.

3. **Consider the fabric.**

   If you're a little bit bigger, look for something with stretch because it will hold you in. If you're super-slim, you can get away with things like raw denim.

4. **Check the waist.**

   If you're a smaller size, you can go high-waisted. If you're a bigger size, a regular rise with a thick waistband is great.

5. **If all else fails . . .**

   A dark wash with a little bit of stretch is always going to be the most flattering jean.

6. **Get them hemmed!**

   If the jean fits you everywhere else but they're dragging around on the ground, that ruins everything. It's only about $15 to have a pair of jeans hemmed. Take them to the dry cleaner and ask the seamstress to match the thread. It's easy and makes a huge difference (same goes for any purchase you make).

The "Style in a Pinch" Chart

I'm a fan of wearing whatever the eff you feel great in, but if you're struggling to put together an outfit in the morning, here are my favorite, no-fail combos:

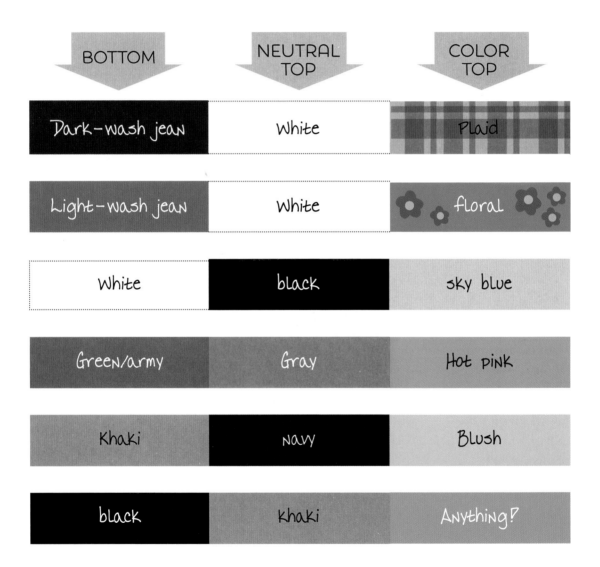

BOTTOM	NEUTRAL TOP	COLOR TOP
Dark-wash jean	White	Plaid
Light-wash jean	White	floral
White	black	sky blue
Green/army	Gray	Hot pink
Khaki	navy	Blush
black	Khaki	Anything!

Annebet's Style Rules

As you continue developing your personal style and shop 'til you drop, remember these quick thangs:

1. **Never judge your body based on models.**

   I really wish people knew what it was like to make a piece of clothing. You go from a sketch to making a muslin on a lifeless form, and then create something from that. Then you go into a fitting with a girl (called a "fit model") whose entire job is to be a human Barbie. And everything is based on this girl's proportions, which are not normal. The process is very unfriendly for the human body. Never feel bad if you try something on and it doesn't fit.

2. **Be honest with yourself.**

   If you have big arms, don't wear anything that's sleeveless. If you're bigger in the middle, don't wear a belt that cuts you off. Show off the parts you love!

3. **Remember that sizes fluctuate from brand to brand.**

   There is a standard scale that designers base their sizes on, but every brand is still different. So if you're buying a double zero from the Gap, it's probably a four. And if you're buying a double zero at Rag & Bone, it's probably a child's size. The point is not to focus so much on the number written inside (which no one else can see anyway!), but instead on what fits. Do that, and you'll end up looking slimmer.

Accessories

Accessorizing is the secret way to update older or classic clothes and make them look modern. Here, Annebet breaks down the three basic levels to daily accessorizing, and I added my two cents, obviously.

PERSONAL JEWELRY

These are pieces that are meaningful to you, like earrings from your mom or a necklace that your boyfriend gave you. Layer on these faves (not too many at once though!) every day.

EVERYDAY JEWELRY

Rotate in any costume jewelry that you're drawn to. I go through phases where I really love bracelets, or I'll have, like, six chains on. But you have to balance it—you don't want to look like Mr. T, so if you have three or four necklaces on, skip the bracelets and big earrings. I also love any kind of cheap cocktail ring. You can wear them during the day or make it a nighttime thing—like three large stones on your fingers.

Note: If you develop a rash from any costume jewelry (sometimes it can irritate your skin), either paint the piece with clear nail polish (I have no idea why this works, but it does) or stop wearing it and instead purchase jewelry that is either stainless steel, nickel-free or a pure metal, like gold, sterling silver or platinum. Refer back to "Personal Jewelry" if this gives you heart palpitations.

A POWERB!TCH TIP: If you're looking for a classic piece of jewelry that will last, but you don't have thousands of dollars to spend on gold, try sterling silver. It's almost a third of the price, won't tarnish and you can usually get some sort of natural stone (maybe not a diamond, but sparkly cubic zirconia or even topaz) in the deal. Otherwise, if you do invest in quality plated jewelry, it will usually say somewhere on the label (24K, 18K, 14K, etc.), which means it's pure gold (versus gold "tone," which is not actual gold).

THE BAG

Annebet believes in quality over quantity when it comes to her bags, so she says save up and buy yourself a nice one. A great bag will last forever. And not only that, it's an outfit-maker. She says you can be wearing a pair of white high-top sneakers and carrying the new "it" bag and you're good to go.

Note: If you're more into the bargain bag than the new "it" bag, make sure the leather at least looks authentic. If it doesn't, don't buy it. Be honest and ask someone with good taste for his opinion (either a rich person or a gay guy—that's where I get my style advice).

And, oops, I came up with a few more . . .

Belts, scarves, hats, gloves, headbands, decorative socks and whatever else you can think of— just make sure they're not too matchy-matchy. These extras are a good way to complement your color palette and add a bit more personality to your look (add a pop of color, tone down that neon sweater, etc.).

BELTS

If a shirt is longer than your pant line or is too loose, add a high-waisted belt to cinch it in. This is also a great way to take a look from school or "work" to date with one piece. I've also been known to make a belt out of a scarf, so don't rule anything out. Be creative and redefine the purpose of each piece, as long as it doesn't involve turning your frozen steak into a meat dress (it's been done . . .).

HATS AND HEADBANDS

Sometimes your hair isn't doing what you want it to. Quick fix: Throw a hat on or a headband over your ponytail to mask the chaotic mane underneath so that you never, ever have a bad hair day.

DECORATIVE SOCKS

The whole decorative sock thing has been coming up a lot recently in fashion. They're great if you're going for the grunge look or a cute retro vibe, but don't try to make your dad's white tube socks work—they won't achieve the same purpose.

GLOVES

Gloves are so freaking fancy. They also keep your third and fourth fingers warm, but if you live in a snowy climate, stick with leather gloves because the knit ones will get wet. If you have unusually small hands, as I do, buy a pair of vintage gloves. It's some sort of scientific fact/observation that women's hands were smaller on average sixty years ago. (Imma take your grandpa's style!)

FAVORITE OUTFIT IDEAS
POUR LE IMPORTANT STUFF

AN INTERVIEW

An amazing pair of black pants and a bright shirt—
button-down or silk—because your personality
should be doing most of the talking. You have
options with the pants: you could go high-waisted
or choose a tighter, cigarette pant. As long as you
look like you'd score well on the SATs.

A DATE

Unlike an interview, there's no dress code for dates.
There's really no need to look fancy (unless he's
taking you to the opera). I love wearing my leopard-
print wrap dress, which I always feel great in.
Annebet's favorite idea is a semi see-through T-shirt
and a neon bra underneath. Then add great hair and
a good lip. Done.

A PARTY

The key is to never be overdressed. LA has taught me a lot about assumptions, and I've learned to always err on the side of looking casual, with formal accessories that I can quickly hide in my purse if they end up feeling like too much. Think a nice pair of dark jeans, a white tank and a sleek black blazer. Add a chunky necklace and cocktail ring with some patent leather pumps and you're totally ready to dress it up or down when you get there.

YOUR PERIOD

Stick to loose shirts that cover your belly but not your butt. I'm also not opposed to elastic waistbands here—they shouldn't be from the '80s, but a pair of pants with a little *wiggle* room will curb any homicidal feelings toward those "other" pants you own. Oh, and steer clear of colors ranging from white to bright yellow (no use gambling with a potential leak situation). Lastly, don't wear shorts or skirts with fringe. Once, I was wearing a pair of Daisy Dukes and then realized that one those of "strings" was my actual tampon string. Don't find out the hard way!

Quality versus Kualitée

Here's how to make sure you're not buying sh!tty stuff:

1. ## Ask where it was made.

   Anything made in the United States is going to be better quality than something that was imported. Bottom line.

2. ## Check the fabric content.

   If you're looking at something that's full of polyester and spandex… ugh, just ugh. Put it down. For jeans, there should be a large cotton content, and then a small amount of knit stretch or spandex. But polyester is your enemy—it's really freaking hot, so avoid anything with high polyester content.

3. ## Note the fabric weight.

   Anything that's made of a super-thin fabric is not going to last, especially if you're wearing it out to parties or to school or work and there's going to be a lot of wear and tear.

4. ## Look for strong seams.

   When you're picking out a piece of clothing, be sure to check for any stray strings or issues with the fabric. This may seem like a no-brainer, but it's always good to gauge the item you buy against other items like it. Meaning, if one silk shirt is 100 percent fine but two of the others in stock look a little worn down, move on. That's a good indication of how well it was made.

5. ## Go for the environmentally friendly bonus.

   Go the extra step and order a few pieces of recycled clothes from a local thrift store or vintage boutique. The fabric is usually made from eco-friendly fabrics in an eco-friendly factory. Some companies even donate a portion of their profits to charity.

BARGAINS VERSUS BRANDS

As I've said before, I sort of hate labels, but the truth is, I have a few select brands that I go back to time and time again because they fit me really well. The key thing to remember: Never buy an item simply because of who made it. After all, the tag is on the inside and nobody else is going to see it. Be open to finding bargains or checking out discount chain stores—girl, you know which ones I'm talking about!

EXPERT SECRET: I've found some of the best things I own at Goodwill. Troll through your local thrift stores and you'll be surprised at what you find. Just dry-clean it or wash it, and you're good to go. eBay is also a great resource that I wish I had known about in college, and Wrapped is a great source if you live in or close to a big city. —Annebet

FORGET-ME-NOTS

1. Don't focus on size (no one else can see the label anyway). When you feel great in your clothes, you'll look great in your clothes.

2. Nab perfect-fitting jeans, a white tee, black pants, a white button-down and a thong. Those are the five basics that will build a great wardrobe.

3. Accessories are the best way to have fun with your personal style without spending a ton of money.

PART

4

YOU BETTERING YOU

Batteries Not Included

CHAPTER 9

ORGANIZING
AND
DECORATING

IT DOESN'T TAKE A VILLAGE TO DESIGN A ROOM

MY EXPERIENCE: GAS MASKS AND
STAPLE GUNS AND STORAGE! OH MY!

WHY HAVEN'T I BEEN FEATURED ON *MTV CRIBS* YET, YOU ASK? For one thing, I don't have gold teeth. But mainly, it's because I live in a three-bedroom condo, 95 percent of which has been decorated in a DIY fashion. Let us flash back to a little more than three years ago, when I decided to move out of my parents' house. *Awkward* had just aired its first season, but between rent, gas (not the farting kind) and my lack of a roomie, I was footing an expensive bill for an eighteen-year-old. Sure, I'd fantasized about chaise longues and five-thousand-thread-count sheets, but in reality I had champagne taste on a boxed wine budget. So, I had to get creative.

I ended up taking a lot of hand-me-downs from my parents and buying the rest of my stuff secondhand. (P.S.: Can I just say that Craigslist is wonderful for selling and buying *material things only*? Not yourself. I was really lonely once and posted an ad for a "friend," and all I got in return was a bunch of penis pictures. Don't do that.) Anywho, moving away from the phallic and back to the furniture: With the exception of my mattress, basically every major thing I purchased for my apartment was through a thrift store or online. The key was keeping an open mind—with a little bit of spray paint, a staple gun and some trial-and-error-minded handyman skills, I did everything from reupholster my dining room chairs to remake my '80s-esque coffee table into a brand-new-looking masterpiece. Not only did I end up with everyday reminders of my hard work and creative ideas, but I had memories of my friends who helped me move and decorate, too. Like how I accidentally spray-painted my balcony blue because the tape on my carpenter's drop cloth wasn't, well, taped down. And yes, the balcony is still a bright blue disaster. But the swimming-pool blue on my swimming-pool-less balcony is well worth the eyesore; in fact, it's a bonus reminder of how amazing my teal-blue coffee table looks inside. I ended up giving the coffee table away to a friend, and even though it was our very first DIY project and has a few "dribbles" rather than "even coating," she loves it because it's like a giant memory box . . . specifically, a reminder of when I sat on a wet table. Now bear in mind, my huge DIY overhaul was a big time commitment, and I couldn't possibly ask my friends to participate in every fume-y moment! So when it came to pieces I was more nervous about messing up, like revamping 1970s, seven-foot-tall, iron bookshelves and painting them a glossy dark finish, I did those on my own to avoid a control-freak freakout and possibly a lost friendship. With every project, I was not only surprised by how much money I saved, but by how much my friends and I were able to accomplish together. The result was an apartment fit for all those magazines that I'd fawned over, but better, it was personal—a reflection of *me*.

MEET YOUR
EXPERT

JENNIFER ELLEN FRANK, New York–based feng shui
practitioner and interior designer

Her Philosophy on Design: I love to look at the way people are dressed—
that's a great way to figure out someone's personal style. Are you more
casual, always preferring to be comfortable? Or do you like to dress up?
That translates into design—your personal space can reflect that as well.

The Art of Feng Shui

The biggest pitfall people make when it comes to decorating is that they just
buy a bunch of crap without considering whether or not it will all work well
together and become friends. To avoid that dreadful IKEA return line, look
to the tried-and-true methods of feng shui.

Don't sweat it if you aren't familiar with
feng shui—neither is Microsoft Word (it keeps
telling me I'm spelling it wrong). Feng shui
is the ancient art of improving your experience based on your surroundings. Have you
ever been in a room and were totally unable
to focus or just felt a weird vibe? Well, ancient
people (holla!) would say that is due to your
chi, or energy flow, in that room being blocked
or hindered by your current floor plan. Here's
how to shui sh!t up:

1. **Outline your space.**

   If you're moving to a dorm or an apartment, measure the dimensions and
   draw a quick outline on a piece of paper.
   Include windows and doors—they'll
   become game changers as you start to
   place your furniture.

EXPERT SECRET: *Feng shui* (pronounced
fung shway) means "wind and water" in Chinese—
you can't live without either one. Way back in time,
when the Chinese were building their houses,
they were looking for this energy flow of wind and
water. They wanted to place their house where
the wind would come through, so the scents in
the kitchen would flow out the door. And they
believed that flowing water brought prosperity.
They used to plant their rice crops near water,
because that's how they made their money.
—Jennifer

2. Use this weird shape-y thing.

As you can see, this looks nothing like a room. Commonly referred to as the "bagua," it's sort of like a stencil, meaning you can pick it up and lay it over your floor plan, designing accordingly.

EXPERT SECRET: *Balance* is a good word to keep in mind you're setting up any space—that's what I strive for when I design. When you walk into your room and feel like it all works together, then you know your job is done.
—Jennifer

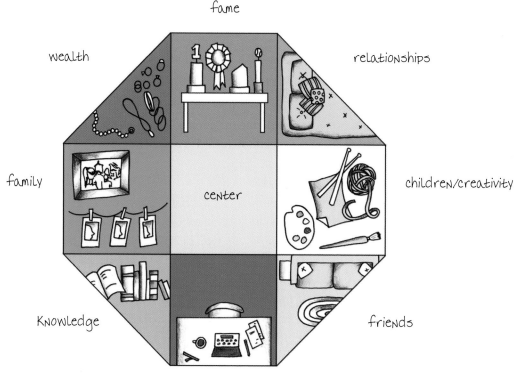

RELATIONSHIPS

This is usually the bedroom (or sleeping area). A properly placed bed is thought to offer security, so put the head of the bed against a wall, not a window. The foot of your bed should be diagonal to the door, never directly in line with it.

CAREER

Your workstation goes here. Power-position the desk so that it is facing a window, which allows creative energy to come through. Avoid placing the desk so that your back is facing a door, as this can be distracting (#Paranoia).

CHILDREN/CREATIVITY

Don't freak out—this space will not get you preggers. It simply represents the purest of creative thinking. Use it as a hobby spot (Do you craft? I heart crafting . . .) or simply as an inspiration-friendly space to brainstorm your ideas from the ground up. This is where your craziest thoughts can be put into action.

KNOWLEDGE

I love *Anchorman*, but in case you don't have "many leather-bound books which smell of rich mahogany," feel free to make this tiny area a storage solution for schoolbooks and other learning tools. Since it's close to your career area, you're able to easily access reference points and past wisdom.

FAMILY

Right next to knowledge and across from your bed is the "family area." This should be a place where you keep pictures from your childhood and photos of your family. Make this spot a comforting place to land when crappy life situations arise. Reminiscing about the happy times can be a huge help in the face of uncertainty.

WEALTH

Personally, I've found that this is a good place to stash your valuables, such as jewelry. It's a nice reminder, looking out from your bed and seeing this delightfully superficial area, that you've accumulated some pretty cool sh!t so far in life.

FRIENDS

Right in between creativity and career is the thing that makes both possible—friends. They'll be there for you during the good times and the bad times and also inspire you, much as this space will. If you're in a dorm or a small apartment, this is where you should have your couch and TV. It's good for socializing and creating new bonds.

FAME

It makes sense that when you walk through the career zone, you can see, as Katy Perry would say, the "fingerprints" you've left on the world. This is the place in my apartment where I keep my fan mail and trophies. It's not vain or purely a matter of ego to congratulate yourself—rather, it's a healthy reminder of how far you've come. Even if the only thing you've ever won in your life is a gold star in kindergarten (or those "Participation Awards"—I have three), show it off proudly.

CENTER

This is the middle of the room, duh. This area is all about health—it affects your general well-being, and is where you want to focus on balance. It's important to keep this space free and clear, that way the chi can flow easily, and you can move from space to space without climbing over random decorative footstools. Plus, I am happiest when I'm running around my apartment thinking about a million things, not having to simultaneously maneuver through an obstacle course of crap on the ground.

CUSTOM JOB: DECORATING AND MAKING YOUR ROOM YOURS

Just as my apartment is a reflection of me, your décor should reflect you from floor to ceiling and everywhere in between (yes, even your hamper). Start with the basics. You probably already have a general sense of styles that you love and hate (#ThanksPinterest), so the next step is translating that into your own real-life space.

Feminine

For a girly girl who prefers the sparkly things in life, this is your oasis. Even though it *looks* like there's a lot to be done here, you really don't need to strategize all that much. (You can just throw a shirt on a hook, hang it from your closet door, and it will seem "placed.") Look for whitewashed pieces of furniture and accents in romantic, pastel colors, like sage green or light pink. Mirrors and translucent, glass pieces (like a crystal chandelier) will add depth to your space. Curtains will also add a certain je ne sais quoi. Pocketbook perk: Most of your girly childhood furniture can make the transition into this makeover. Bottom line: Think of a tea party in the English countryside (#That'sOnMyBucketList)—this is like your fantasy version of that.

ECLECTIC

AUTHOR SECRET: Keep proportion in mind. Don't get a huge-ass couch if you're in a dorm with a mini fridge. That'll just look weird. —Ashley

If you've ever found yourself watching a TV show starring a sexy starving artist dude, à la *New Girl*, you've probably noticed that his hipster bachelor pad is oddly amazing and shabby-chic. That worn leather couch! That antique rug! That organized clutter! That sh!t is called "eclectic"—a combination of everything. For you, it's an opportunity to combine work with play, taking your hoards of supplies and stacks of papers and using that as part of your décor (seriously, even last night's pizza delivery box can be a part of this "well-placed" clutter). Look for furniture that feels earthy and lived in, like a mahogany desk or a light, woven rug, and work in anything that feels important to you—piles of your favorite books, colorful shoeboxes, candles, even a subtle ode to *Anchorman* (guys love that movie. Just saying . . .). Metal touches are a fun way to keep this often old-timey style from looking like your grandpa's study—and think outside the box! Take a random hammer from your dad's toolbox and use it as a paperweight for your homework. If he asks, just tell him it's "art."

I like to call this "IKEA chic." It's a great choice for those of us who like things simple, polished and *very* clutter-free. Keep furniture sleek—focusing on clean lines (no slumpy armchairs allowed!)—with a very streamlined color palette. A black and white color scheme is very sophisticated, while decorating with a few shades of one color, like a range of reds or purples, looks super-modern.

166 organizing and decorating

TRADITIONAL

This style is popularized by girls who prefer a certain straightforwardness to things. You need things to be functional and are OK with putting in a little extra effort to making your space look neat and put-together. Larger furniture with wide surfaces and plush chairs primed for lengthy hours are a great combo for focusing and getting sh!t done. Keep your color palette muted—neutral colors and jewel tones (like deep red or hunter green) are best since you don't want a ton of distractions. Design plus: This style is super-easy to update—just a few accent pieces can change the whole feel in a subtle way.

ZEN

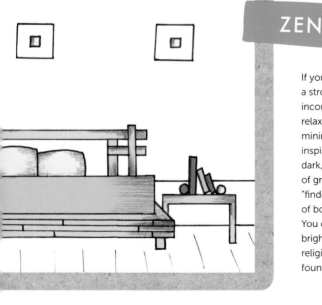

If you consider yourself a spiritual person or have a strong interest in symbolism, this style can incorporate your daily practices into a positive, relaxing space. There are two ways to go here: minimalist (a more free-flowing Japanese-inspired feel), with understated colors—such as dark, low-rising furniture, white linens, and pops of green or bright orange. Then there's the richer "finder's showcase" route—layers upon layers of bold colors, like reds, oranges and golds. You can even play with contrasting colors, like bright orange and turquoise. Add in symbolic or religious pieces of importance, or use them as foundational items to build the room around.

Color Me Mine

So, "color therapy"—it's a real thing! All shades (not just those fifty) have the power to affect your day-to-day mood. I'm not suggesting you paint your room neon yellow if you feel like you need an energy boost (a rave-inspired room just sounds like an anxiety attack waiting to happen), but keep in mind that the color you go with will have lasting effects even after the paint dries. Here's what you'll get from each one.

BLACK

Sophisticated, mysterious and powerful. Beware, though: Too much black and it'll feel like you're living in a funeral home. (If you go this route, one accent wall may be wise.)

GRAY

Strong character, mature and stable. This base color, as opposed to white, adds a hint of warmth in a sophisticated way.

WHITE

Positive (it's like a blank slate!), crisp and fresh. If you change your mind a lot, keep your walls white and leave color to easily interchangeable accent pieces (like pillows!).

RED

Energetic, daring and romantic. You're the boss of your own room, and this is the power color to prove it.

ORANGE

Uplifting and motivating, orange is often overlooked. Use it in moderation—like with a fun, bright duvet cover. A wall of orange can be jolting.

YELLOW

Joyful, cheery and energizing. This is a great choice if you want to trick yourself into thinking that studying is fun.

GREEN

Relaxing, promoting financial well-being, connecting to nature. Green is an awesome go-to from walls to accent pieces. (It's also my favorite color, so I'd be totally flattered if you chose it just because of that.)

BLUE

Tranquil, calming and welcoming, blue is a beauty. But stay away from too many gray-blues—I call that color "depression blue"—LOL.

AUTHOR SECRET: As an actress who depends on good lighting to flatter me on camera, I can safely say I know how important lighting is. Factor in natural light and artificial light. If you have only a few windows, make room for floor lamps and table lamps to add a little extra oomph using warm light. On the flip side, invest in blinds or curtains. You never know when a Friday night may turn into a Saturday morning. Bow-chica-bow-bow! —Ashley

PURPLE

Wise, spiritual and luxurious, this color can be really powerful. After all, it kind of reminds me of Harry Potter (#MagicWithDanielRadcliffe).

PINK

Romantic, compassionate and sensitive, this color is not just restricted to girly girls. Stick to pastels if you're a little hesitant to commit to a hot pink, *Legally Blonde* sitch.

DIY Design

As I said earlier, I pretty much hand-decorated my whole apartment. Everyone who steps inside remarks about how great it is, and when I tell them I did it myself, they really drool. But I learned a lot of this stuff the hard way—from getting fined by the mall across the street for vandalism (long story but just know, it was kind of Bansky of me) to dealing with gas masks, I'm hoping to save you some trouble and chiropractor bills as a result of what I learned.

THE ULTIMATE DIY KIT

- Hammer and nails (best to have two to three sizes of nails on hand)
- Screwdrivers and screws (have different sizes of each, and both a Phillips head and a flat head)
- Paintbrushes (Grab a few different sizes—a big one for large surfaces and a small one for detail.)
- Staple gun and staples
- Upholstery scissors

- Extra-strength double-sided tape
- Painters' tape
- Super Glue
- Tape measure
- Leveler
- Contractor's gloves
- Contractor's respiratory mask
- Protective eyewear
- Crappy clothes
- Shoe guards

- Drop cloths (Old sheets will do.)
- A guy (Yep, you'll need a dude friend or a father figure to help you. They are strong enough to get stuff done and stupid enough to have no idea what they signed up for.)
- Power drill (Maybe let the guy handle this—or at least spot you while you work.)
- Camera

ASHLEY'S SPRAY PAINT INSTRUCTION MANUAL

Don't skimp on paint quality.

You'll have to redo it if it's a cheap or crappy brand. Ask a retailer (who doesn't look like he's been "smell-testing" the paint, though) for recommendations.

Read the label.

You likely want an indoor spray paint. I also like 3-in-1 spray paints, which include primer, paint and gloss in one formula. (Gloss is basically a topcoat that helps prevent the surface from scratching easily.)

Don't spray-paint indoors.

The fumes are way too strong and even a gas mask won't protect you from the harsh chemicals.

Factor in the weather.

If you live in a humid environment, expect to wait longer for the paint to fully dry. And if it is damp outside, don't paint at all. The surfaces of your furniture will turn out bubbly. (All I know is that one time I was painting on a particularly damp day in LA and a bunch of my furniture had to be redone. Rude.)

Clean things up.

Make sure the surfaces you're about to paint are clean—no dust, no residue, nothing. Wash them with warm water and soap (or Windex).

Tape your drop cloths down.

Otherwise, even if you're careful to cover every nook and cranny, the wind will blow all your hard work away.

Do a test strip on a contractor's sheet.
First, shake the paint can really well so that the paint comes out the same shade through the whole can. Perfect your strokes on a vertical piece of contracter's sheeting so you can see what drips, what dries and what coat is the desired color, all without ruining your real piece of furniture.

Make broad, fast paint strokes.
Don't be a baby about it. Keep your hand in constant motion at a fair distance from the piece so as to avoid dripping and an uneven tone.

Pay attention to the drying time on your paint.
This can vary from one hour to forty-eight hours. Always allow at least an hour for paint to dry before doing a second coat.

Inevitably, something will get scratched.
I recommend keeping a few color markers on hand for your darker colors (blacks and browns) and a few acrylic paints that closely match your color for larger touch-ups.

Throw a paint party.
Bribe your friends with pizza (or whatever food they love) and make the DIY process a party, too. Even if things don't turn out perfect or something gets damaged, you'll have fun. After all, it's the memories that count.

REUPHOLSTER A CUSHIONED CHAIR

Step 1 Flip the chair over and, one by one, remove the screws that lock the cushion into place. Keep them all in one place, like in a covered container, so you don't lose any of them.

Step 2 Use thick fabric (many fabric stores will guide you if you explain to them what you're doing—that's what I did), and cut it roughly in the shape of your cushions. Use more fabric than you think you'll need, because it needs to wrap around the bottom of the chair.

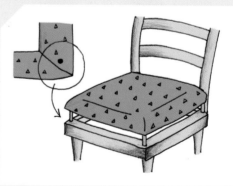

Step 3 Flatten out the fabric and flip the cushion over. Fold the corners, or any angle of the cushion that causes the new fabric to bunch, into a flat piece, as if you're wrapping a present.

Step 4 Then, prepare to use the staple gun (by placing it directly over where the folds on one corner meet). Poke holes in the fabric where the furniture screws were in the chair and align the entire cushion back on the chair base. Screw back in and repeat until you've done each chair.

Jennifer Ellen's Decorating Dos and Don'ts

DON'T! **Skip the small things.** Installing quirky knobs and door handles is so simple and can make a huge difference. Just make sure your landlord or dorm manager allows you to change them, or at least keep the originals on hand for when you move out.

DO! **Embrace mirrors.** Not only will you have a ton of places to do your makeup in the morning, but mirrors instantly make a room feel bigger.

DON'T! **Shy away from flameless candles.** Use them—it's just easier that way.

DO! **Get creative with room dividers.** Bookshelves work wonders to block out roomies.

Organization: Piles Are a Safety Hazard

I didn't realize how big my parents' garage was until they put some of my old boxes and "keepsake" items into the U-Haul for me when I moved. I couldn't fit it all into my new place so, box by box, I had to go a little "Martha Stewart" on my old semi-hoarder ways. It was freaking exhausting. At one point, I was unpacking my photo albums and came across a picture of me, when I was about nine years old, and I realized "Oh my god . . . I just unpacked that shirt in the picture." Which meant I had clothes that were more than ten years old and for some reason was under the impression that sparkly Abercrombie pants were going to make a comeback. I realized I had to do some *major* purging. If you're nodding your head in agreement at this statement, go room by room and run through these six steps:

1. **Prepare to purge.**
   Designate one box as "keep," one box as "trash" and a third box as "give away." You can also keep a small box for "sentimentals."

2. Follow the one-year expiration rule.

A general rule of thumb is that if you haven't used it (clothing, shoes, bags, jewelry, gadgets and gizmos aplenty, hoozits and whatsits galore—#ArielWasAHoarder) in the past year, toss it. If you're really struggling, put it in the giveaway pile for now and ask an objective friend for an opinion later. This process is cathartic and needs to be done almost impulsively.

3. Pack up your donation boxes.

Hopefully, they fit in your car. Also, don't be a dick and put gross sh!t like an old razor or powder buff or old undies in there. Cosmetics in general should be discarded. Goodwill or the Salvation Army won't accept them anyway.

4. Follow the "one in, one out" rule.

As in, for every item you buy, get rid of one. This is what sometimes reins in my shopping addiction, because there is always something better, newer, cooler or whatever, but you have to be willing to part with something you already own to buy it.

5. Purge often.

I try to donate a little every two to three weeks. In fact, keep a small laundry hamper around to toss things in as you find even more random useless stuff or just something other people could use more than you.

6. When donating, get a receipt.

It's tax-deductible based on the value you estimate for your goods.

ROOM BY ROOM

Now it's time to organize all the stuff that made the cut. But putting things away while easily being able to get it back out seems to be the dilemma of anyone who's ever tried vacuum seal storage bags. Here are the world's/my greatest organizational tips on maximizing your space with minimum logic and maximum ease. First we'll tackle the mother lode (and hopefully mother/roomie-free zone): the bedroom.

The Bedroom

EMBRACE DRAWERS AND DRAWER ORGANIZERS

As you can see, this rendering of my closet has a lot of shelves and drawers. Categorize your items by type (jewelry, bags, shoes, coats, tanks, tees, blouses, vests, sweaters, pants, etc.) and put them in separate corresponding bins, making sure that part of each piece is visible upon first sight.

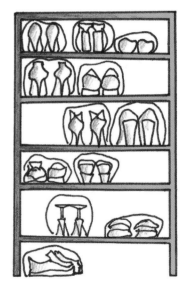

I SEE YOU'VE NOTICED MY SHOE SHELVES

Well, those were relatively cheap (20 bucks for a pack of two at a hardware supply store, and I just stacked three on top of each other). This is where I keep my shoes and bags, all within sight and within reach. A great tip for caring for your shoes and bags is . . . more bags. I keep all my shoes in separate plastic bags so that they don't scratch up against each other and get inadvertently damaged. The bags I use can be found at most wardrobe supply stores or online.

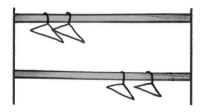

CLOSET

Most apartments or dorms have an insultingly small closet, but there *is* something you can do about it. Head on down to your local hardware store and buy an extra closet rod that you can screw into the wall or buy a tension rod. Install it securely and at a level that your clothes can comfortably hang. As you can see from my closet, I have two extra rods. Note: If you install rods as high as I did on the top level, get a step stool; otherwise, you'll spend an hour a day trying to jump up and grab your good-luck hoodie.

GET A CHEAP GARMENT RACK FOR EXTRA SPACE

This is a lifesaver when I'm trying to decide what to wear on the red carpet or I'm packing for a trip. But if you find you don't have an actual closet in your dorm or need extra space, make it a mobile closet. Perk? You can hide the clothesmobile when guests visit.

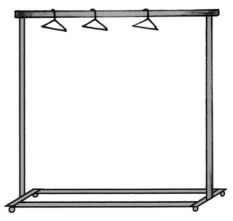

BAG IT

To avoid scratching your shoes and purses, put them inside plastic bags. You won't have to worry about the studded hardware on your black clutch scratching the leather on your boho tote.

BUY NONHEADACHE HANGERS

There are a few things that annoy the crap out of me—one of which is when tank tops fall off hangers randomly or get stuck around five other hangers and then you have pull all of them down, untangle them and put them back. I recommend only buying slim plastic hangers (although wood hangers are nice for heavy coats and such) that have "strap guards" to keep the tanks and boat-necks trapped on that damn thing. And it always helps to hang a tank or boat-neck tee by the garment string that each piece should come with.

BUT HANGING ISN'T JUST FOR CLOTHES!

The best way to keep track of your belts and scarves is to embrace the space on your door. You'll see I have a few contraptions to hang my belts and scarves. They are so easy to remove and easy to put back this way. Invest in a tie rack for your scarves, a belt hoop for your belts, and an over-the-door shoe rack for your thicker scarves.

AVOID CRUSHING STRUCTURED HATS

Beanies and soft hats can be stored anywhere, even in a drawer. But even if you have to add a shelf to store other hats safely, it'll be worth it. Because there is nothing more depressing than a dented cowboy hat.

DO BETTER FOR YOUR JEWELRY THAN A SHOEBOX

I used to store my jewelry this way—my necklaces were tangled, things got damaged and, worst of all, I could never find two of the same earrings. Now, you may or may not know that, aside from acting and writing, my two other passions are horseback riding and jewelry. I am obsessed. A few months ago I started collecting gemstones. I had to keep them in a safe place, so my shoebox storage method had to go. Instead, I invested in some jewelry display options, as well as jewelry inserts. Now I'm able to keep everything organized and protected. Hang your necklaces on necklace racks, bracelets on bracelet racks, and earrings and rings inside a drawer lined with velvet or another protective material. It's the best way to sort and save.

GOT AN EXTRA RACK?

How many times have you lost your sunglasses . . . in your own home? My number was pretty high, until the day I realized I had an extra jewelry rack from my spray-painting adventures that I hadn't known what to do with. Turns out, those things are AWESOME for storing your sunglasses in plain sight. (As long as you remember to put them back at the end of the day.)

SPACE BAGS

I know, I know, I've mentioned them before and they sound so *mom*-ish. But you will love them, I swear! They are the perfect way to store your off-season clothes (meaning if it's summer, all your puffy coats go in the bags and get vacuumed down to the size of a bedsheet like magic).

WHAT TO DO WITH THE INEVITABLE RANDOM PILE OF LEFTOVER CRAP AFTER YOU TRY TO CLEAN YOUR ROOM

Resist the temptation to create the world's largest junk drawer (if you can't shut the drawer fully, you've gone too far). Instead, embrace small baskets or bins, which will motivate you to further divide and conquer.

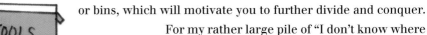

For my rather large pile of "I don't know where to put this but I still need it" stuff, I ended up with seven small bins—one for tools, one for lightbulbs, one for laundry supplies, one for "extra décor," one for keepsakes from on set, one for spare parts to the apartment (I took off the old knobs but have to save them if I move) and another for batteries and small tool parts. I always know where to find what I need.

Workspace

Given the fact that you are most likely working on something very important for school or work (or Facebook), it's crucial to keep your workspace streamlined and clutter-free.

TAKE CARE OF YOUR KEEPSAKES

I'm pretty big into sentimental stuff. While you may forget certain things, souvenirs and special saved items can bring back memories like it was just yesterday. (Plus I like to think my kids will be the first kids in like, ever, to appreciate their parents' weird nostalgia.) The shelf you're seeing (why, yes, I did paint it myself!) is a prime example of how to organize your memories. I have each box labeled, by project or contents. That way you can be as matchy-matchy as I am without losing track of what's in which box. Keep your most treasured stuff in bags for extra protection.

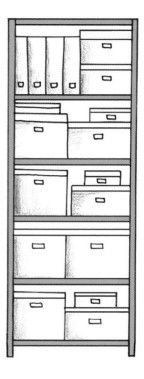

LABELS ARE KEY

I don't believe in piles, but I do have a folder in my desk titled "Misc. papers." It's mostly things I haven't put away yet . . . or just truly miscellaneous papers. But that's as far as I'd suggest in terms of keeping your paperwork together in one giant stack. I keep my most frequently used files in a super easy-to-find place: hanging file holders. They are a lifesaver. I have a few folders in each, from current projects to financial paperwork. In general, here's your "keep" list—everything else can be tossed:

★ **Current Projects:** This should be filled with any printouts related to current projects you're working on, classes you're in or work information that you would need on hand this month.

★ **To-Dos:** Fill this guy up with any bills that need to paid, your to-do lists, random sticky notes that need to be written up, online orders that you are expecting and anything that you need to do or handle and can quickly clear from your counter into the folder to be dealt with another day.

★ **Archives:** As implied, this would hold all the old "Current Folder" materials that are no longer needed this month, such as any important printouts related to past projects that took place within the last twelve months, and classes you took within the past six months.

★ **Financial Documents:** This should hold all your bank statements, bank info, copies of your bills, rent, budget, extra checkbooks and tax documents.

- ★ **Receipts:** This is my favorite. I haven't had to get a store credit since implementing my strategy here. Keep all your receipts organized by store and wrap a rubber band around them. Put the receipts for each month in separate see-through zipper bags. This will help you with taxes and the returns line.

- ★ **Government-Issued Documents:** This should include any government-issued files, such as passports, birth certificates, past residencies, copies of your driver's license and registration—any legal paperwork and insurance paperwork (claims and all!).

- ★ **Medical Paperwork:** Keep records of your doctor visits, medical history, current or past illnesses and injuries (including any surgeries), medications you take, your blood type and a list of your allergies.

SPECIAL PERSONAL MEMENTOS BOX

In this box, separate from your file folders, place anything from birthday cards to travel souvenirs and treasured childhood items. Before putting it into the box, either wrap each item up carefully or put it in a zippered plastic bag.

BOUNCE OFF THE WALLS

These shelves add space to the room without taking up valuable desktop real estate. The less stuff on the floor, or workspace, the better. I installed these babies myself—the hardest part was finding the right design. (Oh, and as you may be figuring out, I really like the color turquoise.)

The Living Area

YOUR BOOKS AND MOVIES MAKE GREAT ROOMIES

Whether you live in a dorm, apartment, house or castle, I'll bet you have a TV. If you have a TV and a million books, as I do, you absolutely need to copy the hybrid bookshelf TV stand. I was on the prowl for a cheap bookshelf on Craigslist and ended up finding three for $100. *Boom*, it was awesome. My books are arranged by genre and author. There are even some vintage books (oh, I love collecting books). Stack some horizontally, some vertically, and dress up your bookshelves with candles and framed photos for a well-designed look. Quick reminder: When guests come over, hide any embarrassing books in an emergency bin (for instance, *How Not to Be a Crazy Person* or your autographed copy of *Fifty Shades of Grey*, which is right next to your *Twilight* collector's edition). I'm not judging!

TABLECLOTHS AND PLACE MATS ARE THE BEST BAND-AID

I had to move my dining room table into my third-story apartment (two girls, 982 pounds of solid wood—you do the math). A stranger offered to help, thank god, but sadly he scratched the surface right in the center. (This is also how many IKEA delivery stories end.) No matter—just put decorative place mats or table runners over the scratched area, as if they were born to be there. Your friends won't even know what they're missing.

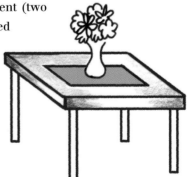

Bathroom

Organizing your toiletries has got to be done (otherwise, you really will spend two hours getting ready in the morning, and wouldn't you rather sleep in?). Start with four main categories: hair, face, body and nails. Then divide those into the following subcategories:

1. FACE

★ Makeup and makeup tools
★ Skin products (cleansing towels, face brushes, etc.)

2. HAIR

★ Cleansing and styling products
★ Styling tools (hair dryers, brushes and clips, etc.)
★ Hair accessories (headbands and such)

3. NAILS

★ Polishes
★ Tools and polish removers

4. BODY

★ In-shower tools (loofahs, razors, etc.)
★ Postshower products (creams and oils)
★ Spa stuff (bath soak, bath salts, bubble bath, etc.)
★ Hair accessories (headbands and such)

You should end up with an easy-to-see system (if it's a stacking system specifically for under-the-sink storage, even better; it will utilize the high space underneath your bathroom sink) that looks kinda like this:

STUFF YOU WANT TO HIDE

You've also got your feminine products, cotton swabs, ear swabs and whatever else you don't necessarily want front and center. Put those in decorative canisters with lids, so people develop FOPAIN (Fear of Poking Around In There) when they see them.

FORGET-ME-NOTS

1. Feng shui will help you feel more at home in your personal space. The biggies—put your bed against a wall and your desk against a window.

2. Just as your clothes reflect your personal style, so does your living space. Bright colors will give you energy, while pastels will calm you down.

3. Organization is everything. When in doubt, buy a bunch of clear bins and start throwing stuff in them. You'll figure it out.

CHAPTER 10

MONEY, MONEY, MONEY, MONEY

THE MOST INVALUABLE RESOURCE THAT MAKES THE PLANET GO 'ROUND

MY EXPERIENCE: GETTING CUT
OFF HAS ITS PERKS

IF ONLINE SHOPPING WERE A PERSON, I would date it, buy it a ring (from itself) and marry it. I've done a wild amount of buying online, and it doesn't just stop with clothes. Oh, my spidey sense is tingling . . . there's a sale somewhere. BRB.

OK, sorry, I ended up at Amazon.com. But I didn't purchase a thing! (Victory is mine!!) Anyway, the main thing I want to tell you here is that money is *real*, y'all. I know that may sound a little . . . *well, duh, of course it's real, Ashley. I paid good money to read this book in my PJs while my cat quietly drools on me.* It's hard to understand how the government can print so much freaking money every day, but somehow it's still not enough to afford new jeans. I still don't get it, but maybe my personal finance expert, Zac Bissonnette, can explain later.

Basically, you're young, and maybe you've relied on your parents for funds, and they've done the best they can. But then comes the day when you're cut off. And that $100 check Grandma used to give you every Christmas isn't enough to pay rent, own a car or even buy a ticket to go back home for Christmas to get another check from Grandma. I've been there, totally f!cking broke, and to make things worse, I was already a working actress.

Long story short, my parents and I got into a huge fight after I'd been living on my own for about a year. They helped out sometimes when I couldn't make the rent, and they still paid my phone bill, but nothing else. Nada. I was also contributing money *back* to my parents as well (sort of a "we all

support each other" kind of thing, which is a disaster, and you'll see why). When we got into this fight, I remember I was in my apartment on the phone with them, while my ex-boyfriend sat on the little blue couch my parents let me have. They liked my ex at first—they liked all my friends and coworkers at first. But now they didn't. I suppose they thought he was stealing me from them (most parents do—and in a sense, he was). I was becoming emotionally independent, but financially, I was still indebted to them. They'd done all they could to keep me "on their side," but a lot of damage had been done. They threatened to stop paying my phone bill on that call, and then hung up on me midcall. I looked at my boyfriend at the time, and he shook his head in disbelief. Then we laughed. It was sort of funny, in a weird way, because I thought everything would be fine and go back to normal. It did not.

I got an email the next day saying I would not be supported by them any longer, that they had taken the money out of our joint account (I did not have my own) and that I needed to come to where they live (a fifty-minute drive away) to close out the accounts at the bank. I felt blackmailed. And I was. But it was their strange way of helping me. Some call it tough love, but I call it $1.74. I had an empty gas tank, my boyfriend was now at work and I had to be up at their bank in thirty minutes. So I found a dollar, put gas in my car with it, hoping I'd make it there. I did. At the bank we didn't talk. I signed the papers and the banker gave me the remaining amount—$1.74.

So at least I knew a buck could get me back home. And I'd have seventy-four cents to spare. Woo-hoo!

I ended up having to learn the hard way that the world as you know it can change in an instant, and while money can't buy you happiness, it sure as hell can buy you a ticket to the survival train. Luckily, *Awkward* would start filming again in a month, so I made an embarrassing call (my then-boyfriend had signed me up on his plan) to my manager, who kindly loaned me enough money to make it through five weeks until my paycheck came. After that day, I didn't talk to my parents for two years.

But I got through it, and a whole lot worse, somehow. I am in touch with my parents again. Anyway, facing life head-on—with my own hard-earned cash—made me braver than ever. I began to watch my money more, and now I accept that I can't simply make dollar bills appear out of thin air when I want something shiny. I have to save, not just for a rainy day, but for any day, because you never know what can happen. And, frankly, even now, with my shopping habit still kind of a problem, I luckily have enough financial PTSD to work through it and try to break some of those habits. (Confession: I did recently buy a diamond ring, but it was almost 90 percent off!) So, dearest readers, know that money doesn't last forever. You'll always feel good about yourself and capable if you save for the important things, like college, your phone bill and maybe even nice little extras like a donation to charity or gifts for others. Do that and you'll feel rich in a way very few people get to understand. I want that for you. (Minus the whole $1.74 part.)

> Anyway, facing life head-on—with my own hard-earned cash—made me braver than ever. I began to watch my money more, and now I accept that I can't simply make dollar bills appear out of thin air when I want something shiny.

MEET YOUR EXPERT

ZAC BISSONNETTE, personal finance expert and author of *Debt-Free U* and *How to Be Richer, Smarter, and Better-Looking Than Your Parents*

His Philosophy on Money: Personal finance isn't just about the cliché of thinking long term; it's about realizing the things that matter *right now,* and recognizing that a lot of the stuff we're being told will lead to a happiness boost won't. For example, studies show that making an income (as an adult) of more than $65,000 per year probably won't make you any happier. People who wear high-end watches are not, on average, happier than people who wear low-end watches. On the other hand, there's some evidence that things like vacations (experiences), in general, lead to a stronger and more lasting happiness boost than stuff. And then there's all kinds of research that debt and inadequate savings lead to stress and misery, while things like having a plan and contributing to retirement lead to feelings of competence and self-worth.

From Zac: A Very, Very Long List of Sneaky, Out-of-the-Box Ideas and Websites That Will Make You Major $$$

Just kidding . . . Most of those are scams. If you have some sort of computer/ technical skill, you can make a little money on sites like Fiverr.com. It's not trendy or sexy or what you want to hear, but if you want to make money, the best thing to do is find a demanding part-time job. And don't worry that you don't have enough experience. For most entry-level jobs, the specifics of what you're doing are taught on the job. So take a lap around the mall or make a few pit stops at local restaurants, and ask who's hiring.

From Me: Five Easy Ways to Make Your Own Money
(SO YOU CAN DO WHATEVER THE HELL YOU WANT WITH IT)

1. Babysit

I know the first thing that comes to mind is poopy diapers, but I'm telling you, this is a great way to rack up serious dough doing almost nothing. (I know Zac said you should get a demanding part-time job, and this is one of them. You'll learn all sorts of values—and then the kid will go to bed at 8 p.m. and you can watch TV.) Plus, you get to choose when you do it and you don't have to watch your paycheck waste away to taxes—it's straight cash in your pocket at the end of the night. The ideal gig is a single one-ish-year-old. She's (let's pretend it's a girl) not a newborn, so she can hold her head up, but she can't talk yet, so she can't tell Mom and Dad that you ate half of her Mac 'n' Cheese. (But don't forget to take care of the kid. That is kind of important.)

2. Hostess at a restaurant

There's a joke in LA that when someone says she's an actress, you should ask her which restaurant she works for. Tons of people have to waitress in their lives, but hostessing is the secret sweet spot. You basically just have to stand there—and you're interacting with the patrons when they first walk in, bright eyed and bushy tailed, before they get cranky because their filet mignon was cooked medium well instead of well done. (Which is doing them a favor, if you ask me.) Plus, some restaurants even hand tips to the hostess at the end of the night. And if you're slightly under twenty-one, you can hostess at a bar and report back to all your friends about what the sloppy old people did while they were drunk.

3. Pimp out your closet

There is money hiding in your closet and you don't even know it. I get that it's tough to part with stuff, but if you open those doors and look at everything as if it's got a big fat price tag on it (that is, you could potentially get $10 for this, $15 for that), your sentimental mind-set will start packing its bags. There's the classic online listing sites, but there are also a bunch of cool apps available, which basically let you post your stuff Instagram-style, creating an online store right from your bedroom. Sell five of those hardly worn cardigans smushed in the back of your closet, and go out and buy yourself some cool leather pants.

4. Wrap gifts around the holidays

No one, I mean no one, likes wrapping Christmas gifts. In fact, I'm willing to bet it's your mom's favorite thing to complain about on Facebook in December. Post your own status update offering to help out any parents in need, and you'll make bank. Tack on a $15 fee for supplying wrapping paper and bows.

5. Set up techy stuff for old people

Fact: Old people are afraid to deal with technology. Additional fact: You are not. If you ever want to convince a sixty-five-year-old that you got into Harvard, just have him watch you navigate an iPad mini. He'll think you're Steve Jobs. So, market yourself around town as a technology wizard—offering to set up new computers, install new software or update apps. You know it basically takes the click of the button, but I'm willing to bet folks will pay you $25 to do it for them.

> **EXPERT SECRET:** Never apply for a store credit card. Sure, every cashier in America will try to convince you that this is a great idea because you'll get 10 percent off your purchase today. Don't give in. You're basically inviting yourself to rack up tons of debt that you can't afford to pay off. —Zac

From Zac: Keeping Track of Your Money via a Macro Budget
(DO YOU REALLY NEED ONE, EVER?)

Here's my position on budgets: It's not that they're a bad way to manage money. It's more that the people who will be inclined to manage money that way are going to do it anyway (it's just a certain mind-set/focus on organization that relatively few people have) and no one who isn't inclined to use a budget is going to use one just because you (or me or *Marie Claire* or President Obama) tell them to.

So, for those of you who aren't inclined to create and live by a spreadsheet: Automate everything that you possibly can (student loan payments,

MONEY MANAGEMENT

In order to best prioritize and manage your money, you need to figure out what your priorities are. This worksheet is here to help. Look to it whenever you're feeling tempted to go off the rails.

What do you know you'll need to be financially responsible for one day? (College, a car, etc.)

ITEM	COST	WHY THIS IS IMPORTANT TO ME

What fun items would you like to buy in the near future? (A designer handbag, the new iPhone, etc.)

ITEM	COST	WHY THIS IS IMPORTANT TO ME

What's the total cost you're looking at here? $

How many hours would you have to work over the next few years to put away enough for the first category?

How many more hours would you have to work over the next year to treat yourself to two or three additional, fun items?

When you need a little motivation, visualize yourself having all of these things. Now, write yourself a message to go back and reread here:

_____

_____

_____

_____

contributions to your savings account, etc.). That way, you have all your real necessities taken care of. Then, whatever's left you can spend on everything else. And since you don't have a credit card, you can't get into debt. And since you automated all the really important stuff, you've forced yourself to prioritize without tracking every package of mints you buy in Excel.

The "Can You Afford It?" Quiz

There are going to be times, many times, when you're tempted to buy something you can't afford. This includes everything from a $4 bottle of water when a perfectly nice bottle of generic is right next to it, to a $200 couture backpack when you could just go with a discount backpack, to a $3,000 spring break trip when you could just go home and pay your family a visit. Sometimes it makes sense to give in, and sometimes—more times—it makes sense to hold back. When these moments take place, grab your brain by the balls and say, *Hey brain, listen to me!* And then ask yourself:

1. **Have you already paid for the basics—or do you have the money set aside to?**

   If you cover your rent, your phone bill or your monthly car payment, that's the first priority. And don't think you can just go to Mom or Dad to help you out if you need to. The problem with doing that over and over is that you're basically the girl who cries wolf. Do it often enough, and they won't be as willing to help you when you are in deep need of their deeper pockets.

2. **Is this getting in the way of things you said you really want (that you really, really want)?**

   If you're staring at a random sweater in the mall, thinking about how cute it would look on you, remember that shiny new car you've had your eye on for months—and how great you'll look it in every goddamn day. Before you're willing to blow your money on something small, think about how it will affect the things you're really working toward.

3. **How are you going to feel afterward?**

   Are you really going to feel that much more amazing after drinking expensive, brand-name water than you would if you drank generic? Tomorrow, are you even going to remember that you drank a bottle of water? Probably not. So don't waste your money on it.

Starting a Savings Account

It's never too early to start saving money. You probably already have a piggy bank or a sock drawer or some means of saving cash. Well, now you're ready for the big time: an actual bank account that you can access through a real, live drive-through window. Follow these guidelines to make the most of it:

1. Consider a CD (Certificate of Deposit).

If you want to start investing and/or have an interest in becoming a billionaire one day (shout-out to Sheryl Sandberg!), certificates of deposit are a good way to dip your toe in the water. All you need is a handful of starter cash—say, from a Bat Mitzvah or a generous check from Grandma—that you realistically won't have to touch for a few months or, better yet, years. By buying a CD at a bank, you're making a low-risk investment, where the bank will pay you a small interest rate, higher than what you'd get from, say, your checking or savings account. Plus, you're guaranteed to get at least whatever you put in. (Even if the bank goes all Lehman Brothers on you, your deposit is protected by the FDIC up to $250,000.) Go for either a traditional CD, which gives you a fixed rate for a limited period, after which you can withdraw your moolah or roll it into another CD, or a liquid CD if you're still squeamish about saving, because it allows you to withdraw money without a penalty. There are other CD options as well, which you can ask your bank about. (And they'll think you're, like, really smart.)

2. No matter where you save, aim to set aside 20 percent
of your income per month in savings.
So if you're handed 100 bucks after a night of babysitting, fork over $20 to your savings account.

3. Don't touch it.

There will be times when you'll look longingly at some expensive, beautiful thing in the mall and think, *Oh, I'll just take [insert price] out of my savings.* But then you'll do it again, and again, and soon you won't have any savings at all. This account gets a giant chastity belt. If you need more money, work more!

From Zac: The Best Ways to Prep Your $$$ for College

This is a biggie—it's different than saving for an iPad or a sparkly dress for New Year's Eve. So, I'm going to let our man Zac take the mic again.

529 PLANS

These education savings plans offered by the states are great—especially if you can contribute early or your parents are helping. If you're in high school, the most important thing is to keep it in a savings or a money market account—you don't have enough time to ride out the potential volatility of the stock market.

FAFSA

This stands for Free Application for Federal Student Aid. It's a form that can be filled out by prospective and current college students to determine how much financial aid you can get from the government. Nearly every student is eligible for some form of financial aid (unless your dad is Warren Buffett), so it's worth filling out a few pieces of paperwork to see what you can get. At the same time, don't rely on this as your sole source of college funding. (The government is stingy like that.)

EXPERT SECRET: When it comes to college, the biggest myth is that where you go to college will matter a lot. More likely, it will matter very little. A while ago, someone told me that she was looking at a couple of colleges and one was ranked like #86 in *U.S. News'* "Guide to America's Best Colleges" and the other was ranked #132, so she was more intrigued by the one ranked #86. And I'm like, "DO YOU THINK THERE IS A SINGLE PERSON IN THE WORLD WHO ISN'T A HIGH SCHOOL STUDENT, PARENT OF A HIGH SCHOOL STUDENT, OR GUIDANCE COUNSELOR WHO KNOWS THAT?" Very, very few HR people are as on top of what colleges are considered to be "good" as upper-middle-class high school students and their parents are. For most students, the best college choice will be the one that allows them to graduate with the least debt. —Zac

SCHOLARSHIPS

Same advice here—don't rely on scholarships, as they are a b!tch to slog through and apply for, when you could be spending that time working a part-time job and saving guaranteed cash. Start with Zinch.com, which allows you to create an online profile that will help the site locate scholarships that are relevant to you. They also dole out a weekly $1,000 scholarship, just for filling out a 280-character essay. (That's two tweets. Girl, you got this.)

From Zac: Dealing with Uncomfortable Money Situations

They're like taxes for young people—you can't avoid them. But you will survive!

SPLITTING THE BILL AT DINNER

This is a big one, especially if, like me, you are a teetotaler. Because then you go out for dinner with four people and they each have three drinks and you just have a $14 salad and the $400 bill comes and they're all like "OK! $120 each! Sounds good! This was fun, let's do it again!" One thing you can do is tell the waiter you want your check separately. It's kind of a dick move, but people will get it.

EVERYTHING ELSE

Other problems will come up when you have friends who have more money to spend than you do (or are just dumb and insensitive) and there's pressure to spend outside your comfort zone. My advice is to just be honest: people will respect that. And if they don't, they're not very good friends. "Listen guys, I just really don't have the money to do this; I'm saving for college/a car/etc." Just tell people. Chances are, some of your friends will be in the same position and they'll appreciate your breaking the ice.

WHEN FRIENDS ASK TO BORROW MONEY FROM YOU

This can happen in oh-so-subtle ways. You're at the mall or at lunch with a friend, and she forgot cash or is just $10 short, so she asks you if you mind spotting her this one time. Problem is, $10 basically equals a million dollars out of your budget, so while you may not have visible pit stains, inside you're sweating. If it's a good friend, this is the first time she's asking and you have the cash, lend it to her with the following script: "Sure—but I'm super-tight on cash, so don't hate me when I text you before school tomorrow and remind you to bring money to pay me back." But if this is a habit of hers, you've gotta shut this b!tch down. And there's no need to be apologetic about it (odds are, she knows what she's doing—manipulating you!). Say to her: "I wish I could help you out, but I really can't this time."

That's it—it's her problem, her job to solve it. On the flip side, if your friend has been tight on cash, has never asked you for money and calls you freaking out because she doesn't want to call her parents, you have two choices. The first one is tricky. You have to make sure you are and will be financially stable, understand that the loan may not get paid back quickly, if at all, and then figure out how that could complicate or deepen your friendship. You'll know what to do. Ask her if she wouldn't rather borrow money from you now and deal with her parents later. Settle on a date for payback or cash in your karmic goodwill and give her it as a gift (just don't wrap it). The second one is kind of tough. Try calming and coaching her through how to have a healthy talk with her parents, how to dismantle their negative or guilt-laden remarks. Just being there for her to lean on during and after makes you a great friend. You can help her deal with the next options later.

Owning a Credit Card

This is risky business. Having one can help you build credit (important down the road when you're trying to rent an apartment, buy a car, etc.), but you have to really be honest with yourself and figure out whether or not you're financially responsible enough to have one. Will you be able to pay the bill in full *every* month? If you can answer yes without a doubt, go for it. If the answer is maybe or let me just try it or no, forget it. Massive credit card debt is not your friend.

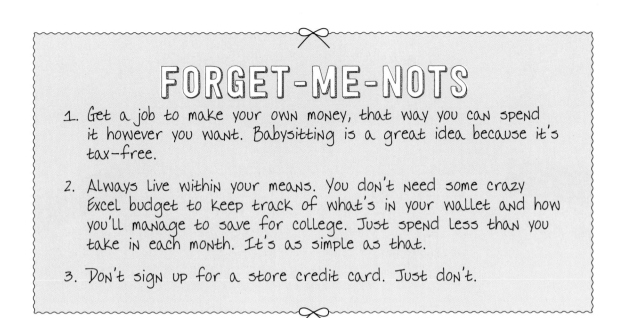

FORGET-ME-NOTS

1. Get a job to make your own money, that way you can spend it however you want. Babysitting is a great idea because it's tax-free.

2. Always live within your means. You don't need some crazy Excel budget to keep track of what's in your wallet and how you'll manage to save for college. Just spend less than you take in each month. It's as simple as that.

3. Don't sign up for a store credit card. Just don't.

CHAPTER 11

TIME MANAGEMENT

YOUR ALARM CLOCK DOESN'T TAKE BRIBES

MY EXPERIENCE: BATTERIES NOT INCLUDED

LET ME PREFACE THIS SECTION WITH A LITTLE CONFESSION: I procrastinated and mismanaged my time before writing this chapter about procrastination and time management (#MomDon'tYellAtMe). OK, now that that's off my chest, I will begin. But first let me paint my nails.

OK. So, when I first sold this book, I started out with good intentions and a Herculean schedule. Problem was, it was totally unrealistic and nearly impossible to keep up with. (Thanks, Hercules.) I ended up in a world of frustration every time life threw something at me (metaphorically speaking, of course) that I hadn't "planned for," like a parking ticket or a late night of filming. I tried sneaking in a bit of writing on the *Awkward* set, but it was impossible to focus. I would be on my laptop squeezing out little snippets at a time, but then I had a tough time recalling my lines while we were shooting a scene, and then when I went back to writing, I had forgotten my train of thought and everything I was trying to say felt disjointed. I was trying so hard to control my schedule based on unrealistic expectations that everything I did was mediocre and had to be redone, costing me even more time.

By this point it was summertime, and I sort of let things just . . . fall away a little. The whole book was already sort of written in my head, so I'd come up with a thousand excuses, distractions and legitimate/nonlegitimate reasons to postpone actually writing any words (looking back, it was because it felt so freaking overwhelming to do so!). I realized I had to stop with all

the bullsh!t (my room is a mess! my nails need painting! my couch pillows need fluffing!) and *just do it*. Or, as I like to say, "Nike it." So instead of a crazy schedule, I started making a detailed checklist (which I will show you later). It helped me keep things flexible so that I was able to reprioritize as needed while standing up for my own needs and saying, "No, I need to focus on this" if other things popped up. Once I did that, it felt like there were so many more hours in the day. And once I actually sat down at my desk, writing this book was kind of . . . *fun*. (Note to publisher: It was fun the *whole* time! Totally fun! I LOVED it!) And now here you are, reading it. And that's way more rewarding than fluffy couch pillows.

MEET YOUR EXPERT

Nicole Williams, career expert and author of *Girl on Top: Your Guide to Turning Dating Rules into Career Success*

Her Philosophy on Time Management: It's easy to get bogged down by a massive project that has many moving parts. The best way to tackle a time-consuming amount of work is always to dissect it—and focus on smaller increments.

Three Starter Rules for Staying Productive

Here are the main, big-picture lessons I've learned—and still have to remember at times—that helped me write this book and maintain über-productive days.

1. Having a routine helps.

For instance, every day I wake up and make the bed, feed the cat and dog, take some supplements, shower and meditate. If I don't do this, I feel out of control no matter what happens throughout the rest of my day. (P.S.: Here is a brainy reminder: control is an illusion. Action is the only truth!)

2. Remember why you're doing this.

When you're struggling to get the ball rolling, think about why you wanted to do this in the first place. It's because one of your life dreams is to become a published author or make the varsity soccer team or get into college. Remind yourself of that goal. Write it down on a heart-shaped post-it if you have to. Whatever it takes to get going.

3. You'll always win if you learn the lesson.

I had an audition recently that I almost passed on, but I didn't. I did the work and I did as well as I could on it. I didn't end up getting the part, but, hey, life is a constant learning experience if you're open-minded. There are no such things as mistakes, only lessons. And as long as you work as hard as you can, the experience will be worth the effort put forth.

How Candy Taught Me
to Set Realistic Goals

One of the best ways to achieve your day-to-day goals is to set realistic ones. I don't say this because I don't believe you can't do it; rather, I believe you can *over*do it (#BlairWaldorfWasCrazy).

You know the phrase *too much of a good thing*? I'll tell you a quick and distractingly funny story before I get to my goal of talking about goals.

An old attorney of mine (he wasn't actually that old—I just have a new one now) invited me over for dinner one night. I went, and it was nice. His kid was jumping over couches and playing pretend "attack" with the walls. Anyway, the kid kept looking at me and laughing. A piece of candy suddenly flew by my head and over to him, and he finally calmed down and came to dinner. I don't have kids (unless Maury knows something I don't), but I was amazed at how well that worked. The boy asked for more candy and his father said, "No, why don't you tell me what too much candy does?" The kid was like *bursting* out of his chair and suddenly proclaimed, "DIABETES!!" While this was slightly offensive (myself being a former round child and having two relatives who do have diabetes), I will say this: that attorney taught me something. He had a short-term goal: to get his kid to STFU. And a long-term goal: to get his kid to grow up healthy and happy. Our main goal can interfere with our day-to-day tasks and before you know it, you'll look back and realize you didn't get any closer to your big goal because you got impatient and skipped over the smaller goals. Rome wasn't built in a day, so, you know, don't develop scoliosis trying to.

Don't applaud just yet (seriously, you'll freak people out if you just start clapping). There's another part of this, which, sadly, I really relate to. It's called perfectionism. I hate when people say perfectionism is a good thing or is rare—I don't feel that way. Truth is, we are all perfectionists at something, and lazy as hell at other things, which is fine. That's life. You don't have to be pumped about doing the laundry to be a hard worker. Procrastination isn't your pitfall; it's just your excuse to fall into a self-pity pit. Sorry! Tough love coming right at ya here.

Basically, those things we just discussed up there—the goals and post marks—do need some prep to get there, but don't waste your whole day prepping for something you're not actually going to do. I say this with extreme expertise in this area. If I had a nickel (make that a quarter; street parking doesn't take nickels) for every time I said I was going to do this or that or write a chapter on procrastination or a sentence about it or just a long joke like I'm doing now as I move my head back and forth for no reason because I feel like I have to use that melody of exasperation. Wait, what was I saying?

Oh, right, no amount of lead time or stretching will ever make the big goals easier to accomplish than they are right now. I used to always say, "It will never be less scary to [insert goal here] than it is right now." That's true. In fact it's like super-true. Have I made my point? Nope. But I'll stop trying to be funny and say it like it is: have ambition, do as much as you can as best as you can *now*—that way you can enjoy a long-ass TV marathon later, totally guilt-free.

Nicole's Productivity Pitfall Quiz

IF IMAGINING THE PROJECT AS A WHOLE FREEZES YOU WITH FEAR . . . THINK SMALL.

You're much more likely to put everything off since it seems like such an overwhelming task. Plan ahead and put it on paper. Map out your plan and schedule work for twenty-minute intervals. Set a timer on your iPhone and stick to working hard for that period. Getting a lot accomplished in the amount of time it takes to watch two episodes of a TV show on Netflix will amaze you.

YOU CONSISTENTLY MISS THE DEADLINES YOU SET FOR YOURSELF . . . DON'T BE AN OVERACHIEVER.

Saying you'll have a project done in half the time allotted won't do anyone any good if you can't realistically meet that deadline. Set reasonable goals—especially if this is something new to you and if you are working with a group of people.

YOU WORK UNTIL YOU BURN YOURSELF OUT . . .
PENCIL IN BREAKS.

While it might seem counterintuitive to plan for breaks, it will actually help you work faster. After completing twenty minutes of nonstop chemistry problem solving, you're bound to need a creativity breather. Knowing you have five minutes to read the latest celebrity gossip post on Facebook or chat on gchat will help you work better. Scheduling breaks will help energize you and keep your project running on time. If you completed a large, time-consuming project, treat yourself to dinner at your favorite restaurant or a relaxing massage.

YOU PUSH THINGS OFF BECAUSE YOU "WORK BETTER UNDER PRESSURE" . . .
TELL A WHITE LIE.

Are you one of those people who often pulls all-nighters? Do you think working under pressure builds up your adrenaline and makes you work smarter? Reality check: This is one of the worst ways to work. Working until the last minute often means you don't have a chance to edit your copy or have a coworker proof it for errors. If you absolutely need the ticking clock to complete tasks, you need to start making up fake early deadlines so you build in some padding. Mentally schedule deadlines two to three days before a project is due and work toward those earlier deadlines.

YOU'RE STUCK IN THE "PREP" PHASE . . .
DON'T SPEND TOO MUCH TIME "PLANNING."

New project folder: check. New highlighter: check. New fancy engraved executive pen: check. Spending too much time preplanning can often kill your project's mojo. Spending time and money on these "essentials" will often set you over budget and behind schedule. The most important item you need is your hands—put them on the keyboard and just start doing.

How to Steal More Time Out of Your Day

(WITHOUT GETTING DETAINED BY MALL SECURITY GUARDS)

All right, so now that you're done rereading those last few paragraphs over and over again, let's move on to exactly how to structure your day, through my own little creation called "check that stellar sh!t." Scan or copy the checklist. You'll need a new one each day. (Sorry, trees.) Now, behold my checklist.

Disclaimer: This is my own, real-life checklist that I use to start the day. It's up to you to decide what to put down instead. Dun, dun, dun . . . OK, now I'll explain all this. Stick with me here, because this stuff is so freaking gratifying.

ROUTINE

As I've said before, starting the day with a routine helps me stay grounded and reduces stress like whoa. Feel free to add in or customize yours, but the things that should go in this column are super-basic—it's all about taking care of yourself and making time for the little things that we forget to do when we're feeling overwhelmed.

TO-DOS

Here's where you write down what you need to get done that day, from a hair appointment to your chemistry homework to buying your best friend's birthday present. These few minutes of prep will save you time in the end because you won't be rushing around in a panic when you realize you left your chem book in your locker—again. Depending on the day, I'll organize the tasks at hand in sequential order or by priority.

TO SCHEDULE

Use this space for nonimmediate things that need to get done eventually—anything from reminders to birthdays to a lofty project you want to start soon.

PHONE, TEXTS AND WHATEVER ELSE

This is for those of us who don't use pagers (so, yes, that should be just about everyone reading this), but have a tendency to forget to return phone calls, texts, emails or whatever the hell else. This is sort of like asking yourself, "Who do I need to get back to or reach out to today?"

YESTERDAY'S POINT

This is just a friendly reminder about a fun thing that happened yesterday or an important lesson you learned. Your past will always play a role in your present. Acknowledging it gives it less power, more purpose.

The Checklist

ROUTINE

- ☐ ....
- ☐ ....
- ☐ ....
- ☐ ....
- ☐ ....
- ☐ ....
- ☐ ....
- ☐ ....

TO DO

- ☐ ....
- ☐ ....
- ☐ ....
- ☐ ....
- ☐ ....
- ☐ ....
- ☐ ....
- ☐ ....

TO SCHEDULE

- ☐ ....
- ☐ ....
- ☐ ....
- ☐ ....
- ☐ ....
- ☐ ....
- ☐ ....

PHONE, TEXTS, ETC.

- ☐ ....
- ☐ ....
- ☐ ....
- ☐ ....
- ☐ ....
- ☐ ....
- ☐ ....

Reflections & Recollections

YESTERDAY'S POINT

- ....
- ....
- ....
- ....
- ....
- ....

FOOD & WORKOUT LOG

- ....
- ....
- ....
- ....
- ....
- ....

DREAMS

- ....
- ....
- ....
- ....
- ....
- ....

COULDA DONE BETTER

- ....
- ....
- ....
- ....
- ....
- ....

HIGHLIGHTS

- ....
- ....
- ....

DREAMS

Call me crazy, but I really do believe that dreams are our souls trying to tell us truths. I personally have gained a lot by recounting my dreams (some I just forget and that's OK, too). They can help you follow a gut feeling or just make you ROFLOL over that weird dream you had about the penguins and the mangos. (I haven't had a dream like that yet, but I would sure like to.)

FOOD AND WORKOUT LOG

Sounds tedious, but you'll thank me later. We all have bad habits in one of these areas (#Guilty), and it's important to reflect on our progress and pitfalls if we want to establish better habits in the future. (Refer back to the fitness and nutrition chapters for more on this.)

COULDA DONE BETTER

This is not a place for you to call yourself an asshole, but it is a place where you should call yourself out. Whether it's road rage, laziness or a telling a lie, this is the spot where you write down what—you guessed it—you could've done better. Use this not only to identify what went wrong but also to pinpoint how you can make it right the next day and avoid doing it in the future.

HIGHLIGHTS

This is like a quickie diary. I do like the idea of everyone free-flowing their deepest thoughts every day, but this is a good place to CliffsNotes it. For example, today's highlights were: packed for vacation, finished reading a book and had a great massage.

FORGET-ME-NOTS

1. Procrastination is an excuse to let yourself down.

2. Don't set unrealistic deadlines for yourself. Think reasonably about how long each task will take and pencil in breaks to keep yourself from burning out.

3. Don't dismiss all the hard work you did each day as "unimportant." Take time to celebrate your achievements and think about how the next day could be even better.

The Dos and Don'ts of Keeping Your Game Face On

Now that you know how to get started, here's how to keep going like the freaking Energizer bunny:

DO! **Factor in time.**

Use a calendar app (or if you happen to have a Zooey Deschanel sense, write in your vintage planner) and put in a realistic time frame (padding for traffic) for each task or event. This will help you designate what can and cannot be accomplished each day. (Time won't stop, so don't try to avoid sleep . . . seriously, I did that for a while and I ended up like a friggin' zombie.) For extra punctuation, set mini-alarms on your phone. They'll help remind you when you need to power down the computer and start the next task.

> **EXPERT SECRET:**
> Padding in extra time can actually encourage you to work a little faster to beat a promised project deadline.
> —Nicole

DON'T! **Be afraid to ask for help.**

Some people just aren't wired to do certain things. I don't have enough time in the day to focus on driving only, so it's very tempting to multi-task. To curb my enthusiasm, I carpool most days so a better driver than I am can take care of the navigating while I do adult things like participating in conference calls and tweeting. Maybe this isn't your exact case, but whether you need a tutor, a hug or a friendly ear, never burden yourself with too much. Ask for help when you need it. Trust me, everyone will be better off if you do.

DO! **Have fun.**

All work and no play makes a girl a b!tch. Sorry, but it's true. If you don't factor in time with your friends and family, or just a fun solo outing, you're going to start to be bitter and resentful, your work quality will suffer and you will purposefully try to trip anyone who walks by you.

YOU PURSUING YOU

Nike It!

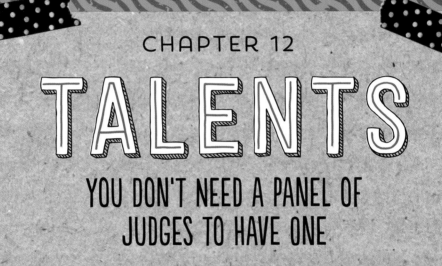

CHAPTER 12

TALENTS

YOU DON'T NEED A PANEL OF
JUDGES TO HAVE ONE

MY EXPERIENCE: I OWED MYSELF
A CHANCE TO TRY IT

IN A WORLD WHERE GRADES WERE KING and ten-year-olds played Mozart by memory, there was one girl with one tissue box. That girl was me, playing said tissue box as if it were a violin. (My teacher deemed me so horrible at playing that she decided to spare my audience the sound of strings and already had tissues on hand in case anyone's ears started bleeding.)

Where I grew up, there was a strong emphasis on the arts, including a very prestigious school for "gifted" children. My poor parents assumed that the gifted school was a long shot, since their child would rather make "carpet angels" (you know, like snow angels, but in Florida) during piano lessons. After nine years on the planet, I had only shown a real talent for the '90s ball-and-chain type toy known as the Skip-It. (That love promptly died when my parents threw me a Skip-It-themed birthday party, even renting two U-Hauls to pick up the herd of attendees from my school, but no one showed up. My mom told me, "You're just special.")

But my parents were determined to help me discover my true potential. So, after ditching the tissue box and the Skip-It, my parents secretly got my IQ tested. They would tell you to this day that they knew I was smart and it wasn't really a secret that my IQ was being tested, but they also lied to me about Santa, so I don't believe them. In truth, my parents took me to the only IQ tester in the county who wasn't accepting bribes from parents to get their kids into that accelerated learning school. And great news: I'm a legit motha-f!ckin' genius! I got into Mensa, an elite club for those with an IQ in the top 2 percent.

Bad news: I was still a dork without any particular talent. (Which, side note, is actually very normal for high-IQ individuals. Supposedly the smarty-pants of the world have a statistically lower chance at nabbing the high-paying jobs, a large social network or even a clean criminal record.) As a certified smarty-pants, I would argue that the world just doesn't understand because I'm-so-smart-and-everyone-else-is-so-dumb-so-there, but the truth is I'm not a "purebred" smarty-pants, so I still have a chance at a private plane. (Yay?)

What I mean is that I have ADD (attention deficit disorder) and am LD (learning disabled). Which, as I would come to find out, feels less like a deficiency or disability but more like a "difference," and a damn good one. Which is clinically proven to be good for your ego. The only reason I bring this up is because I really dislike the way the public views these and other "disabilities." Oh, you know what? Sorry, my LD prevented me from wording that right. What I meant to say was: KISS MY SUCCESSFUL A** B!TCHES!! If that distracted you, don't worry, you didn't catch my ADD. You just caught yourself secretly appreciating what makes you different, too.

But back to discovering my true potential. So far I had nothing, aside from a need to always be doing more than one thing at once. And being sensitive. And being fearless. Those would all turn out to be vital characteristics in becoming an actress, but before I got there, my parents and I had to rule out everything else. Here is my reject pile, along with notes:

GOLF: team member injured by my rogue golf club

TENNIS: did NOT like tennis skirts or jumping

BASKETBALL: kept giving the ball to the other team

ICE SKATING: butt hurt

ROLLERBLADING: cement, butt hurt

SOCCER: NOT a contact sport, whoops

IRISH DANCING: I'm NOT a ginger

BAKING: I used salt instead of sugar

PIANO: Never made it past "Chopsticks"

COOKING: bad with knives

ATVS: flipped it

RAISING A COW FOR SLAUGHTER: set it free in the suburbs

CRAFTS: ate the glue-y Cheerios

MODELING: I accidentally threw up the food the company had me posing with

Eventually, I found my way to horseback riding and swimming. Horses became a huge hobby of mine and eventually I was showing them competitively. My parents, going full force to help me embrace a talent, any talent, soon moved to a horse farm and made it their business to make horses "get busy" (aka breed). I had a blast, and so did the horses who were getting it on.

When I first cantered on a horse, I had an aha moment. It was a moment of utter clarity. I was one with the horse—the smooth near-galloping gait carried me gently and with a relaxing speed as I felt the wind in my hair (and the smell of manure in a strong gust of wind). Horses, then, were my first passion. I soon became obsessed and to this day am still involved in the equestrian community. As you know, my next love was acting.

Frankly, I didn't start out very good at it. (I was even told to get another career at one point!) But I kept trying, meeting with every acting coach I could find, studying every movie and closely following my role models' careers. After all the hard work and slowly working through the stigmas of LD and ADD, I finally began to figure out my flow, or the way I work.

What I found was that not only do I learn differently, but how my brain works is so different from the rest of the non-LD/ADD community that it actually works to my advantage. My crazy ideas are praised, I am less afraid to take risks and I am able to see everything from a different perspective than those around me. Yes, I did have to form my own way of memorizing lines (saying each line seven times and slowly adding another line to each repeat—eventually, I'll have gone through the whole scene about forty times), but soon, I found myself gaining skills and I even started getting referred to as talented! I'd turned those "weaknesses," the ones I thought had guaranteed that my future wouldn't be so remarkable (I feared I would never be able to retain information, never learn a language and so on and so forth), into incredible strengths that would open so many doors.

And here we are, years later. I am fluent in Polish, and I memorize pages of dialogue every day for a living. (I'm even told I'm a quick learner!) In addition to being an actress and a Polish speaker, I'm also an author, a director and a living, breathing example of someone who can benefit from something that is perceived by most as a weakness. I'm sure this is going to tick some people off or not accord with some clinical bullsh!t, but I stopped caring about that a while ago. Through the years, I learned to embrace what made me different; I didn't "work through it" or "work around it," I worked *with* it. I can confidently say that my LD and ADD have made me a unique person, and a strong motherf!cker, too. I'll never listen to anyone who tells me, "You can't do that," because when I face adversity, I just remember where I came from and all that I've learned. My mom was right—I am special. But I'm no more special than all those folks out there who, like me, have stopped trying to "be" something they are not and are instead the best version of themselves.

NICOLE WILLIAMS, career expert and author of *Girl on Top: Your Guide to Turning Dating Rules into Career Success*

RE-MEET YOUR **EXPERT**

Her Philosophy on Talents and Dreams: We tend to discount what we love as too easy to be a job or a career. Think back to what you wanted to do when you were a kid—a newscaster, a model, etc. What are the elements of the job, and where do your skills or talents fit into today's job market? In high school and in college, that's when you want to go as far and wide as possible. What would be impossible/unthinkable for you? Train your mind in that direction, and keep your eyes on that path.

Nicole's "Get Your Sh!t Together" Story

I grew up in a very small, working-class town. My mom worked at a paint factory, and she *hated* it. By virtue of that, she kind of hated the rest of her life. She would come home, drop off McDonald's and go to bingo. We had a foster sister whose primary purpose was to take care of us.

At a very young age, (a) I thought, *There's no way that this is going to be my life* and (b) it inspired me to want to help other people in their career. My mom was working eight-hour shifts, but it consumed her life. Your career *so* relates to the qualify of your life in terms of your income, in terms of the time you get to spend with your family—your overall satisfaction with life has so much to do with your career.

I think that my mother's parents taught her that there's a divide between your personal life and your professional life, and you're not supposed to like your professional life. That's just what you do from 8 a.m. to 5 at night. Your job isn't something you're supposed to love. But actually, career *is* your life. This is something that you're going to spend 70 percent of your waking life doing, and by virtue of that, it's something you really do want to invest in for your sake, for your partner's sake, for your kids' sake, for your family's sake. Obviously, seeing my mom do work that she absolutely despised really taught me very early and in a very hands-on way just how much it sucks to have the wrong job. So I look at career as kind of a lifestyle issue, not just a compartment in your life.

If you think of it as something to enhance your life, it's not this horrible thing that's inherently so hard and so bad. That's not to say that it isn't challenging or that you don't have bad days, but it really is the foundation of a great life. So it's worth investing in and worth taking the reins on.

Keeping the Door Wiiiiide Open

If we defined our talents based on *America's Got Talent*, we would be limited to either swallowing swords or becoming an eight-year-old musical prodigy. Luckily, we can be a little more opened-minded than that. Would you want to limit yourself based on what other people define as a talent? Or worse, why would you want to let someone else tell you what you're good at? Those are very common pitfalls, but I'm hoping you don't close off your opportunities like this by letting other people pick and choose what you decide to do with your life. It's *your* life—take control before someone else takes control for you! Focus on being completely open to any possibility, considering any skill or any quirky talent that you enjoy pursuing, and making it your full-on thing. After all, if you enjoy doing it, keep freaking doing it. Nobody else has to understand or enjoy what you do. That's just letting a little bit of poison in to dampen your happiness. Even if there's a bit of a learning curve (which there always will be), stick to it. You won't truly know the depth of your talents unless you give everything a fair shot. Look how many things I had to try before I even began to grasp what it felt like to love horseback riding or acting! It's not a race. Rome wasn't built in a day, and neither is your potential. (You can totally tweet that and I won't even try to take credit.)

LET'S DISCOVER YOUR TALENTS, WHY DON'T WE?

Talents come in lots of shapes and sizes, and you have more than you think. To get a semi-quarter-kind-of-accurate count, I've included a worksheet to help you determine your best qualities, what things—big or small—you're great at and love to do most, and then we'll talk about how to develop those talents a bit further.

Name five things you know how to do really well.
This might include a subject in school, a sport, being a good friend or even quoting lines from *Bridesmaids*. Anything you feel well-versed in.

....

....

....

Hold up—were you worried about sounding boring or nerdy? Stop it.
Perhaps you know a lot about math, or Native American history, or makeup and fashion. Whatever it is, I think it's cool, and I could probably learn a thing or two from you. (Why weren't you around when I was writing this book?!) Keep tabs on the list above. It can be a great launching pad to build from and help you discover even more areas of interest. And, if not, you'll at least need this worksheet again later in this chapter.

Name five *new* things you'd like to learn how to do really well.
This might include a subject in school, a sport or even quoting lines from *War and Peace*. Anything you're not well-versed in but want to be.

....

....

....

This is a great way to remind yourself that there are so many ways for you to grow and expand your knowledge. I try to make a list like this once a year in order to gain some novice skills outside my comfort zone. It keeps life colorful and gives you the opportunity to develop more passions and hidden talents, or just become a more well-rounded individual.

Name five things you like to do for fun—
whether you know how to do them well or not!

....

....

....

....

....

Paying attention to your hobbies may sound like a no-brainer way to discover your true talents, but what if your hobbies include watching TV, online shopping or playing video games? Well, those guilty pleasures can become careers too, you know: producer, personal shopper, digital animator—look 'em up! If you love TV, read books about and/or by critics and start watching shows as if you're a critic in real life. Take notes on what you liked and didn't like about each program, and eventually you could even start a blog with your reviews. Are you an online shopping fan? There are a *ton* of lucrative careers in retail—think buyers, stylists or even working in finance and trolling the stock market for the next "big thing." (OK, that doesn't have anything to do with clothes, but you *are* looking for trends...and you'd make enough money to go shopping a lot, so...) And gaming, well, you basically hit the jackpot. It's the biggest sector in the entertainment industry, more than ten times the profits and market range than movies and television combined!

Name the top five things people compliment you on the most.

....

....

....

....

....

Noting what other people say about you (the positive stuff) can give you an even better and unbiased clue as to some of your strong suits, and perhaps even a skill set that comes so naturally you forgot it was there (like making Kraft Macaroni & Cheese without burning the cheese—you may think anyone can do it, but you would be dead wrong).

Expert Secret

Try out a bunch of different things. You're not meant to know what exactly you want to do with your life yet— it's OK to switch paths.

—NICOLE

I ABSOLUTELY AGREE WITH NICOLE HERE—in fact, her advice can be taken a little further. For example, when I first started in the entertainment industry, I had no intention of being a writer or a director. Nor did I have any dreams of being a designer or having my own "brand." But what I've learned is that if you constantly apply yourself and make it your mission to grow and evolve (for me that means cultivating both on- and off-screen skills), you never know where it could lead you. Hell, I didn't expect to be writing a book, or directing TV episodes, but here I am, doing all of that. I never closed myself off from any opportunity to grow. Maybe I'm naive, but if I am, I attribute my success to that naïveté. Because if I knew how hard some of this stuff would be, I probably wouldn't have tried it in the first place, but I'm glad I did!

QUIZ: THE WAY YOU WORK

Everyone learns differently. Understanding what makes *your* wheels turn can help you discover hidden talents.

If you were to start learning something new tomorrow (like the guitar), your main plan of action would be . . .

A Take a class. That way a teacher can show you the ropes, step by step.

B Watch videos online over and over until you master it yourself.

C Do tons of reading on the subject so that when you do give it a try, you feel super-prepared.

D Try it right off the bat, learning from your mistakes.

If you chose A, you learn best through auditory means. Hearing the information first helps you to digest it faster.

If you chose B, you're a visual learner. You master a skill when you can watch someone else doing something and then mimic her actions yourself.

If you chose C, you're a studious learner and like to prepare, prepare, prepare. Being able to read things on a page helps you fully grasp every aspect of it.

If you chose D, you're not afraid to make mistakes and learn as you go. Your interest is piqued when you're engaged in the activity 110 percent, even if you're not a pro.

Which of these abstract skills do you currently find yourself excelling in most?

A Memorization (retaining and recalling information without much effort)

B Adaptability (the ability to respond well to change)

C Communication (conveying your opinions while also listening to others)

D Gathering information (researching and studying)

E **Organization** (a love for organization and attention to detail)

F **Problem solving** (thinking through a multitude of scenarios in order to come to the best conclusion)

G **Creativity** (thinking outside the box)

H **Leadership** (having a vision and guiding a team through its execution)

Now that you have a better idea of your personality traits and strengths, you can use this to pinpoint what fields might be a perfect match for you.

If you chose A, you're like a human encyclopedia and have an insane ability to soak up information. You'd excel in medicine or law, where you need to recall a great deal of info at once—helping lots of people along the way.

If you chose B, you love to experience new things and respond well to change, so a career that allows you to travel would keep you constantly engaged. How much fun would it be to see the world as a professional photographer? (There are even professional smartphone photographers! You could get paid to Instagram!)

If you chose C, you're a people person—always the social butterfly talking at parties and in the hallway. You'd do well with a career in social work or counseling, since people gravitate toward you and even trust you with their problems. Also consider sales and real estate, where you need to be likable so that people want to buy from you!

If you chose D, you're a curious person who wants to get to the bottom of everything. You'd make a great reporter or detective, where it'd be your job to uncover the truth!

If you chose E, you pay attention to details, a skill not everybody has. You'd make a great event planner or office manager, where you're in charge of keeping track of even the smallest details and maintaining order.

If you chose F, you're very analytical, using logic over "gut instincts" to come to a conclusion. You'd excel in the finance, science or tech fields. (Hello, Facebook!)

If you chose G, solving an algebra equation makes you want to blow your brains out— you'd rather be in art class working with your hands. You'd make a great architect or graphic designer, where you can really push the limits.

If you chose H, you don't get nervous speaking in front of a group or giving directions; rather, you thrive on it. You're always the one organizing group events or giving suggestions to others, which means you'd make a great manager or entrepreneur.

Nicole's Career-Planning Dos and Don'ts

DO! **Take all the risks you can now.**

If there's something you want to try, try it. You're more likely to be forgiven and will have more time to recover.

DO! **Take every job seriously.**

My first job was as a hostess wiping tables, but you never know who's watching, or who is going to move to a different industry, or become best friends with someone at your dream company. Do the best work you can, always!

DON'T! **Beat yourself up over a mistake.**

Apologize by explaining what you've learned and why it won't happen again. Then move on. Don't belabor it.

FORGET-ME-NOTS

1. The hobbies you love—even if you can't imagine them becoming an actual career—can always be turned into an actual career.

2. Never stop trying new things—even the things that don't come easily will teach you something and bring you closer to your goals.

3. Your passions can always change. What you like this year doesn't have to be what you like next year, and what you love now doesn't have to be what you loved yesterday.

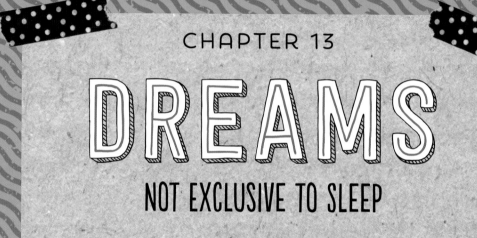

CHAPTER 13

DREAMS

NOT EXCLUSIVE TO SLEEP

MY EXPERIENCE: TO SELL OUT
OR NOT TO SELL OUT

AS I'VE MENTIONED BEFORE, about nine years ago I had just begun my venture
into professional acting. Kind of. I mean, I had just signed up for a little
showcase in Orlando, but I was so excited. I thought, *Everything is going
to change—I'm going to be a star!* (Yes, I sounded just like Molly Shannon's
character in *Superstar.*) That was partially true, but if you'd told me back
then, "In nine years you'll look back on this moment and realize that everything you know and want for yourself will change, and for the most part
what you hope for in your career won't happen just how you want it to,"
you would've broken my heart and made me cry. Maybe people did tell me
that back then, in a way, but I didn't listen. I guess I just kept dreaming, and
it wasn't until years later that I would notice I'd become jaded enough to
think dreaming was stupid.

Not too long ago, I was offered a role in a big studio movie. I was sitting
outside on my balcony, when one of my reps called to tell me that I would
be getting the official offer soon.

Before I got that call, I got another call from someone on my team,
explaining to me that I didn't have to take this role if I didn't want it. Sure, I
knew that, but, at that point, my career had consisted mostly of indie films
and cable TV and, as many actors and actresses in my shoes can attest, the
promises that a studio can offer are outstanding. Bigger paycheck, wider
audience, usually a heightened appeal to the opposite sex and, most of all,
your chance to join the very glamorous and very elite A-Listers of Hollywood
Club. Who wouldn't want that, right? *F!ck it*, I thought. I was tired of being

the bridesmaid and never the bride. Of course I wanted to do it.

As often happens with Google stalking, what started as an enthusiastic Google search about my big new job turned into a big new buzzkill. Turns out, a well-known Disney actress (let's call her Disney Channel Queen) had originally signed on to do the movie but then backed out. It happens all the time in this business, but it was a bummer to find out I'd been second string. I tried to cheer up by reminding myself that I'd be starring against a big-name movie actor (let's call him Big-Name Movie Actor) in the screen adaptation of a novel with a large and fanatic fan base. But somehow at that moment, I remembered just how god-awful the script was. I don't know if it was my ego or my gut, but suddenly this project had a whole lot fewer pros than cons.

PROS

Starring against Big-Name Movie Actor would be awesome!?

CONS

The director hadn't done a movie since the early '90s.

It filmed in the South during the hottest month of the summer.

The script wasn't my favorite, to put it nicely.

I'd have to cut my current salary in half, thus lowering my future pay.

My "love interest"—I'd worked with him back in the day—was talented but just not someone I felt I had a lot of "chemistry" with in this role.

Then came another call from my team: "They'll give you the offer if you go meet with them." I was hesitant to string the production along any further. "You can interview them and ask them whatever you want! This isn't something you need to beg for. They'd be lucky to have you," my team told me, among other statements, which made me feel very confident that I could really gain some clarity from a meeting. So, I agreed.

Cut to me, a push-up bra and this meeting. I was in the waiting room, chumming it up with a receptionist (those guys are the coolest—assistants and interns are so underappreciated in this town), when the casting director called me in. As I walked in the room, I noticed that there were only two other people there. Apparently, the director and the writer were doing some location scouting out of town, but they were the ones I was most interested in talking to. Still, I remained hopeful.

As I sat down on the couch, the producer asked me what I thought about the script. In my normal, funny manner, I replied, "Well, I'm here, aren't I?" Total silence. Ugh. #Fail.

Slowly, the conversation reached a point where I would normally sing the praises of the project. But I couldn't think of anything else to say, so I started talking about my vacuum. Yes, my *vacuum cleaner*. It was weird.

Another producer walked in, a friend of one of my reps who had been responsible for bringing me into the mix, and thankfully broke up all the forced conversation. Once he was there, I felt that I had the opportunity to ask more technical questions, particularly about the cast's openness to improvisation on set.

"Big-Name Movie Actor *loves* to improv. He's such an actor's actor."

That was exactly what I wanted to hear. This was turning out well, I thought. So I did my normal spiel about how I work, my in-depth process and all the stuff that usually gets both the business side of the room excited about my commitment while enticing the creative team's curiosity. I always humbly end it with, "At the end of the day, I'm just here to work for *you*. It's my job to acclimate to your style and give you the best I have."

I mean all of this when I say it, always. However, nobody was even remotely concerned about how I'd factor into the cast and crew. It was strange—assuming that these guys were more nuts and bolts than I may have signed up for, I determined it was time to just ask for what I wanted.

"I really want to be working on the other side of the camera at some point and, clearly, you guys are really good at the business side of this and I don't want to overstep my bounds, so if I do, understand that I really am just interested in the production side of things," I said as I clocked the room.

"No, of course, that's fantastic. Ask away!" a producer assured me.

"Well, I guess I'd love to know what happened with Disney Channel Queen. She's great, and I guess I'm just curious about what led to all of this and how I got here."

They explained it right away: "Basically, we were just caught up with Twitter followers, and she has so many that we really banked on that to widen our appeal." I nodded; I totally understood that. "But we found . . . well, you know, we love you for this role. You gave a great read and at the end of the day, Disney Channel Queen had a conflict with her schedule and we took that opportunity to come back around to what would really set the project up for being more than just a commercial success."

This was all music to my ears. All was well. We wrapped up the meeting and I left feeling really empowered as a businesswoman.

The weekend came, and as I sat on my porch downloading the new ALT-J album, I realized that I *still* felt hesitant about the whole thing.

Right then and there, I forced myself to be honest about all the issues I'd been brushing to the side: I had become fixated on the money and the fame I'd garner from being the face of this already well-established franchise, as well as the future roles I could get from using this as a stepping-stone.

I thought to myself, *I've come so far, and yet this project—while right for some—feels so far away from what I stand for in this career.* I want to make an impact on the world through my work and my daily habits and choices. I want to inspire people. And what could possibly be less inspiring to my generation, to you guys, than throwing away the ethics and principles I've built a career on just for a quick paycheck? I feel an oddly maternal responsibility to inspire you, my readers, to be the best you can be. Taking that role would make me a hypocrite. I reconnected with all I stood for, back when I first realized that this industry was for me. That means having fun and challenging myself in the job I love, being a part of other TV shows and movies with a purpose and a message so that maybe, just maybe, I could make an impact on someone's life.

My mind was made up: come Monday I would have to pass on the project, hoping that I wouldn't burn any bridges in the process. I didn't want to let my manager down, as he had gone above and beyond for me, as he always does (seriously, he's like my extended family). For this project, he had put his word, his reputation and a very important relationship with a very important person on the line for me. He had called someone he knew who knew the lead actor (a very successful, talented and long sought-after A-lister) and had worked hard to get me the offer because he thought I wanted the role, and because he thought it was the right move. I felt a lot of guilt as I wrote him an email telling him I wanted to pass. I wouldn't have blamed him if he had been mad at me. Admittedly, it had taken me too long to come to the decision.

I got a response from my manager. He felt that he had to relay to me some of the feedback about my "passing on the project" . . . and it was not good. The now-pissed-off producers were saying the meeting didn't go well at all (#VacuumHaters). But the real icing on my karma cake was that Big-Name Movie Actor was offended that I'd passed on the opportunity to star in a movie with him. And that he'd never heard of me before. As my manager told me the first part, I felt even sh!ttier. I really *did* want to star in a movie with Big-Name Movie Actor. I never meant to offend him. (Hey, I'm totally not offended that he's never heard of me. He's not really in the demographic.) I just hope that he continues to forget about me until the day we *do* get to work together on something and have a great time, and hopefully a do-over. And I'd be wishing for a unicorn if I thought the people I pissed off actually cared about why I did it.

> Because here I am, doing what I love to do, for the right reasons, every day. I've been through a sh!t ton, I've worked my ass off, I've made mistakes and I've felt the ups and downs, but not one moment of this journey has been wasted.

In the words of Oprah, "Real integrity is doing the right thing, knowing that nobody's going to know whether you did it or not." So, the morning after the last of the sh!tstorm landed, I made a promise to myself: *I will never stop dreaming.* So, if you were to tell me now, in reference to the next ten years of my life, "In nine years you'll look back on this moment and realize that everything you wanted would change, and that, for the most part, what you hope for in your career won't happen exactly the way you want it to," you would be speaking to my heart and I'd still cry, but they'd be happy tears. Because here I am, doing what I love to do, for the right reasons, every day. I've been through a sh!t ton, I've worked my ass off, I've made mistakes and I've felt the ups and downs, but not one moment of this journey has been wasted. Not one dream of mine has actually died, and along the way, I've developed new interests and new dreams and I've had new and unexpected accomplishments. As long as I stay true to myself and my dreams, I'll draw something valuable from every situation—a rejection at tryouts or an angry A-lister ranting at me, whatever. Nothing in life is random. There's always some lesson to be learned or reason behind it, even if it's not immediately apparent. This outlook makes me feel strong, ready to take on the world. And the world now, well, it's a hell of a lot better than I could've ever dreamed.

The Meaning of Dharma

Though the word itself has many meanings and interpretations, I was taught that dharma is, in a broad sense, your destiny. It's the ancient Hindu tradition of living according to a code of ethics in this world while being true to your nature. It is designed to unveil your life's purpose, leading to a sort of concrete "meaning" for your life. To me, this stands out from the other definitions of dreams and success.

The way I understand and try to live by dharma is this: if you know that you have a passion for something, and you use that passion as a vehicle for your life's work, you will then accomplish a destiny that isn't limited to one absolute and narrowly defined peak of success. Rather, you'll find yourself constantly fulfilled as you pay tribute to your basic truth.

I'm not suggesting that you don't dream big. But I don't think anyone should live for "one moment." I try to live for *every* moment and, like my understanding of dharma and my life principles, I try to stay very true to my greater purpose, which is to help make the world a better place. At the end of the day, I believe that should be everyone's goal. No matter what, whether you're a member of the Peace Corps, rescuing people from the world's evils day after day, or an entertainer who sings for a living to bring joy and distraction to our daily grind, in some way, shape or form, you are not only contributing to a better world, but along the way, embracing a core element of your being, which makes you feel fulfilled on the inside.

Simply put: Dreams are a calling outside of ourselves that we are meant to answer with the talents inside ourselves, which leads to careers, yes, but ends in an ongoing purpose in life that is greater than ourselves.

Goals, Goals and More Goals

It's important to set the bar high—it speaks to how much you believe in yourself, but with a big goal comes the need for patience. Setting a time limit or any other restrictions can easily turn any large, inspiring goal into an intimidatingly impossible one.

I started off with little to no plan. I literally got on a plane in Florida and landed in LA. My mother was able to navigate a lot of the business decisions (thank god, because I was only fourteen!!) but, as you probably know, there comes a time when you can't depend on your parents to get you everywhere. Sorry, Helicopter Moms.

I have to credit a lot of my methods to happenstance. Meaning, I wandered around for a long time wondering why things weren't going "according to plan," when I eventually realized, "Oh sh!t, I don't have a plan!" I came up with a rough list, narrowing down my huge goals into really small steps to work toward every month. Then I was able to conceptualize a more specific plan in order to reach these goals. An onslaught of New Year's resolutions almost guarantees that you forget them by February—you need realistic, achievable goals. Here is the basic formula: divide your goals for different areas of your life into a loose list of monthly accomplishments to help you realize them in the long run.

In Ten Years

CAREER GOALS

....

....

....

....

....

PERSONAL GOALS

....

....

....

....

....

This Year

CAREER GOALS

....

....

....

....

PERSONAL GOALS

....

....

....

....

This Month

CAREER GOALS

....

....

....

PERSONAL GOALS

....

....

....

More Get-Ahead Dos and Don'ts

DO! **Pat yourself on the back.**

Every victory deserves a celebration. I'm not suggesting you throw your-self a party for handing in a book report on time (I am suggesting that you text your friends a series of six dancing lady emojis, however). But I like to create self-rewarding rituals for the big stuff, like totally zoning out with *Sex and the City* and a box of truffles the day after your last midterm.

DO! **Make a list of pros and cons when you don't know what to do.**

Ask yourself concrete questions: What are the benefits? What are the downsides? Is this something I will be eventually proud of or is this some-thing that will make me want to move to Mexico? Go as in-depth as you want to. If you have more pros than cons, go for it. If not, well, steer clear.

DON'T! **Compare yourself to others.**

This is a recipe for self-loathing and disappointment. It's a difficult thing to master, but if you think of yourself as a moving part of a team, you can be happy for your classmate/friend/etc. For instance, if your goal in life is to make people laugh and your friend (or someone you know) goes on a super-successful comedy tour, there's no reason you should be jealous. Because even though you weren't the one making those people laugh, someone did and, in a sense, that's also part of your goal being realized. (Yes, this happened to me. Don't judge my jealousy! Kay, thanks!)

My Top Three Ways of Coping with Disappointments

When things don't turn out the way I'd hoped, here's how I deal:

1. **Help someone else.**
   This always helps me. It brings me out of my own bubble and sometimes I find myself giving the very advice I needed to give myself.

2. **Make notes for next time.**
   Having my own CliffsNotes on hand is key to a successful and time-conscious review.

3. **Always have something positive to say about the experience.**
   Otherwise, if it's all negative, you're going to subconsciously avoid the hurdle again and never actually improve.

workbook

LEARN FROM YOUR MISTAKES

Think about the last time something didn't go as planned and you were disappointed. You'll win if you can walk away from it having learned a lesson. So, here, write down the following:

1. What you could have done better:

....

....

2. One reason this disappointment turned out to be a good thing:

....

....

3. One thing you'll do differently next time:

....

....

The Details: Nicole's Tips on Putting Yourself Out There and Setting Yourself Up for Success

Chart a course and rip out the rearview mirror:

1. **Build your résumé on LinkedIn (or paper) and be specific.**

   Find a company you love, and go on their website. Learn the language of that company, read their mission statement and mirror that language as closely as possible when you're writing your profile on LinkedIn or creating a formal résumé. Include links to your projects, your volunteer experience and any other relevant details about your background. That way, when hiring managers search for potential job candidates online, you're more likely to come up!

2. **Use your knowledge of social media to your advantage.**

   Their comfort level is not the same as your comfort level, so whether it's Twitter or a blog, get online and show off your expertise in your desired industry. The first thing a company is going to do is Google you. If they can't find you—if there's no blog, no online presence—they're going to think that you're out of the loop, and you're likely going to get passed over.

3. **Reach out.**

   Identify people who have a life that you want. Go on LinkedIn, find those people and ask them how they did it. (Don't approach someone on Facebook—that's like approaching someone in Disney World—they're in "fun" mode, not business—and they won't want to answer.) Send out a standard connection request, and put in your message that you really admire what they've done. Try to mention something that links the two of you—like an article of theirs that you love—and ask if you could take ten minutes of their day to ask them a few questions over the phone. Come prepared. This isn't about shooting the sh!t—ask them three questions, and then allow them to dismiss themselves once you've hit that ten-minute mark.

My Tips on Sending Really Important Emails
(BECAUSE I'VE HAD TO SEND A LOT OF EMAILS TO REALLY IMPORTANT PEOPLE)

I'll assume you know that your email signature should be void of <3 and ;), but the other subtle differences between your social life and your work life may be harder to discern. Here are a few key things I've learned about sending emails, including a really freaking great example at the bottom.

Address the person formally by name. As in, "Dear Ms. Smith." This little detail makes a difference. It's basic etiquette that people tend to overlook in our modern and rushed world.

Introduce yourself. The person you're emailing may not know who you are, and even if it's someone you know through a mutual friend or someone you met briefly, it's just a good refresher.

Mention where or how you got her contact information. Don't be a freakin' creeper. I once got a handwritten letter from the CEO of an office supply company I'd recently purchased some stuff from, but he didn't tell me where he got my info, so I freaked out and thought I had a stalker who somehow knew that I had all teal office supplies.

Give her a genuine compliment. Or at least include why you chose to contact her (or him!). This is where you get her attention and prep her for what you want to ask.

Thank her for reading your email. At this point she has spent twenty seconds reading and she has probably already realized that, so thank her for taking the time to do so and let her know it's appreciated. This will give her ego enough fluff to keep reading.

Tell her why you're different. Talk up your drive and skill level with a quick mention of your accomplishments and where to find more of your work—links are always a great, fast idea.

Ask for what you want. Here's where you put what you want on the table, but give her a little room to come to you. If you're hoping to meet for coffee, ask for "a bit of her time," which allows her to come up with a meeting plan that she feels comfortable with. You're more likely to get what you want if she feels that you're flexible.

Make a joke. You can do this anywhere in the email, but a clean and PC joke (don't be contrived) can make the whole interaction seem less robotic and more human.

A POWERB!TCH'S USE OF POWERB!TCH TECHNIQUES

Dear Ms. Smith,

My name is Ashley Rickards, from MTV's Awkward. I got your information from my coworker Ryan Johnson, who mentioned that you were involved in _____. Not only am I a big fan of _____, but I would love to work with you. Thank you in advance for taking the time to read this; I know you must be very busy. It's just in my nature to surround myself with people I respect. In fact, your research on autism really impacted my performance in Fly Away, where I played Mandy, a teenager on the autism spectrum. I would really love to pick your brain a bit and get some advice on how to get involved in _____. Any advice or tips you have would be much appreciated. Again, thank you so much for taking the time to read this and for all your contributions to the autism community. I look forward to hearing from you.

All my best,
Ashley Rickards
Cell: XXX-XXX-XXXX

So, let's say Ms. Smith, who doesn't actually exist, calls you. Obviously, you won't know when she calls, but make sure to keep an eye for any unsaved numbers in your phone. If a potential call from Ms. Smith comes in, don't answer it if you aren't in a place where you can have the conversation. Keep it short, use a similar approach to the email format and schedule a time that works to meet, remembering to be flexible. If she can only meet at a certain time and you have a nail appointment then, agree to the time that works for her and move your manicure to a later date. This is more important, I assume.

Thank her again for reading your email. This is a good way to wrap it up. You don't want this email to become a 900-page novel.

Sign off with strength. A simple, "All my best," works wonders.

Put the ball in her court. Give her your contact info (a standard signature with your phone number and email underneath is a good way to go). She will respond when/if she can.

Spell-Check!!! A misspelling in an email is like having a missing tooth—it's impossible to ignore.

PERFECT YOUR BODY LANGUAGE

This is where a lot of girls undermine themselves without realizing it. I've found it really helpful to know how I come across to others and the vibes I give off in person; that way I can either fake my way through a nerve-racking interview or state my case in a nonintimidating way. Here are some key moves to embrace and avoid:

Maintain good posture.
It makes you look so much more confident. Slouching hints that you're feeling insecure or overwhelmed.

Minimize the nodding.
Too much nodding and non-verbal agreement signals can rub people the wrong way. I personally feel that it makes people seem stuck up.

Keep your arms uncrossed and at your sides (or in your lap if you're sitting).
Folding them shows hostility; fidgeting makes you look nervous. And talking with your hands too much may seem theatrical. Try to only use your hands when describing a complex or highly visual situation. Hold a notebook if it helps keep those hands occupied.

Minimize the smiling.
You don't want to come across as a Barbie doll. Instead, try to keep your face natural and focused. Smile when it feels natural, not forced.

Give a solid, strong handshake.
That immediately gives off a powerful vibe. It shows you're strong, mature and not easily intimidated.

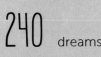

The Dos and Don'ts of Talking to Really Important People

DO! **Upgrade your vocabulary.**

If you tend to overuse words such as *like* or *totally*, try to replace them with more professional phrases, such as *absolutely* or *of course*.

DON'T! Swear.

It's f*&%* distasteful.

DO! **Pay attention to their cues.**

If your potential boss seems uninterested, move the conversation away from yourself and instead ask questions about him. ("What is your favorite thing about working here?") People love to talk about themselves, and a little curiosity goes a long way.

DON'T! Gossip.

Sh!t-talking a former boss, teacher or coworker does nothing but provide your prospective boss with a clear warning sign that you aren't always a team player.

DO! **Ask smart questions.**

Sometimes when we're young and relatively inexperienced, we're afraid to reveal our rookie status. You'll never know if you don't ask—and when you're young, that's when people want to teach you.

DON'T! **Talk about the game.**

When you're with employers, don't talk about how many interviews you've been on. Talk about your skills and talents, and they'll know you're in demand.

Criticism:
Constructive versus Cruel

Trust me, I've met my fair share of haters. It can be difficult to tell the difference between what is constructive criticism and what is negative energy. Luckily (thanks to Nicole!), I've learned a few easy ways to take in the positive and filter out the negative.

Be sure to choose your friends/associations wisely—it's that whole "birds of a feather flock together" thing. Surround yourself with people you admire and make you want to be better. If you want to write a book, join the literary club at school. If you want to paint, take more art classes and go to art exhibits.

Steer clear of people who bring you down or make you feel ashamed of your talents. People's negativity may be a reflection of their own insecurities about not having accomplished their own dreams.

Constructive criticism, though, is often a huge compliment—it means someone cares enough to invest the time and energy to help you, and listening to what they have to say can be hugely important. Don't be the girl who cries when someone suggests that you update your wardrobe to respect the dress code or pay more attention to detail. If your boss suggests these things, it's because she cares and wants to help you succeed. Rejecting criticism can hurt you down the road.

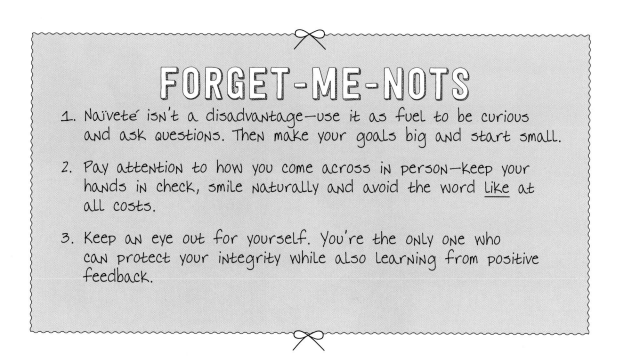

FORGET-ME-NOTS

1. Naïveté isn't a disadvantage—use it as fuel to be curious and ask questions. Then make your goals big and start small.

2. Pay attention to how you come across in person—keep your hands in check, smile naturally and avoid the word Like at all costs.

3. Keep an eye out for yourself. You're the only one who can protect your integrity while also learning from positive feedback.

PART
6

YOU AND OTHERS

Barney Was Clingy

CHAPTER 14

FRIENDS

WHO DOESN'T LOVE THOSE TACKY LOCKETS FROM CLAIRE'S?!

MY EXPERIENCE: BARFING ON COMPUTERS AND CRYING IN PALACES

AS A LARGE NUMBER OF STUDIES and blah blah blah show that, by nature women are more intuitive than men. We're also more sensitive, and more resourceful and capable of managing a crisis. All that aside, we also tear each other apart. And I'm not sure why we think that is getting us anywhere or making us feel better along the way—it's not.

It was a cold day in Florida, which means it was about seventy degrees outside. Nevertheless, I was at school, fourth grade at the time, and even though my chair was in the back of the room, I felt like I was smack in the center and everyone was staring at me. And they were, because I looked green in the face and very ill.

BLECHHH.

I threw up all over my computer. We were learning about Macs back then, and pictures of those huge, brightly colored iMac G3s lined the walls. And, now, my barf did, too. I stood up, as I felt another vomit session coming. I was paralyzed with embarrassment—there's no way to quell your nerves after you've barfed, because you're just nervous about barfing again.

"Gross," I heard a voice say. I assumed it was just some kid in my class making fun of me, but when I turned around, I realized that the voice didn't belong to a student. It belonged to my middle-aged computer teacher.

Great, now even the adults don't like me, I thought. (I now refer to him as an "adult" loosely.) I grabbed my arctic-blue backpack from under my desk (arctic blue was still a cool color back then!), while also trying to keep my

next barf down, and ran. My '90s-era Sketchers that my mom gave me for Christmas took me as far as I could from that classroom, which wasn't too far. I hadn't exactly been giving PE my best shot. I made it to the playground and hid inside a plastic castle. My impenetrable playschool fortress wasn't actually very sturdy, though. I felt it creak under me as I decided to let it all out and just cry. It was a full-on sobfest in there—me, a big-little girl with two pigtail braids, my barf-covered floppy disk, and the Furbies that were simultaneously going off in my backpack.

The school bell rang a half hour or so later, so I emerged from my castle and went to the parking lot to find my mom's car. I quickly explained what had just transpired and then didn't say another word the rest of the way home—and I wouldn't let my mom say a word to me, either. I mean, what could my mom or anyone else say after something like that? I wasn't going to let anyone get a word in edgewise, if you even tried to coddle me. So we just left it alone and, thus, I was alone.

A few months ago, I found myself in the throes of things here in LA. I'd been disappointed, to say the least. And just like that afternoon in school, all I wanted to do was run away and cry. That plastic castle surrounded by mulchy bits of grass on the playground had been replaced with a castlelike hotel room. But that night ended much differently, and much better, than those postbarf hours spent in hiding years before.

There, in my home away from home (hotels are kind of like a reprieve for me), I sat down and started to cry in a little puddle of disillusionment. Same little-big girl, but with side bangs and a silky PJ set. Then I felt my friend's arms surround me, and I hugged back. This time, I didn't want to be alone, because I knew I wouldn't find relief if I didn't let anyone in. This time, I had my best friend in the whole world holding me up. And just as she had my back then, I will have her back. Always.

The moral of the story is that jobs, money, boys and whatever else you can think up will come and go. They will, trust me. But good friends will never allow you to feel alone. Have a friend. Have as many as you want, or just a few close ones. Find the last girl you saw who looked just as alone as you may feel, and make sure the two of you aren't alone anymore. Be a ruthlessly caring woman. If you put yourself out there in full disclosure, just being open to a helping hand, someone will come and love you not just for all that you are, but in spite of it, too. That's a bestie. I've had a few women impact me like that; I can't give out their names, but they know who they are. And you, you already know who you are, too.

Finding a true friend—one who can really pick you up when you fall—is hard to find, but don't give up trying. And once you have them, nurture that relationship. It's one of the most rewarding ones you'll ever have.

MEET YOUR
EXPERT

BRANDON AKI, relationship expert (he's the real-life "Hitch," people!), author and the intimidatingly tall guy I bring around with me to scare off photographers.

His Philosophy on Friendships: It's so important to understand who you are and who you want to become, first. A lot of people get into friendships and relationships alike without understanding who they truly are. If you don't do that, when it comes to surrounding yourself with great people, your surroundings are not open to receiving the best people in your life.

Attracting Awesome People into Your Life

Making new friends may seem difficult and scary, but it doesn't have to be. The first step is forcing yourself to meet lots of different types of people, which will up the odds that you'll find someone (or lots of someones) whom you truly "click" with and want to be BFFs with. Here's an action plan to get you started:

1. Choose your location wisely.

In order to meet people you really love hanging out with, take a class in an area that interests you. It's easiest for people to bond at first over a common interest, so if you like to read, go to a bookstore and reach out to someone interesting by asking what she's reading. By starting off the conversation that way, you avoid any random, awkward one-liners.

2. Just go for it!

Deepak Chopra's book, *Teens Ask Deepak*, talks about how to start a friendship. He suggests that, rather than worrying about how best to approach a new friend, sometimes it's best to just reach out and ask if she wants to be friends. I can attest to this working. In fact, after meeting Deepak for the first time, I sent him an email where I basically said how much I admire him and that I'd like to be friends. Now, I buy him shoes and send him pictures of my cat. He's one of my closer friends today.

3. Don't fear rejection.

If someone rejects your friendship, just think of it this way: clearly they suck. But seriously, they obviously wouldn't have made a good friend! Be grateful for their honesty or at least how easy they made the decision for you—it'll save you a lot of time and frustration. The people who deserve your friendship will be open to you from the start.

4. Be clear to your guy friends.

If you want to be friends with a dude, make sure your friendship is clearly mutually platonic. Unless you're open to it becoming something more, you should be able to have a conversation about it with him, or at least judge the situation honestly and decipher if you're setting yourself up for hurt or for hurting him.

5. Make the first (real) move.

If you're the one who initiated the friendship, follow up and invite them to a movie or something you're both interested in. Don't overwhelm them with a barrage of texts—just ask and see what they say. Based on their response, use your judgment to determine how to proceed from there.

6. Take it easy.

Don't burden a new friend right off the bat with your deepest, darkest secrets. Not only will you run the risk of an unexpected betrayal because you haven't tested the trust waters yet, but it's possible you might scare her off. Eventually, a time will come when you can open yourself up, and you'll know in your heart when the time is right.

> **EXPERT SECRET:**
> Never be afraid of rejection when you're trying to make new friends. Rejection is just part of finding the right people for you. It's well worth it when you find great friends who can last for years—even a lifetime! —Brandon

Receiving Awesome People into Your Life

Just as you'll try to approach people you want to be friends with, people are going to approach *you* for the same reason. Attract the best kinds of people by doing the following:

1. Put yourself first.

If you start off by focusing on your happiness, dreams and inner peace, you'll find yourself in a much better place to attract likeminded friends. Those who see your light will flock to it like a moth because they relate to you, and you'll find a really rewarding friendship in someone who respects you right off the bat.

2. Be friendly to everyone.

You never know when a potential friend is watching, so if you're rude to the busboy at a restaurant, your potential bestie will assume you're just mean.

3. Think about your body language.

If you're always scowling or rolling your eyes at your phone, those signals will send out a pretty unapproachable vibe.

4. Don't go online to find friends. Seriously.

I know I sound like a broken record, but it's so dangerous. I can't stress enough how bad an idea this is. Not only could you get catfished but you're risking your safety and potentially your life. There are a lot of crazies out there—not worth it!

Don't Lose Yourself
(CONTRARY TO WHAT EMINEM SAYS)

Brandon and I both agree that in order to have a successful friendship, you've got to know what you *want* in a friendship. And that old saying is true: you are who you surround yourself with. But if your friends aren't onboard, or don't support you in being the best version of yourself, you run the risk of losing hold of who you are. You never want to fall into that super-draining cycle of trying to be something you're not while turning into something you don't want to be.

> **EXPERT SECRET:**
> Maintaining solid friendships is about understanding who you are and staying focused on the friends who support your goals. If you're afraid you might forget who you are along the way, write those goals down. When I was growing up, I kept a journal. That can be a very important tool. Write down your feelings about your friendships, and then look back on that and see how far you've come as your friendships progress. Ask yourself regularly: Have you gone off into a different direction where you don't want to be? —Brandon

SETTING UP YOUR FRIENDSHIP CRITERIA

It's important to identify what you want out of a friendship and how that can support you in reaching your goals (while sharing some really amazing moments with someone who's equally amazing!). Here's a little guide, similar to the journal Brandon mentioned—but more fun—to help you identify what you want and what you need.

What are five core values that are important to you in another person? (beliefs, spirituality, ethics, a passion for *Game of Thrones*, etc.)

....

....

....

Name five emotional needs you require most in a friendship. (support, honesty, availability, trust, etc.)

....

....

....

What are five qualities you cannot tolerate in a friend? (dishonesty, laziness, manipulativeness, obsessive, gossiping, etc.)

....

....

....

Name five instances in the past that have damaged or ended a friendship.

....

....

....

Name five hobbies or interests you would like to have in common with a friend.

....

....

....

Do you want to have a few very close friends or a wide social circle?

....

....

....

IF YOU'RE BEGINNING A NEW FRIENDSHIP, REFER BACK TO THIS LIST.

However, when you do, it's important to remember that no one is perfect, so keep your expectations realistic. As long as she meets *most* of your criteria, you may find that you still want to be friends with this person, which is fine as long as she supports you in your goals. I've had a lot of "friends" in the past who just turned out to be total b!tches. There are always a few bad apples in the bunch, and it's almost impossible to avoid them. Oftentimes, you may not even know when you have a "good" or "bad" friend in the mix. So, next, Brandon breaks down how to judge the finer point of a friendship.

Expert Secret

Never pretend to be someone you're not. Pretending to be somebody else is exhausting and, eventually, it will fall apart. You'll save yourself time and you'll open yourself up to better people by being who you are.

—BRANDON

A Healthy Friendship, Defined

A healthy friendship is one that inspires you and makes you want to keep growing. For instance, if somebody picks up a great book and says, "Hey, I thought about you when I read this. What do you think?"—that's somebody who is going to help you grow knowledgewise. Good friends are going to make us feel better about the paths we're taking and make us want to keep growing in a very positive way.

HEALTHY FRIENDSHIP TRAITS

- You have a general "good feeling" when in their company.

- Their life or outlook on life inspires you.

- You respect them.

- They respect you.

- They stay true to their word.

- Their desire to gossip is minimal and doesn't become a bonding point for you two.

- They don't exploit you or your confidence in them.

- They're nonviolent.

- They like you for who you are—right *now*.

- They don't want to gain anything from you (money, popularity, etc.).

- They wouldn't put you in harm's way (by driving drunk, asking you to cheat or lie for them, etc.).

- They have gone out of their way at least a few times for you, especially in a crisis.

- They have a cat (that's a joke—but cat people are way cooler than dog people; it's a scientific fact).

An Unhealthy Friendship, Defined

An unhealthy friendship exists when you're constantly feeling bad about yourself—when you're consistently around somebody and have this "down" feeling, or just the thought of them makes you feel bad. If they say demeaning things to you, or gossip, or start rumors behind your back, that's a red flag.

UNHEALTHY FRIENDSHIP TRAITS

- You feel uneasy around them.

- You filter yourself around them (not speaking your mind or being afraid to).

- They're violent.

- They disrespect you by talking behind your back or being rude/cruel to you.

- They lie to you often.

- You do not trust them.

- They gossip most of the time and that has become a hobby for you two.

- They put themselves in harm's way.

- They put you in harm's way.

- They engage in criminal activity (seriously, avoid this . . . unless you're already in jail, of course).

- They use you for means other than your friendship.

- They share your secrets.

- They have never gone out of their way for you.

- They like you for who they *think* you are, not who you actually are.

- You do not feel safe around them.

- They have a dog (again, a joke . . . but, seriously, if they aren't allergic, get them a cat!).

Speaking Up for Yourself

There are obviously going to be times when you feel hurt or sad in a friend-ship, but you can't expect anyone to read your mind, so give them a fair shot and respectfully communicate what you need. Here are the key ways to make sure any issues are effectively and productively resolved, drama-free, whether you're feeling hurt or someone says you've hurt her.

WHEN YOU'RE UPSET WITH A FRIEND . . .

1. **See your actions through your friend's eyes.**
   This can be difficult to do, but when you put yourself in the other per-son's shoes, you start empathizing. Once you've tried to see things from their point of view, reach out and tell them how much they mean to you—and simply that you care about them and want them in your life. That will help them empathize with you and see where you're coming from.

2. **Cool down.**
   As you begin this conversation with them, remind yourself not to play the blame game or raise your voice. Doing so will only alienate them and make them feel guarded, unable to hear your side of the story.

3. **Start with the facts.**
   Bring up the situation or a specific instance that hurt your feelings (not plural—pointing out multiple situations at once will just make them feel under attack), using as many specific facts as you can, and remind them of what it was specifically that is triggering this conversation.

4. **Then explain your feelings.**
   Tell them how their actions in that instance affected your thoughts, and the feelings that resulted from that.

5. **And specify why you reacted the way you did.**
   Most likely this is where you may have to admit something you did, either by explaining why you b!tched them out that day or your reac-tion to the situation. If you didn't do anything and instead told them right away that it wasn't cool, use that here.

A POWERB!TCH'S CODE FOR CONFRONTATION

Here's a totally perfect fill-in-the-blank worksheet we've created as an easy go-to when you need to have this conversation:

"When _____ happened and you _____,
I thought _____. It made me feel _____
and I then _____. In the future, I hope we
can avoid this. The next time something like this happens, we
could _____ or _____
or _____. Do you feel comfortable with any
of those solutions?"

6. Give 'em a guide:

Don't just expect them to fix it blindly. Before you even have this conversation, really think about what you want them to do differently. Keep your requests reasonable and explain that you're only trying to safeguard your feelings or ease your interactions in the future. Bring up a few solutions and, with your friend, decide on a reasonable one that you both feel comfortable with.

WHEN A FRIEND IS UPSET WITH YOU . . .

1. See your actions through your friend's eyes.

Repeat step 1 from "When You're Upset with a Friend . . ." (Empathizing goes both ways.)

2. Remember who you're talking to.

Remind yourself that this is your friend—she's hurt and is taking a chance by opening up to you. Even if her approach is defensive or blame-y, try not to take it personally (she might not have read this incredibly helpful chapter first, as you did).

3. Listen up.

As much as you may want to jump in and defend yourself, try not to interrupt. Hear her out fully before speaking.

4. Evaluate her position.

Determine (honestly) what is true about her side of the story and what isn't. If something comes up that you feel is exaggerated or assumed, ask yourself how untrue it is. Is it just a difference of opinion or is it a flat-out lie?

5. Reflect on what she says.

If what she is saying is true, be sure to really open yourself up and absorb what her feelings were about it. Then listen to your own feelings about it, too.

> **EXPERT SECRET:** Forgive *yourself*. It's OK to make mistakes. We all fall short. We just need to learn how to get back up.
> —Brandon

6. Ask for more specifics.

Don't be afraid to ask for more information or details about something she mentioned. Once she is done sharing or venting, simply thank her for sharing (don't patronize). Praise here is really key—it makes people feel listened to and more respected, plus your friend will be more open to hearing your questions.

7. Clarify your position.

If what she said is questionable or untrue, calmly explain your side of the story. Remember that the negative feelings she has may not even be about you personally. She could be going through something else and is taking out her anger on you.

8. Defend your position.

Here you either have to defend yourself by pointing out that something they said isn't true or explain why you think or feel that it is wrong to blame you. At this point, offer support and suggest a solution to the issue.

9. Resolve the issue.

Ask for forgiveness, if you feel like you owe it. Even if you don't, but they seem inconsolable, you may want to take one for the team and momentarily calm them or take a little undue blame for the greater good of the friendship.

Can This Friendship Be Saved?

If another three months go by and your friend has shown zero effort in contributing to your friendship, or you have not felt comfortable continuing to work on a friendship with her, it's time to move on.

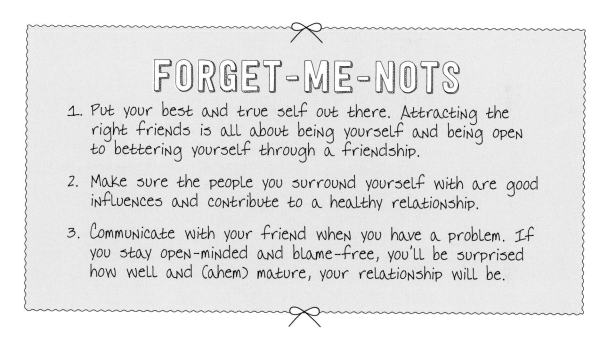

FORGET-ME-NOTS

1. Put your best and true self out there. Attracting the right friends is all about being yourself and being open to bettering yourself through a friendship.

2. Make sure the people you surround yourself with are good influences and contribute to a healthy relationship.

3. Communicate with your friend when you have a problem. If you stay open-minded and blame-free, you'll be surprised how well and (ahem) mature, your relationship will be.

CHAPTER 15

THE FAM

DON'T BE FACEBOOK BUDDIES

MY EXPERIENCE: THE IRISH GOODBYE

To me, home smells like hairspray and chaos. At least, it used to. Back when I lived with my parents, it was always a frenzy—and an unnecessary one at that. And given my not-so-huge social calendar, I had plenty of family time. Lots and *lots* of family time . . . yay.

My mother and I were always very close. We still are. But back then, about three years ago, we were *too* close. She was my best friend and I was hers. It sounds really sweet and whimsical to be that close with your mom, but in reality, how could I expect my best friend (my equal) to be my parent (my superior)? I couldn't. But it took one very glamorously tragic party at the European Music Awards in Belfast to bring us to our breaking point.

"ASHLEY?!?! DO YOU HAVE YOUR PASSPORT???" my mom yelled to me in the middle of the Los Angeles International Airport. (Apparently, she was under the impression that I was in a different terminal.)

"I'm standing right here, and, yes, I do have my passport," I said as I laid it down on the linoleum counter of the check-in desk.

"OH, OK! SHOOT! I dropped my sunglasses. Have you seen them?" she continued, still under the assumption that I was three terminals away.

As I watched my mom go through her usual spaz attack, searching her bags for the sunglasses she had on her head, I texted my friends and tried to appear as if I wasn't traveling with her, because in that stress test, she's my mom, and moms are embarrassing sometimes. But we eventually got through security, my mom continuing to give people nervous little half grins and mumbling hellos the whole way as we made it onto the plane.

We were flying first-class international, which was pretty cool, since the chairs in those planes lie completely flat. I mean, I could've spent the whole freaking plane ride playing with the chair's five hundred switches and modes, but I wanted to seem like I'd done this whole "jet-setting thing" before, so I quickly decided not to mess with the buttons. Then I looked over and saw that my mom was busy doing exactly what I thought I was too cool to do—adjusting her chair frantically.

"ASH?? DO YOU HAVE YOUR SEAT BELT ON?? I THINK MY CHAIR IS BROKEN," she yelled over at me, again as if I'm in another country.

With no help from me, she eventually figured out how to turn her chair back into its upright position, yet she followed up by jumping at every small creak or sound the plane made during the forty-five-minute boarding and takeoff process. It was going to be one long, loud and anxious plane ride to Dublin. Luckily, she took her Nyquil as we put on our sleep masks, then calmed down a bit. Once we got to that point, it really felt like I was with my best friend. We were so happy and excited to go to the European Music Awards in Ireland! It's a miracle I slept on the plane at all.

But, thankfully, I slept through most of the plane ride, only waking up to my mother's snoring a couple times. I got a coffee right before we landed to ward off any time-difference-induced sleepiness. (I really hate to acknowledge my jet lag because then I end up napping instead of exploring.) By touchdown, I was practically jumping out of the plane, and my mother was back to her nervous smiles and half nods. We got to Baggage Claim, and after a strange customs interaction (the agent thought I was Selena Gomez . . . awkward), we were embarking upon a very scenic two-hour ride with a taxi driver who would not stop talking.

"Ey! This is a field o'er ther and around the wee hours you can catch a ripe part of dee sun! Oh, I took me wife to dees coast once . . ." Of course, my mother was totally enchanted by him. After an eternity, we arrived at the hotel. Again, I practically jumped out of the car and onto the cobblestone streets of Belfast. It was amazing—I'd never seen anything so pretty. Naturally, I wanted to drop my bags and go exploring right away. However, my mother, who had forgone the free coffee on the plane, was tired as hell and needed a nap.

So I dropped off my bags and immediately went exploring solo. Being that young and alone in a beautiful city is something I will never forget. The freedom was invigorating. After years of being the overprotected only child of a small-town couple from Maine, this was heaven (plus, they had a Topshop). After I walked around for a couple hours, grabbing food and buying some handmade jewelry, my mom finally caught up with me. We grabbed a coffee and munchies at McDonald's. (Yes, they have those there!) But a McD's breakfast in Ireland wasn't a sausage-and-egg McMuffin. It was potato waffles with cream and shredded cheese and it tasted amazing.

Throughout the rest of the day, I was stopped every couple of feet by Irish screams of "JENNA!!!" which made me feel *so* cool. I mean, I'd never even been to this country before, but they knew me! My mother could not have been prouder. And she expressed this thoroughly by the number of pictures she took. (It was worse than a mom on prom night . . .).

I had rehearsal around 1 p.m., followed by the awards show. I'd do my thing and present the EMA for best male artist (the Biebs won) and watch the performances. Afterward, the plan was to go back to the fancy hotel, get room service and gossip.

Soon after the actual rehearsal, hair, makeup and red carpet, my mother and I were guided to our seats by security. It was an amazing show and seeing it together, her watching me, that was her favorite thing. Making her proud, that was my favorite thing. We were total equals in this moment—just two friends having fun in Europe.

> It was an amazing show and seeing it together, her watching me, that was her favorite thing. Making her proud, that was my favorite thing. We were total equals in this moment—just two friends having fun in Europe.

As the show began to wrap up, though, the champagne started to take effect. I was feeling like a million bucks and wanted to abandon our old plans and go to the after party instead. (I was convinced that Bruno Mars and I would end up talking/bonding/dating.) But she felt a little too tipsy and wanted to go rewatch the awards show on TV at the hotel.

"Are you sure?" I asked, hoping she would in fact go, since I wanted to hang with awesome famous people and be as fake and chic as my heart desired.

"I'm only staying for a little bit!" I assured her, not wanting to make her feel bad or left out. "I just want to check it out."

Well, turns out Bruno Mars did not go to the party—in fact, I didn't know anyone there at all. Even though I had my "super-fancy celebrity" face on, my fake pretentious ways were no match for the truly pretentious nature of that party. The place was full of neon lights, posh white couches and multiple levels of party. I caught myself looking a little too outwardly uncomfortable, so I decided to warm myself up a bit. (Plus, I was embarrassingly early.)

I sat down with a drink and struck up a conversation with one of the employees. We went on about how the other A-list attendees were so clearly hung up on where their "section" was in regard to their friends' or former flames'. It was kind of a riot to watch from afar. Anyway, I had a couple drinks and chatted with some friendly natives, danced a little, but as soon as my feet started to hurt/bleed, I quickly noticed the party was getting a little too outta control for me (but mostly my feet just hurt). So I made my way down to the lobby and got in a cab.

Back at the hotel I tipsily stepped into the elevator. I wasn't drunk, but I was damn close. I smoothed back my hair and tried to appear a little more graceful, as I didn't want to look like pre-rehab Ke$ha if my mother caught a glimpse of me. And, even though my mother and I had separate rooms, she'd also gotten a key to mine (classic codependent move). There she was, waiting patiently for her best friend/daughter to come home and hang out with her. I changed into my PJs and got those freaking heels off my poor, sore feet. We spent our evening just as we had planned (just a little later), watching reruns, googling red carpet pictures and ordering room service.

When the fried food arrived, my mom broke out some champagne and poured me a glass. Then my stomach started to churn. My mom insisted I eat something (fried) before finishing my glass.

"Drink that slow or else you'll get drunk and puke," she urged. That was what I should've done, but you know how sometimes a friendly warning can seem like a friendly challenge to ignore it and see what happens? Well, that's what I did.

I was so new to the whole "bubbly and vodka" adult life. It was like giving a three-year-old a giant cookie and saying, "Stop eating this amazing cookie at some point!" But I went on and eventually, I don't know what happened.

The morning after hit me like a freight train from hell. As I opened one eye to check for daylight, I immediately felt a pounding headache in the front of my skull. I had absolutely no intention of coming out from under these soft covers—until I smelled something *really* gross. Bracing myself for whatever I was about to find, I pulled the covers away, sat up, and as I

stepped toward the bathroom . . . *squishhhhh*. I looked down to see what my foot was in, and OH MY GOD.

I had puked right next to the bed. And then stepped in it. Karma isn't a b!tch; karma is a gross, evil, twisted b!tch who totally owes me a pedicure. Needless to say, I was panicked. We had to be out of the hotel room by 10 a.m. It was 9, and now I was using some very thin toilet paper (*not* a good picker upper) to pick up my own party foul and flush it down the toilet. But I started to panic again and I decided to confess what I'd done to my mom.

She'd been up for hours and looked so together and refreshed. We were supposed to go on a bus tour of the city in twenty minutes. Clearly, in my current state, that wasn't happening. She looked at me for a second and then I came in the room and said/cried to her, "I puked! It was gross and it was on my foot!"

My mom's face registered three things in that moment. One, that she shouldn't have been "partying" *with* me. Two, that she should have done a better job of defining her expectations for me in Ireland. And three, empathy for her little girl, who made a mistake.

She gave me a hug and told me it would be OK. (I still had puke in my hair, which she would later point out to me once the embarrassment faded from my very flushed faced.) We went into my room and she assessed the damage.

"OK . . . let's . . . uhm . . ." She didn't know what to do any more than I did. I felt so guilty.

"I've just been using toilet paper," I replied.

Well, she really stepped up to the postparty plate, and minutes later we were cleaning the carpet with the hotel's freebie shampoo and expensive towels, then drying it with a blow-dryer. The whole time, my mom was talking me down from hysterics. "This is so embarrassing . . . oh my god . . ." I said, over and over.

"It's OK. It's over, and you're not the first young person to do this. You'll learn for next time," she said, over and over.

In that moment, in that hotel room, in that mess of me trying to grow up too quickly, we both recognized how our relationship was going to have to change and mature, for the better. She wasn't my bestie in this moment. She was my mom. And that was exactly what I needed.

So . . . here's the thing about this chapter. In *A Real Guide to Really Getting It Together Once and for All (Really)*, you've gone on a (very personal) journey with me—and along the way you've heard from lots of smart people who've helped me get my sh!t together. But now, it's just you and me talking. This chapter is about family, those closest to you, who will forever stick by your side—whether they're literal relatives or the ones you choose for yourself—and I want you to consider me, and this book, someone and something that will always be there for you. And what follows are the roles and relationships that I hope you'll use to create your inner *A Real Guide to Really Getting It Together Once and for All (Really)* circle.

Roles and Expectations

While I get that there are a million types of relationships each person has with his or her family, I'm a firm believer in the idea that if we all just stick to our roles, the show will be fine. As with my mom, our relationship became difficult to manage. It was a power struggle between mother and daughter through my mom's eyes, but during several occasions it felt like she was a friend who was trying to control me. Worse, I missed out on the chance to make friends and confide in people my own age—which is absolutely necessary when you're young—because I allowed my mom to be my *only* friend. That incident in Ireland was the beginning of us working together to have a healthier mother/daughter relationship, which we have today (even though she still freaks out a lot at the airport).

Here's my larger point: your family is not stupid. They're just very, very nervous about messing up the most priceless thing they've ever had—you. They will go to extremes, make mistakes and then (or at the same time) they'll probably suggest you avoid extremes and mistakes altogether (like how your dad jokes about becoming a nun—he's joking, but kind of not really).

Generally speaking, adults can be more childish than children (they've lost their innocent naiveté, after all), and your parents are no exception to that. But before you go tell your mom that I said she's a baby (which I did not say!), take a deep breath. I'm not suggesting you dismiss the rents or grand-rents. I'm putting a bigger emphasis on *you* to be the responsible one, because family (especially parents) can't always live up to your expectations or even their own, for that matter.

Your aunt or uncle, your brother or sister, or mother (I'm really tempted to continue to Dr. Seussify this!) each has a role, and if your relationship is healthy, each of them will be there for you in the exact way they need to be. I don't think there are many nuclear families left these days (aka a mom, dad, two kids and a white picket fence), but this chapter is *not* a checklist or a scale to rate your family on. This is for *you* to understand what a healthy interaction with your bloodline looks like and, if possible, to set goals for improving any soured or dysfunctional relationships. Also, if you've got a single mother, divorced parents or any relatives whom you don't speak to (for whatever reason), don't let the idea of this chapter freak you out. It's merely meant to offer suggestions, not condemn anyone, and can include nonrelatives who fill these roles. Wherever you are in life, and whoever is in your life now, as long as you feel safe and happy, that's enough. That's a family. Don't worry about being "normal," because NOBODY'S family is normal. That being said, here is a quick guide to the healthy, sufficient and proper role of each of your homies.

Mother Dearest
HER ROLE: THE INTUITIVE PROTECTOR

Biological or not, she's going to watch out for you as if you're a little bunny who is always two steps away from venturing into the snake pen. She will be

on high alert and not only do her best to protect you physically, but emotionally as well. In a literal sense, she will provide a safe home environment—food, water and shelter. The modern mom is the boss of the family.

Your mom is someone you can look to for constant support and guidance on life's ups and downs (aka listening patiently as you cry over the phone during your lunch break so you don't freak out at your teacher). And, odds are, she's been through the same sh!t, so it's in your best interest to listen to her. She'll also be your cheerleader—and your biggest one. While she may push you to try new things that are outside your comfort zone, she'll root for you every step of the way. She wants you to be the best you can be, and she

wants that more than anything else in the world. And if you look closely, you'll probably notice that she's sacrificing a lot to do so.

She will be protective, she will have opinions and she may have a hard time seeing your friends or your boyfriends in the same light as you do. But from an early age she has probably been one of your most trusted sources of true, selfless advice. She always can and will be, and that's a wonderful thing. However, adulthood is when this really comes into play. (You might overshare in your teens and she may ground you.)

Just don't let your social circle dwindle and allow yourself to become her bestie. It removes a lot of necessary boundaries in the mother/daughter dynamic. While she may have flaws in her screening process (especially with style; not pointing fingers, Talbots or Chico's . . .), take it all with a grain of salt. Even if she isn't IL with your current Prince Charming just yet, listen to her concerns; but that doesn't mean you have to end all communication with someone until *you're* sure about how you feel.

THE HEALTHY MOTHER/DAUGHTER RELATIONSHIP CHECKLIST

- She listens to your opinions.
- You don't talk back to her or disrespect her authority.
- She lets you live your life free of judgment or bias.
- You help make her life just a little easier—putting away the groceries or cleaning up your room once in a while.
- She does not exploit you or your secrets.
- She makes you and your health a priority.
- She provides you with choices and a wide perspective on life and beliefs.
- She has confidence in you and your ability to be your own person.
- She worries about you if you don't call when you say you will. (And even though you'll never admit it, you do the same.)

Your Pops
HIS ROLE: THE OVERREACTING HERO

Your dad was probably terrified when he found out he was having a girl. And why wouldn't he be? We all know how much we can rack up at the mall.

Dads are sort of classically the breadwinner of the family, providing the major income for food, housing, college and whatever else you can "puppy-eye" him into buying for you. And because we aren't in the freaking '50s anymore, some dads are the stay-at-home parent. He'll be all domestic during the day and make sure that at night you *are* home.

Luckily, these days it's illegal to shoot your daughter's boyfriend. (Well, it was always illegal, but you get my point). Being territorial and overly masculine when there is a threat of an outsider disturbing the nest is a biological given. He won't fully trust anyone with his spawn (that is, you). As long as he doesn't hold money over your head or, in my case, buy you tiny little dogs to make sure you don't have time to date guys, you're totally fine.

THE HEALTHY FATHER/ DAUGHTER RELATIONSHIP CHECKLIST

- He provides you with your basic needs.

- He makes you aware of the dangers and risks in life.

- He forgives you without too much of a grudge if you mess up.

- He's advised you on how to pay for college (or has set up a college fund).

- He does not make you feel bad about yourself.

- He tries to be a neutral force if you and your mom or a sibling are fighting.

- He does not make you choose or have a favorite parent.

I can promise you, post–ten years of age, it may be awkward with your dad for a decade or so, but after college, the father/daughter relationship is sappier than any movie you or your mom could ever make him sit through. Also, if something bad happens to you, or you get a paper cut and there is someone to blame, he will blame them and either sue them or slowly drive by the offender's home every day and stare him down for an hour . . . or two.

He doesn't hate fun per se, but if that fun is reckless, crazy expensive, illegal or could come back to haunt you later in your adult life, he will hate that fun. Mothers may be aware of all the dangers around you, but fathers have more of a tendency to actually think everyone is trying to kidnap you. Now, if you're not close with your dad or he is just sort of removed when it comes to your life, the good news is this: you get to have all the dangerous fun you want! (You should probably just think twice before playing leapfrog across the freeway.) On the other hand, you might get the softie dad who lets you get away with whatever you want—and that's because he doesn't want to be the bad guy.

Both parents discipline their kids but, at least in my family, my mother sort of let my dad enforce the law and be the bad guy. Even on a primal level (and, unfortunately, society's stereotype), men can be a little tougher and come across as simply stricter. You shouldn't hate your dad for providing consequences to your actions. It's like that old saying—as long as you still live with him, under his roof, it's his law.

Whereas your mom will typically help you by supporting your goals and ideals, in my experience, your dad may be more of a guide for helping you set high expectations and respecting yourself. Clearly, you're more likely to relate to the parent of the same sex, but your dad has a very good chance of being the best guy you'll ever know, because he wants nothing from you—just your happiness and success, to see his little baby all grown up and safe.

Sisters and Bros

A SISTER'S ROLE: THE TRUE FOREVER FRIEND

Depending on the age gap between you and you sister(s), you're most likely going to be going through similar things, just at different times. Whereas she might steal clothes, embarrass you at school and/or tattletale to your parents, hang the eff in there. It'll usually work itself out. After all, if you're under the same roof or she's in the same city, avoidance can only last so long. Despite the rivalry and potential jealousy, you two have the potential to be the best of friends. I know, it sounds crazy, but the number of years you'll spend together, the good and the bad, will bring with them a bond that truly blossoms around the college years and later. As you confide in her and develop more of a friendship, you're going to be rewarded with a bond that extends far beyond even your parents' lifetime, even if you grow to be very different people.

THE BROTHER'S ROLE: THE CONSTANT WATCHDOG

If you've got a brother, well, he could either be an embarrassing dweeb (younger) or he could be your protector (older). Depending on that, one of you will become a real source of practical advice in the social realm. If he's older than you, it's easier to respect his opinion because he was so recently in your shoes. Your brother may ask you for advice on girls, and you may ask him for a little hint about whether or not your crush likes you, too. At

THE HEALTHY SIBLING RELATIONSHIP CHECKLIST

- You're able to trust them with your secrets (mostly).
- You come before their friends.
- They do not try to pressure you to do anything outside your comfort zone.
- They express interest in including you in their lives beyond the home.
- They make you feel comfortable confiding in them.
- They guide you in figuring out what's cool—and what's not—and can be a source of inspiration.
- You share similar views on household events.
- You can reach a mutual understanding and offer each other forgiveness after a disagreement.

THE HEALTHY
GRANDPARENT/
GRANDDAUGHTER
RELATIONSHIP CHECKLIST

- They spend time with you and attend your major milestones (graduation, wedding, etc).

- Their peeps know all about you because your grandparents are so proud and can't stop bragging.

- They're willing to try a hobby of yours in order to bond.

- They express interest in meeting your friends.

- They provide a home away from home to support your parents' "alone time."

- They love you unconditionally, no matter what your relationship is like with your parents.

the end of the day, you guys are going to balance each other out like ying and yang.

If you are close in age, you may become actual friends. Hanging out at home past curfew (because you're in your bedroom) or bringing him along to an outing with your friends could take some effort at first. Embrace any similarities or hobbies you two have in common, though. It will give you something to bond over (other than complaining about your parents). A close brother will always have your back, no matter how old you are or how bad your back is.

The G-rents
THEIR ROLE: THE HAPPY SPOILERS

Grandparents are like parents, except they only *have* to be around for the fun and exciting parts. And you get a lot of perks out of them. Birthday checks, all-expenses-paid spring breaks in Florida and presents for *every* holiday (including St. Patrick's Day) are practically part of their retirement plan.

A grandparent's job isn't to be the parent (though it can be in some circumstances, of course), but simply to support your parents. They usually won't punish you unless your parents would or have. Instead, they may offer your parents suggestions about avoiding the pitfalls they themselves made as parents.

Gramps and Grandma are obviously on the older side, so if they are super-conservative, don't go out of your way to shock them into becoming open to your ideas and lifestyle. Instead, your grand-rents should do their best to find common interests with you, as well as impart their own life-learned wisdom to you—and you should listen! They've been around for a super-long time, and have experienced a gazillion things so they know some stuff.

The Extended Familia

THEIR ROLE: VARIETY

Extended family—aunts, uncles, nephews, cousins and whomever else you can fit into your legal bloodline—usually provide a wide variety of personalities and family dynamics to "spice up your life." Depending on your culture or your extended family's culture, you may be locationally obligated to hang with them frequently. Along the way, you'll learn to appreciate all that makes people different, because there's no return policy on family.

In the event of terrible news (a divorce, a serious illness, a death in the family), your extended family is going to be there for you and invite you into their lives during this dark time. So, depending on the dynamics, if you're ever on the outs with both your parents *and* your landlord, Auntie Sue may let you crash in her basement for a couple days or months.

You're likely to start some traditions together, and nothing is more comforting and familiar than a family gathering at the same time every year. This is where you can learn a lot about commitment, too. You'll see your parents work very hard and travel the distance, if necessary, to keep in touch with their own siblings and loved ones. Having this stability and a large network of people you can trust to selflessly have your back is a gift that should never be taken for granted.

> ### THE HEALTHY EXTENDED FAMILY RELATIONSHIP CHECKLIST
>
> - They help you appreciate all types of personalities.
> - They are welcoming to your family.
> - They do not put you in the middle of "adult" fights.
> - They make an effort to include you and your family in special occasions, regardless of distance.

Setting Boundaries

There are certain religions that believe children "choose" their parents-to-be before taking up residence in the womb. Well, if that's the case, there are certainly days that I wish I could find my receipt. Of course, it's hard to get along with your family during your transition into adulthood (Spoiler alert: Your mom will never *not* think of you as her baby.), but it doesn't have to be painful. You can avoid a lot of miscommunication, grounding and unpleasant situations by enforcing boundaries with your family members.

Using the roles laid out above, and factoring in your own personal relationship with the given family member, use the breakup/fight guide in the friendship chapter as a template to improve any issues with that relationship.

Ask yourself:

What can I expect from them?

Are my expectations realistic?

How might they feel when I ask them to respect these boundaries?

How can I help them improve our relationship (aka what can I do for them)?

How might my behavior be affecting the way they treat me?

What would I do if I were in their position?

My mom once said to me, "If you act like a child, I will treat you like one." So, I started to take ownership of my mistakes, go the extra mile and depend less on her, thus showing her that I was mature enough to be treated like a bona fide grown-up. With a little respect for your elders (Trust me: they *do* know more than you do), you'll win them over faster than a sob story on *American Idol*. However, just as with other relationships, make sure to check back on this. If the situation hasn't improved, bring up the conversation again. I won't tell you to cut ties with your family, because that's a big decision and not something I recommend unless it's totally necessary. Have patience with them and try to understand where they are coming from. Chances are, you could gain something (like an extended curfew).

FORGET-ME-NOTS

1. Roles and expectations are unique within each family, but the basic functions are usually the same. As long as you have an idea of what they are, you can work toward true understanding and a lasting bond.

2. Boundaries are what you use to protect yourself from someone who isn't willing to change or make a relationship manageable.

3. Fighting with your parents is a different dynamic than fighting with your friends. Your family is your bloodline, meaning they deserve a little more respect and sometimes require blind faith.

CHAPTER 16

RELATIONSHIPS

GLASS SLIPPERS SOUND REALLY DANGEROUS

MY EXPERIENCE: SEEKING OUT THE MISSING PARTS OF ME IN OTHERS, WHILE MISSING OUT ON ME AND OTHERS

"WHO *ARE* YOU?" I ASKED, looking at my soon-to-be-ex. The question of what had happened to land us here, a final goodbye in the hallway of our new loft, exploded from my pained chest. Without answering, he turned away sadly and I shut the door on another happily-ever-after. I'll put it like this: one night one boy, with whom I lived at the time, didn't come home . . . and the next morning when he tried to come home, his sh!t was to the left, to the left, everything he owned in a box to the left.

Fast-forward through two and a half months of sleepless nights, strange indie films and the purging of romantic and sentimental items, and this very intense two-year relationship finally felt like a thing of the past. I was in the best shape of my life, knocking it out of the park at work, and all I needed was a piece of arm candy. I thought, "I'm ready!"

You see, my ex and I were really close. He knew I was the newly appointed Queen of Single Street, so we made plans. And by *we*, I mean *I*. I made plans. I decided that I was going to cook dinner for him, even though I had just gotten my wisdom teeth out and could barely eat ice cream. I decided to make a cheese platter, and I asked my ex to bring caviar, mostly because it's always been a fancy-sounding, mysterious thing and I wanted to try it. Plus, it seemed like such a romantic idea (and it is, as long as you don't have four giant holes in your mouth where your teeth used to be). More now-obvious mistakes entered the picture: (1) I pretended to be

flexible with his arrival time because I wanted to appear "chill" and (2) I lied. He asked me where to buy the caviar, since he didn't know of a place to buy it himself, which surprised me since he always seemed so sophisticated. I said, "Oh, I think Whole Foods has it." Translation: "I know Whole Foods has it—imported (expensive) and American (cheap)—but I'll be the judge of your palate/wallet and see which one you pick." Yup, it was shallow. But then again I had just gotten four teeth ripped out of my mouth, so let's cut me some slack.

It was eight o'clock on the dot—and he wasn't at the door as promised. I huffed and took off my heels, picking away at the cheese tray I'd set up carefully in clear pairings of two. *If I'm going to be kept waiting, in my "casual" chiffon kimono and matching silk skirt, then I'm going to make sure he knows it*, I b!tchily thought to myself. So I nibbled and pouted away like a jaded housewife on an unnamed reality show. Then I realized I'd gotten some cheese in my wisdom teeth surgery "wound," so I had to run to the bathroom and dunk a huge syringe thingy into my prescription mouthwash and "flush out the hole."

DING DONG!

Sh!t.

I flushed out the rest of my weird cheese residue in the sink and went over to the front door.

"Hey, I didn't keep you waiting, did I?"

"Not at all," I said.

He brushed past me and said, "How have you been?"

"Great! Just working and stuff," I attempted to say back casually, while making myself look busy by going through the Whole Foods bag. "You?" I replied, realizing he'd purchased the cheap caviar, a sign in my mind that signaled the end value of this date.

Sure, my goal was to get back into the dating game, but what was I thinking? Oh, I'll just invite my ex over to my house at 8 p.m., ask him to bring caviar, and everything will be like a do over?! Uh, no!

So I started crying. Needless to say, that was the end of that disaster date. But when I think back to that night, I am keenly aware of what my meltdown really was all about: it was the first time in a long time that I had no relationship to define myself within and no love to clean up or console my emotional mess. Just me, alone.

"Who *are you?* I asked. This time, I asked myself. "And what the hell did I do wrong?"

I was devastated that another great love had ended, ashamed of my part in it, guilty that I hadn't done enough, angry that I couldn't save the relationship or him and most of all betrayed—by myself. The biggest liar in this whole thing was me, pretending that I had been ready to go into another relationship and depriving myself of proper healing time. I couldn't go back in time and make that glass slipper fit again. (I'd tried fitting into that relationship too many times without success.)

The answer to my questions was simple, yet as any heartbreak victim knows, not easy. So I took a hiatus from the dating scene and delved into a solo-centered journey of self-healing and self-acceptance. It was about growing up and growing through my old scars that, unexamined, are reopened in each new relationship. I sought help through friends and professionals alike. I occupied my time finding new creative outlets, like painting, cooking and reading a couple new books on topics I'm interested in learning about so I can better myself along the way. Relying on *me* to make myself happy was a powerful thing.

Which led to the next two parts of healing—self-acceptance and self-love. They go hand in hand and are crucial life skills. While we have to be careful to nurture ourselves during delicate times, we also have to take a *very* proactive role in our own personal evolution. It's impossible to be truly loved and known by someone else without loving and knowing yourself.

> The truth is, for better or for worse, you cannot change or fix anyone, and you shouldn't be asked to change in order to be loved.

The truth is, for better or for worse, you cannot change or fix anyone, and you shouldn't be asked to change in order to be loved.

The key to getting back on the dating track (or even just taking your first lap), as with the healing process, is not easy but it is simple: stay relentlessly true to yourself.

The very next guy might not be the one, or the next one after that. But with patience and growth, constant growth, the right person for you will come at exactly the right time. Meantime, I will continue to strive to be the best version of myself, for Ashley. I'm waiting for my Prince Charming, one who is ready *to bring it all and put it all in. And when that time comes, the glass slipper will slide right on.*

MEET YOUR
EXPERT

BRANDON AKI (He's baaack!)

His Philosophy on Relationships: Dating isn't about finding a person. Dating is about finding the *right* person. The more time you spend with the wrong people, the less time you have to spend with the right one.

The Four Ws
WHERE YOU ARE, WHAT MAKES YOU HAPPY, WHAT YOU NEED AND WHY

In most of my early relationships, I hadn't really thought about "my type" or what I was looking for in another person. Back then, I blindly threw darts at a board, hoping one would hit an Abercrombie model look-alike bull's-eye. (In fact, I didn't even know if I wanted to date a *guy*. For a short time, I dated a girl—who actually *did* look like she could be an Abercrombie model.) Looking back on all the figuring out I had to do in my earlier years, I don't have any regrets about the people I dated. They were all amazing people whom I had similarly amazing experiences with. At least in my experience, avoiding my "mistakes" would've deprived me of bringing more quality and depth into my next relationship and eventually "the" relationship with "the" one.

Until I got my sh!t together, I had no idea who I was, so there was no way to figure out what I actually needed—let alone what kind of person I wanted to be with. Luckily, I went to a wonderful workshop with personal growth and relationship expert Arielle Ford last year, and she introduced my friend and me to something very special.

She showed us, in a conference room filled with women of all ages, how to acknowledge all the things we want in a partner, visualize that person and, in essence, "manifest" him or her. So I went along and decided to make a list of this sort. Not a list of demands or superficial perks, but qualities that really support me in being the best version of myself. But before you make my version of this list, which is basically the romantic version of the earlier friendship questionnaire, make sure you're in a quiet place where you can keep your list away from any unwelcome snooping (don't hide it under your bed—parents always look there).

> EXPERT SECRET: Every guy is different. There is nothing else that I can stress more than that. As a guy—knowing all the different conversations we have—it's amazing how misunderstood a lot of guys are, and how girls think that guys are all so simple, because that's just not the case! So don't generalize. Get to know different people and keep an open mind. —Brandon

RELATIONSHIP CRITERIA GUIDE

Describe yourself in five words.

....

....

....

....

Describe your ideal match in five words.

....

....

....

....

What are your goals for your next relationship (just have fun; a long-term commitment; to experiment, etc.)?

....

....

....

....

List some core values that you want to have in common with your partner (morals, religion, family, academics, etc.).

....

....

....

....

Name five archetypes you find yourself physically attracted to (bookworms, athletes, musicians, etc.).

....

....

....

....

Name five hobbies or interests you would like to have in common with your (more than just a) friend.

....

....

....

....

What are the five most important emotional needs that you want to be met in your next relationship (support, honesty, availability, trust, etc.)?

....

....

....

....

....

List five behaviors or habits that would be deal-breakers in a future partner. (These can be anything from location, to partying too much, to too clingy.)

....

....

....

....

....

Where do you want to be in the next few years—and how could you see your next relationship fitting into that plan?

....

....

....

....

HOPEFULLY, YOU NOW HAVE A CLEARER GOAL TO AIM FOR IN THE DATING GAME, AND NOW YOU JUST HAVE TO PLAN TO PLAY.

But even though you made this nice, long list, don't be too quick to write someone off just because they don't meet every single criterion—you might be cutting yourself off from something you didn't even know you wanted. So keep an open mind! I have found some amazing people this way. And even if the date or the vibe isn't right, you can always become friends (you never know—maybe he has a hotter friend who is perfect for you). Bottom line: Ken dolls make bad boyfriends because they are too perfect (and also lack genitalia, but you get my point). Without a few charming flaws, we can't really claim it's true love, can we?

And this is how you really know it's real: Would you be willing to take care of this person through a cold—snot and all? Or would you only be there when they greet you with flowers? Don't judge yourself, but this answer is revealing. So before you go out on the town for the cream of the crop, remember that most crops need a little TLC to grow before they come to life fully. On the flip side, trying to change somebody to fit the mold you're looking for never works, either. (You can't "change" anyone—I've learned that the hard way.) Nobody is perfect, or even close!

Attracting Someone Awesome

Chances are, some of the qualities you listed in the questionnaire you just filled out are things you've been looking for—whether subconsciously or not—for a long time. And chances are, you've settled and sacrificed some of those important things just to be "in a relationship." At the end of the day, we've all veered off track, winding up with someone who wasn't all that, and then were made to feel like (a) what we "want" doesn't exist or (b) we don't deserve what we "want."

But that's just not the case. So in order to avoid waking up one day and realizing that you don't actually like the guy you're with, let's take the next step toward finding your match: making it easier for your match to find you.

Brandon and I broke down four groups of guys who are most likely to be in your dating pool, based on age and stage of development. Attraction involves mystery (what to reveal and when to share, so as not to overwhelm anyone just yet), presentation (letting your "type" find his "type" via your honest and accurate appearance), an X-factor (flirting, being interested and developing a bond) and, of course, it's all a journey. These are the key ideas to remember as you learn how to get the guy you want (aka the guy who deserves you!). I want to be very clear, though: I'm not suggesting that you play games with anyone. The only "trick" you have to remember is that guys are different beasts, depending on their age and circumstances (and just in general), and you need to factor that into the equation to help you get what makes you happy in life. Trust me: once that's ingrained, everything becomes much easier. Oh, and even better news: If you're into girls, there's a good chance you'll be able to tell right away if she's your type. Guys aren't always in tune with their intuition, but since most girls are, we also have a harder time masking how we really feel or even what we are looking for. This will help you gracefully part ways if she isn't your type or you didn't quite click right away (womp womp), rather than going on a few more dates and forcing something that isn't there.

1 SIXTEEN TO NINETEEN YEARS OLD

TRAITS: Since they have very little experience in the relationships department, they don't have a huge backlog of regrets or mistakes—aka baggage. This can be a great thing and generally means they are more open to learning new things. Guys at this age have a thirst for understanding their place in the world and how they want to fit into it.

PROS: The great thing about this age is that guys are still learning how to treat girls. Which means you have a huge opportunity to teach him how you want to be treated (calling you before bed, coming to your volleyball matches, etc.) Don't mother him, but he should be treating you with R-E-S-P-E-C-T.

CONS: The flip side is that guys at this age can be a little immature, especially given the age-old hunch-turned-proven fact that women do mature faster than men. (Muahaha.) Immaturity can surface in a few ways: most often it's shown via a lack of empathy (aka, they don't understand why you're crying and suddenly get super awk), a lack of common sense (otherwise known as hormones) or just some good old childlike shyness (he may be too nervous to approach you or lean in to kiss you).

THEIR STAGE IN LIFE: It's hard to gauge how he will mature or who he will become later in life. But everyone is going through a bit of an identity crisis at this age, so keep that in mind when you're looking for a long-term relationship. You'll either have to be open to growing and changing *with* him or loving the one you're with while you're with each other at this age. Things change for girls, too, and you wouldn't want to rob anyone of the person he is destined (or determined) to become.

2 TWENTY TO TWENTY-THREE YEARS OLD

TRAITS: These guys have the legal standing of adults and all the terrifying things that come with that. As Brandon says, "If you find a guy with a squeaky-clean record, he's doing pretty well at this age." After all, some descend, or rather cannonball, into young adulthood. Having learned a few lessons about themselves along the way, responsibility and risks have a *slightly* more realistic meaning for these guys.

PROS: A bit more experienced and self-confident, college boys will definitely not have an issue letting it be known that they like you. They'll text you frequently, invite you out, hit you up on Facebook and so on and so forth.

CONS: A little too self-confident and "second-hand experienced" (interpret that however you will, either innuendo makes my point), they don't necessarily know how to put all that into action when there is a real, live girl in the picture. They can come off as arrogant, when they are really just insecure. As long as you encourage him, you can boost his confidence enough so that he can drop the act.

THEIR STAGE IN LIFE: With some still in college, this is a hard age to place any hard bets on. However, they can sometimes be more open to long-term relationships and expanding their viewpoints and beliefs into a lifestyle and action plan. The same goes with their taste in girls. They want a girl they respect and who values her own opinions.

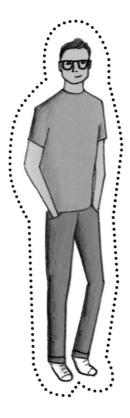

3 MID- TO LATE TWENTIES

TRAITS: A looooooot of change happens during these years, so there's a pretty general state of panic across the board. By this point, guys have entered the workforce and really begun to sink their teeth into their careers. That may still make guys uninterested in a serious relationship, but it's a bit more complicated than that. What could otherwise be seen as self-involved and immature is actually a sign of maturity here, whether we like it or not. See, while the idea of our "biological clock" starts surfacing around our late twenties to early thirties, men tend to be more focused on the fact that their youth is vanishing before their very eyes, so they are often either in a rush to make up for lost time or clean up their act before they feel it's too late.

PROS: At this point, guys have been on plenty of dates and most likely have been in some sort of a relationship with a few kinds of girls (hopefully not all at once, ew). They should know how to approach you respectfully and take you on a proper date, and they are also aware that girls don't wake up naturally flawless. It can be refreshing to date someone who has it all figured out—or at least comparatively speaking. But keep in mind that when a guy is set in his ways, he is set. At this age, men are more stubborn and less willing to give up their game-day routine and gross protein shakes. After all, it's worked for them for this long!

CONS: Many guys I've met at this age are very set in their ways. The classically good-looking guy isn't used to working to get a girl—girls have always come flocking to him and do all the heavy relationship lifting while he just stands there looking pretty. There's also the workaholic, who is so driven by the idea of "getting ahead" that he won't even realize he hasn't called you in three days. Sadly, the workaholic will usually end up with a case of not knowing what he has until it's gone.

THEIR STAGE IN LIFE: These guys can have some pretty concrete goals set for the next five to ten years of their life, and since their hairline isn't receding any slower, well, they don't want to slow down in the race, either. Luckily, these guys support themselves financially and may even have some spare cash to spend recreationally. But while they may have every intention of excelling at work and settling down eventually, unless you're both willing to juggle this hectic time together and be flexible for each other, that family he genuinely wants one day may not happen as soon as you'd like. That being said, if he is the guy you want to be with (healthy two- to three-year relationships happen more frequently at this stage), he'll be worth the wait. Just know that, as a guy, it's in his genetic code to want to provide, so pulling long hours at work or pursuing a risky new career path are usually done with the best of intentions for his family's future, and he's going to do his best in his own way to strike some balance in his life.

Brandon's Relationship Tips

THE HOOK-UP VERSUS THE BOYFRIEND

There are some guys who just want to have fun and date lots of girls, especially when they're in high school and college. But many guys who have the highest scholastic aptitude, who really want to push harder academically and are already thinking about their careers, will likely have a different mind-set than the guy who is just worried about right now and personal accomplishments in the short run.

The best way to know what a guy wants is simply by asking. Whether you believe me or not, guys *want* to be honest. And it's very important to ask early. By the third or fourth date, don't be afraid to say, "Hey, are you looking for a relationship? What do you want?" If a guy really wants to be in a relationship, why would he be afraid of that question? It's important for both people to be on the same page. If you avoid asking the question, you could be setting yourself up for failure and heartbreak. You might as well ask early and see what happens.

THE "FIRST MOVE" (GENERALLY SPEAKING)

It may be old-fashioned, but the truth is, guys *do like to make the first move. But you can and should create opportunities for him.* Let's face it: men usually need a little push. So, say you know where he's normally going to be at lunchtime: sit in his vicinity. That gives him the opportunity to say hi—or at least notice you're in the room. Give yourself three opportunities like this. If you're sitting across from him, make eye contact. That third time, start a conversation. That doesn't mean you're hitting on him or anything—it could just be something like, "Hey, I'm thinking about joining Key Club—how do you like it?" Help him out. After that, if he doesn't keep the conversation going (or brings up "key parties"), cut your losses and move on.

GETTING THROUGH A FIGHT

Normally, relationship fights come about when you feel as if you're being taken for granted. Here's how to speak up and resolve one maturely, without any boxing gloves:

1. The most important thing to remember is to not play the blame game.

Start with an open-ended question: "Why did you do [insert issue here]?" Give him a chance to answer, and then respond with how you're feeling—not what you think of him. So instead of, "You were such an a**hole for saying that in front of my friends!" say to him, "It really hurt my feelings when you said that in front of my friends."

2. Pay attention to how he responds.

If he doesn't care how you're feeling, he'll shut down and move on. And that's a great sign that you're probably not with the right person. But if he says, "Oh, I didn't know I was making you feel that way. I'm so sorry and I'll try not to do that again, blah, blah, blah . . ." well, then you're growing as a couple.

3. Practice active listening.

As you're talking, repeat what you hear him say. A lot of times—and this is true in almost all communica-tion—people will think of what they're going to say next instead of hearing what the other person is saying at that moment. When you do that, you're not truly communi-cating because there is no real back-and-forth, just peo-ple talking at each other. Listen to what he says and then repeat what you heard. It will avoid so much confusion and will help you resolve the issue much faster.

> **EXPERT SECRET:** Take time to ask if the other person is happy. That's something that I find is very, very important. When you're having a casual conversation and just sprinkle it in there, that's a great time to find out where he's at and avoid an argument down the road. If you pull it out of the blue when you're both happy, you can talk about things in a much better way.
> —Brandon

ARE YOU HEADED FOR A BREAKUP?

Normally, things start to go downhill when one person ends up asking for something over and over and over again and the other person isn't giving in. If you find yourself repeatedly struggling with the same issue, that means your partner doesn't want to make a serious effort to address the problem.

Brandon says the first sign a relationship is truly over is when you think seriously about ending it. So, if you find yourself thinking, *Man, I don't know if I want to be in this anymore*, then you might be dealing with more cons than pros when it comes to being with this person. The second and more intuitive sign that a relationship has run its course is when you're feeling as if you're not growing anymore.

Personally, I know how hard it can be to end a relationship just like that. To make it a bit easier and really double-check that this is what you want, write down all the pros about your partner and all the cons about him or her and the relationship. If you find that you've got more cons than pros, it's time to have a talk. Using the same format as with chapter 14, "Friends," keep your message clear and straightforward—the fewer accusations and exaggerations the better, people. If, at the end of the conversation, the two of you haven't agreed to try to improve the weaker parts of the relationship, you either need to accept that he's not going to make an effort or be willing to walk away if staying with him means you'd have to compromise yourself in any way. Three words to keep in mind, though: *Do not settle*. If he doesn't make you feel like a rock star or you don't feel like you're the best version of yourself, then save yourself some heartache and end it peacefully.

Parting Ways and Getting Over Him

Breaking up is hard to do. Trust me: I've been that girl who sh!t-talks her exes and goes rebound-crazy. But I'll save you some of that pain by giving you a step-by-step process for a classy separation. After all, it's a small world—burning bridges to the ground never did anyone any good. Here's my tried-and-true plan for a classy and clean breakup.

HAVE "THE TALK"

The only thing worse than a text message breakup is a handwritten note breakup. Neither is remotely acceptable. Grow a pair. If the relationship is over, you need to maintain respect for each other and do it in person. And don't add salt to the breakup wound by blaming him or being mean. Give him closure by sharing what caused you to make this decision and why you need to move on. And even if you don't mean it, always ask to remain friends. It ends things in a more amicable way, and you never know when your paths might cross again. It's just best to leave things on a positive note.

DON'T TALK (FOR THE NEXT TWENTY-FOUR HOURS)

After your breakup, you may feel tempted to talk/tweet/Facebook/Instagram everyone and tell them all about it. I'm all for talking things out, but airing your dirty laundry won't do you any good or help you get over him any faster (in fact, telling 500–plus people that you broke up is likely going to *prolong* how long you have to deal with it). Gossiping or sh!t-talking him to your friends is also bound to come back and bite you in the ass. Instead, trust one person with the nitty-gritty, and make a rule that you can only complain about the same problem (like the fact that he already changed his relationship status to "single") three times before you can't talk about it anymore. By that point, if you're still struggling with it, I've found it's most helpful to start a handwritten journal. Continuing to rant is only going to make you sound insecure and petty—as well as like a legit cyber-bully if you're doing it online. Take the high road and work through your thoughts in a private place.

PAMPER YOURSELF

During that first week after your breakup, indulge in anything you want—solo or with a good friend. My personal favorite is a cliché recipe for girlie greatness: rom-coms, sweet and salty snacks, and lots of dancing. The rom-coms will distract you and remind you that there's more fish in the sea. (Hello, Mr. Gosling!) Ice cream and a bag of chips is pretty cliché, but who cares . . . it works! Treat yourself to your favorite snacks (go crazy on the garlic if you want to) for a few days. And pamper yourself! A little self-care, like updating your highlights or getting a manicure, goes a long way and will make you feel like a million bucks. Doing so over the weekend is perfect timing, so that your new look makes a real statement when you go back to class or work on Monday.

ACCEPT THAT IT'S REALLY OVER

After a few weeks, it really starts to sink in that it's really over. You may want to reach out to him and try to mend fences or get "closure." But before you do that, reflect and make sure that you genuinely want to rehash things. Often, your ex will either get defensive and exaggerate your part in it, or tell you something you didn't want or need to hear. And when your wounds are still raw, that can really sting and make you unexpectedly flip the f!ck out (speaking from experience). If you're having trouble moving on or breaking the bond, ask for some space. Instead of blindsiding your ex and avoiding him like the plague, explain to him that you need space and have to "detox" for a while to gather yourself and find yourself again. Chances are, he will respect that and you'll have an easier time letting go. A solid six weeks of no communication and "you time" can heal a lot more than dragging unnecessary information out of the other person.

ACCEPTING THAT IT'S REALLY, REALLY OVER

A month or two after your breakup, if you're still friends with him on Facebook or share some mutual friends, you may start to get hints that your ex is moving on. He may have hooked up with someone new or is even in a new relationship (or just being a flirty douche online), and now you have to fight the urge to fight the girl he's seeing. It's a weird thing when you see someone who used to be "yours" and is now "hers." And it's an even more difficult thing to watch! Just remember, that person *did* care for you, and they, just like you, will find plenty of other fish in the sea. That being said, while it's a controversial opinion and some people may disagree with me, I'm all for (after spending some time alone) harpooning the next fish—aka rebounding. It can give you a sense of control and a temporary confidence boost to get you back on your fabulous feet. But make sure you're not hooking up with someone to get revenge or invoke jealousy in your ex—that will only make you feel empty inside and hurt a lot of other people.

> **EXPERT SECRET:** The absolute worst way to get over an ex is to be with somebody else. The only way to get over this person is to have a healthy dose of yourself. It's so, so, so important. You can't escape the problems of your past relationship until you come to grips with the role that you played in creating them. —Brandon

YOU'RE OVER IT

Eventually, the skies will clear and you'll find yourself ready to move on in a healthy way with a new person. Before you do so, make sure you've really worked through and learned from your last relationship so that history doesn't repeat itself. Ask yourself:

★ What do you feel you could do better this time?

★ What can you no longer tolerate in a relationship?

★ How will you handle a fight with this person?

Asking yourself these questions is a great way to set yourself up for a happier and healthier relationship next time. You'll know a bit more, have experienced a bit more and, if you expect more, ask for more! You're worth it.

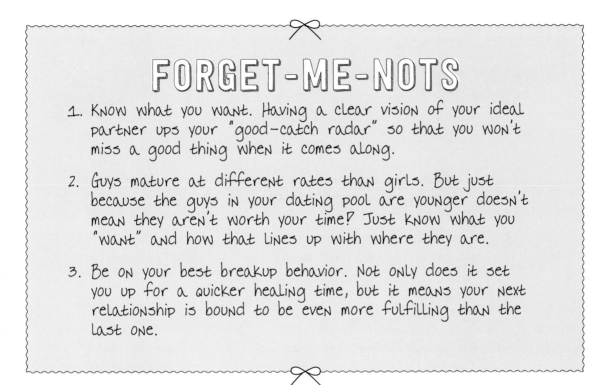

FORGET-ME-NOTS

1. Know what you want. Having a clear vision of your ideal partner ups your "good-catch radar" so that you won't miss a good thing when it comes along.

2. Guys mature at different rates than girls. But just because the guys in your dating pool are younger doesn't mean they aren't worth your time! Just know what you "want" and how that lines up with where they are.

3. Be on your best breakup behavior. Not only does it set you up for a quicker healing time, but it means your next relationship is bound to be even more fulfilling than the last one.

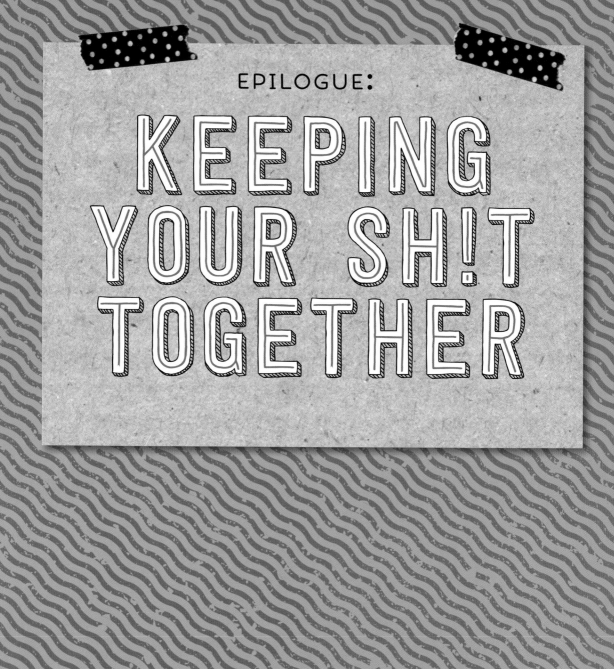

EPILOGUE:

KEEPING YOUR SH!T TOGETHER

Who I was then, who I am now and who I can be—that is exactly who I was meant to be, right now, in this moment simply because it is. I'm able to share with you what I learned, what I believe and what I am learning and relearning every day, as perfectly imperfect as it's meant to be.

After I got my sh!t together, I started the next journey: keeping my sh!t together. In keeping it, I noticed a major obvi: it was really important to consistently make my *true* self *completely* show up for life, no matter how hard (or how good) it gets, so that no matter what happens or doesn't happen I will always have me—the real, true, together and perfectly imperfect *me*. (Super obvi, right?)

But it doesn't always feel that easy or simple. The only simple part would be the two choices you and I have to simply survive the day or thrive. The first, and minimal, option is subtle and sometimes a slow build. Some negative thought, interaction or external setback takes place and instead of using the simple tools and lessons I've learned, I choose to dwell on the negativity. I let the negativity fester and grow until almost every positive thought or action/solution is overrun and I surrender. Soon enough, the things I used to handle gracefully now seem nearly impossible. (Ugh, these nachos are soooo hard to eat!!) But I have the power, tools and knowledge to stop myself from continuing to make the same mistakes and, through my choices, redirect my thoughts and my life so I thrive. Then I make the only choice there ever was: *try*.

That said, and with the real purpose of *A Real Guide to Really Getting It Together Once and for All (Really)* in mind, always remember the most important and most constant—your innermost self. There's a girl staring back at you in your mirror, too. She wants to be happy, and she deserves peace. And over time, she will become less of a distorted reflection in a mirror and more of a clear reminder of how freakin' loved you are. You've gotten your sh!t together from the ground up (really). The mold you defined for yourself here was based on your inner truth. Honor that and pay tribute to the girl in the mirror by always letting your inner self guide the outer stuff. This is your life, your truth and your own unique purpose. Nobody else in this world can give it to you or steal it from you. You are you—let yourself thrive.

Who you were then, who you are now and who you can be are exactly who you are meant to be, right now, in this moment. Simply because it is. *And that is perfect.* So there's one last exercise I want you to do: start screaming. And I do not care where you are, who you are with, what you are wearing or what time of day it is. Just scream loud, proud and as if there were no one listening. This may look like you're losing your sh!t but you're actually celebrating getting your sh!t together and taking the next step: *keeping your sh!t together (really)*.

—Ashley

(FORMER GIRL IN THE MIRROR, CURRENT POWERB!TCH)

GLOSSARY

All the important terms in this book that will stand the test of time, but that you'll never, ever be pop-quizzed on. So, I guess, just read this if you feel like it.

Acne (adult female): Pimples that appear from the nose down to the mouth, but are not as red and aggressive as other forms of acne.

Acne (cystic): A set of pimples that are sore and inflamed. They're large bumps—also known as nodules—that are filled with a weird liquid (come on, I know you've tried to pop one before . . .) and form deep inside the skin.

Acne (hormonal): Large pimples around your jawline that last for an eternity. These suckers can occur at any age, but most often occur during your period, when you're lacking estrogen and are more likely to break out.

Acne (teenage): Violent, harsh, red pimples that surface in the middle of the face.

Affirmations: The practice of thinking more positively. Affirmations work because you introduce a thought that influences your perception, your thinking and your behavior (via Deepak Chopra).

BMI (body mass index): This is a simple equation to measure fatness that is calculated using height and weight only. BMI classifies people into four different weight ranges: underweight, normal, overweight and obese.

BMR (basal metabolic rate): This is the number of calories your body burns each day while at rest.

Body language: The vibes you give off in person.

CD (certificate of deposit): A low-risk investment, where the bank will pay you a low interest rate higher than what you'd get from, say, your checking or savings account.

Constructive criticism: Advice on how you can improve on something. This is often a huge compliment—it means people care enough to invest time and energy to help you, and listening to what they have to say can be hugely important.

Dharma: The ancient Hindu tradition of living according to a code of ethics in this world while being true to your nature in life, to unveil your life's purpose, leading to a sort of concrete "meaning" for your life.

Ectomorph: A body type that is narrow-boned, with small wrists and a small neck.

Endomorph: A body type with a wide bone structure and defined curves.

Face shape (diamond/triangle):
Characterized by a narrow hairline, and a
jawline that comes to a point around the chin,
starting below the ears.

Face shape (heart): Characterized by a widow's peak and cheeks that are slightly wider
than the hairline and drop to the chin.

Face shape (oblong or rectangle): Longer
than it is wide, with a structured jawline (if you
have a curved jawline, yours is oblong).

Face shape (oval): Longer than wide, but with
a smooth—as opposed to a rigid—structure.

Face shape (round): About the same width
the entire way around, with no major corners
around the jaw.

Face shape (square): Equal width both ways,
but with a structured jawline.

**FAFSA (Free Application for Federal Student
Aid):** A form that can be filled out by prospective and current college students to determine
how much financial aid you can get from the
government.

Fear conditioning: Being conditioned to fear
something through experience. If a bee stung
you in the past, you may still fear bees to this
day. This is because you associate the sight of
bees with the painful sting you encountered
in the past and therefore recoil as a result of
that negative experience.

Fear extinction: The process of creating
another conditioned response to counter the
original "conditioned fear" response.

Feng shui: Feng shui is the ancient art of
improving your experience based on your
surroundings.

529 plans: Higher education savings plans
offered by the States.

"Freeze" technique: Taking a second to
connect your mind with the muscle(s) you
want to emphasize while doing each exercise
move.

Meditation: The practice of spending time in
quiet thought. On an immediate level, meditation decreases stress, brings down your blood
pressure, boosts your immune system, gives
you better-quality sleep and harnesses your
creativity and intuition.

Mesomorph: A body type that is not "petite"
per se, but the bone structure is relatively
narrow.

Metabolism: A collection of chemical reactions that convert the energy from food
(calories) into energy that the body needs to
perform daily activities and bodily functions.

Organic: From start to finish, this food is
grown, processed and preserved using only
natural ingredients and is free of human-
made or manufactured ingredients (such as
preservatives, genetically modified organisms
[GMOs], and artificial dyes and flavors).

Papules: Pimples that do not contain pus—
they live beneath the epidermis (the outermost layers of your skin) and are hard and
stubborn as hell.

Pustules: Pimples that contain pus and will generally turn into a whitehead the night before a first date.

Self-esteem: Knowing yourself and seeing that you are empowered just as you are (according to Deepak Chopra).

Self-image: What other people think of you (according to Deepak Chopra).

Skin tone (cool): A skin's undertone, identified by the veins on your wrist having a slightly blue/purple color.

Skin tone (warm): A skin's undertone, identified by the veins on your wrist having a slightly blue/green color.

SPF (sun protection factor): A way for consumers to understand the amount of UVA and UVB rays that they may be vulnerable to. A measure of how well a skin care product protects against ultraviolet rays from the sun.

Style: The process of wearing what you feel good about yourself in (according to Annebet Duvall).

Vegan: A diet free of any animal products—meat, cheese, butter and even eggs.

Vegetarian: A dietary lifestyle that excludes meat.

Well-dressed girl: Someone who is wearing something that suits her and has the confidence that comes from that (according to Annebet Duvall).

ACKNOWLEDGMENTS

To my incredible team of representatives and coconspirators: Thank you for your incredible support over the years and for never failing to go above and beyond for me every day.

To my colleagues and coworkers: It is no small feat to survive this industry, let alone thrive in it as you have. Thank you for inspiring me each day with all that you do.

To my friends: Just one good friend is hard to come by and I consider myself very lucky to have so many great friends, as you have been with me through thick and thin. Thank you for loving me as I am, no matter what.

To my family: The huge sacrifices you made in the name of helping me achieve my dreams is without compare. Thank you for being my rock, always and forever.

To my fans: Your love and dedication from around the world touches my heart and keeps me going. Thank you for enjoying my work and supporting me throughout the years.

Whether in a big way or a small way, directly or indirectly, in good and not-so-good ways, each and every person who has touched my life has made me who I am today and allowed me to do what I do. For that, and to each and every one of you, I am eternally grateful.

INDEX